# ISTANBUL

By Colin Thubron
and the Editors of Time-Life Books

THE GREAT CITIES · TIME-LIFE BOOKS · AMSTERDAM

**The Author:** Colin Thubron, born in London in 1939 and a descendant of the first English Poet Laureate, John Dryden, is a writer and documentary film-maker with a profound knowledge of the Middle East. His extensive travels throughout the area have resulted in several books, including *Mirror to Damascus*, *The Hills of Adonis* (about Lebanon), *Journey into Cyprus* and—for this Great Cities series —*Jerusalem*. He is a Fellow of the Royal Society of Literature.

TIME-LIFE INTERNATIONAL
*EUROPEAN EDITOR*: George Constable
*Assistant European Editor*: Kit van Tulleken
*Design Consultant*: Louis Klein
*Chief Designer*: Graham Davis
*Director of Photography*: Pamela Marke
*Chief of Research*: Vanessa Kramer

THE GREAT CITIES
Editorial Staff for Istanbul
*Editor*: Tony Allan
*Designer*: Derek Copsey
*Picture Editor*: Christine Hinze
*Staff Writer*: Mike Brown
*Text Researchers*: Jackie Matthews, Milly Trowbridge
*Design Assistant*: Mary Staples

Editorial Production
*Production Editor*: Ellen Brush
*Art Department*: Julia West
*Editorial Department*: Joanne Holland, Ajaib Singh Gill
*Picture Department*: Lynn Farr, Gina Marfell, Belinda Stewart Cox

The captions and the texts accompanying the photographs in this volume were prepared by the editors of TIME-LIFE Books.

Published by TIME-LIFE International (Nederland) B.V. Ottho Heldringstraat 5, Amsterdam 1018.

© 1978 TIME-LIFE International (Nederland) B.V. All rights reserved. First printing in English.

No part of this book may be reproduced in any form or by any electronic or mechanical means, including information storage and retrieval devices or systems without prior written permission from the publisher, except that brief passages may be quoted for reviews.

ISBN 7054 0496 X

*Cover*: In the haze of an Istanbul sunset, the massed domes and minarets of the Yeni Mosque and of the Süleymaniye Mosque beyond it are silhouetted against a sky of burnished gold.

*First end paper*: Exquisite paintings of flower displays and bowls of fruit glow on the walls of a room in Istanbul's Topkapi Palace, seat of the Ottoman sultans for four and a half centuries. The room was created during the reign of Ahmet III, a cultivated and pleasure-loving 18th-Century ruler.

*Last end paper*: In this 6th-Century mosaic panel, a donkey driver offers a nosebag to his reluctant charge. The panel was once part of the flooring of the Sacred Palace of the Byzantine emperors.

**TIME LIFE BOOKS**

THE TIME-LIFE ENCYCLOPAEDIA
  OF GARDENING
HUMAN BEHAVIOUR
THE GREAT CITIES
THE ART OF SEWING
THE OLD WEST
THE WORLD'S WILD PLACES
THE EMERGENCE OF MAN
LIFE LIBRARY OF PHOTOGRAPHY
FOODS OF THE WORLD
TIME-LIFE LIBRARY OF ART
GREAT AGES OF MAN
LIFE SCIENCE LIBRARY
LIFE NATURE LIBRARY
YOUNG READERS LIBRARY

# Contents

# Crossroads of Two Continents

Of all structures, a bridge is at once the most civilizing and the most perilous. It may carry merchandise, armies, knowledge—a million humble or momentous exchanges—but it appears to stand only by the grace of chance and time. For some two thousand years, the metropolis of Istanbul, astride the narrow neck of water that divides Europe and Asia, has been such a bridge. The only city in the world to span two continents, it gathers the overland traffic of East and West, and guards the Bosphorus, one of the key waterways of the Earth.

These north-eastern shores of the Mediterranean are different from those to the west or south. The harsh brilliance of Syria and the clarity of Greece are gone. Instead, a traveller approaching Istanbul from the Aegean Sea notices how the very air changes. As his boat passes through the slender channel of the Dardanelles into the Sea of Marmara, he finds mists, cold rain. The land is blurred, the sea often choppy. The rich yellow of more southerly buildings has faded and a new colour appears: stone that is a wintry grey.

Where the Sea of Marmara presses northwards, the straits of the Bosphorus begin. Almost 20 miles long, they wind among steep hills scattered with castles and villages. Beyond them, the huge, landlocked expanse of the Black Sea, humid in summer and blustery in winter, receives the outflow of the great rivers of the Balkans and Russia.

In ancient times, these waterways were wrapped in legend. Through the Bosphorus, Jason and his Argonauts sailed in search of the Golden Fleece; its shores were said to be the haunt of the monstrous Harpies—women with the bodies of vultures; and beyond the narrows lay the land of the Cimmerians, whom Homer described as living in perpetual mist.

Even the early history of this region is crowded with half-miracles. In 512 B.C., Darius, King of Persia, spanned the straits with a chain of boats and sat on a hillside throne watching his huge army march across to attack the Scythians in the steppe lands to the north. More than 30 years later his son Xerxes led the largest force of antiquity, some 200,000 strong, over the Dardanelles to invade Greece. And in 334 B.C., Alexander the Great, moving against Persia, shipped his army over the other way, and poured out wine to propitiate the nymphs of the sea.

It is hard to envisage a time when the headland at the mouth of the Bosphorus stood empty. "The Bosphorus with one key opens and closes two worlds, two seas," wrote an early traveller; and even in ancient days it linked Russia's resources of timber and grain to a civilized Mediterranean.

**Beyond the towering minarets of Istanbul's Yeni Mosque, commuter ferryboats converge on berths near the mouth of the five-mile inlet called the Golden Horn. The ferries carry some 100,000 people daily on a network of routes that links European Istanbul with its Asian sector on the opposite side of the Bosphorus.**

Today Istanbul dominates this strategic channel between the U.S.S.R and the West. An immense new bridge—the first across the Bosphorus since the boat-span of Darius—joins Europe and Asia through the northern outskirts of the city; and the early caravan routes to the city have become the Grand Trunk Road, burgeoning with lorries.

Istanbul itself is divided twice by water, so that the one city has three parts—each almost a city by itself. On the Asiatic side of the straits lies Üsküdar, a rambling quarter of pink roofs and white walls, of new industries and old graveyards. But the core of Istanbul is not here; it is on the populous European side, where two distinct districts—Stamboul and Beyoğlu—are separated by the five-mile inlet of the Golden Horn, which curves inland from the mouth of the Bosphorus.

The younger of the two, Beyoğlu, covers the slopes above the Horn's northern shore. It is traditionally the home of commerce and of minority racial groups; but it is growing and changing all the time and has a sordid panache of its own. On one side of its hill, it tumbles towards the Horn in down-at-the-heel alleys, shops and offices. On the other, it diffuses into modern suburbs and high-rise hotels, and ends where the new suspension bridge is drawn over the Bosphorus with a remote, geometric grace.

But the older European quarter—Stamboul, lying between the Golden Horn and the Sea of Marmara—is the city's heart. A huge, triangular promontory locked on the landward side by ancient ramparts, it was once the capital of the Byzantine Empire and presided over the flowering and decay of the Ottoman world.

Standing recently among the streets of Beyoğlu, I looked across at it with awe. There was no wind. The smoke from steamers in the Golden Horn rose in pillars of waning blue. Beyond the cape, the Marmara lay like flattened steel, broken only by the humps of small islands. And beyond these, the sky and sea were misted together in a single span, white and horizonless, where a liner sailed into nothing.

Something of this hallucinatory loveliness haunted Stamboul, too. Although only a quarter of a mile distant, it appeared to be farther away than it was. So densely built up are its slopes that no streets showed, no cars, no people. Nothing moved at all. It was like a painted backdrop to the clangour of the traffic-filled bridges at its feet, linking it to Beyoğlu.

But it is a backdrop of visionary beauty. Stamboul's buildings merge in a curtain of delicate colour; and out of them, crowning the summits of unseen hills, great mosques lift their minarets to a quiet sky. They have the repose of buildings natural in their places, because the Ottoman architects were sensitive to landscape. The mosques' minarets, sharp and soaring, give an effect of abstract serenity; their cascades of domes and semi-domes intensify the feel of buildings becalmed forever on their predestined hills.

This skyline is to the East what New York's skyline is to the West—almost the parody of a civilization. The city's myriad spires might be the fantasy of

On a whistle-stop tour of the country in 1928, Kemal Atatürk—the general who, as President from 1923 to 1938, founded modern Turkey and promoted Westernization—explains to a village audience the rudiments of the newly adopted Roman alphabet. Arabic script, which Atatürk regarded as an unnecessary hindrance to progress, was outlawed by him in that year.

As seen in an aerial view, waterways divide Istanbul into three sections. The Golden Horn inlet, spanned by the Galata Bridge in the foreground, separates the district of Beyoğlu (left) from Stamboul, site of the Byzantine city of Constantinople. Across the placid, boat-speckled Bosphorus lies Asia (top) and the sprawling district of Üsküdar.

some theatre-loving giant. Can men possibly live here? Surely, the traveller feels, a curtain must go up and reality appear. But after a while, his eye starts to pick out the giant's stranger conceits: a Roman aqueduct, a Byzantine church. And he sees, high on its cape above the Marmara yet almost hidden in a cloud of plane trees, the towers and pavilions of the sultans' seraglio—once the most secret and inaccessible palace on earth.

Cities, like people, grow more complex with acquaintance. Today, Istanbul seems to be the realized dream of the Ottoman Turks. But their vision disguises an older one, and that an older one still. For the tripartite geography of the city is matched by its history; a trinity of names—Byzantium, Constantinople, Istanbul—lend their differing cadences to its past.

Some 2,600 years ago, the shores of the Bosphorus were settled by Greeks. The first of them were blind to the advantages of Stamboul's site, and settled instead at Chalcedon, near modern Üsküdar. But legend has it that the oracle of Delphi instructed a second expedition to found a colony opposite the "city of the blind", and these men, seeing the Chalcedonians' mistake, decided to make their home on the soil of the future city. Byzas, their leader, is said to have given the name Byzantium to the little town he built on the headland in about 660 B.C. But this, too, may be legend.

Far into Roman times the history of Byzantium remained unmomentous, although the emperor Severus sacked the city in A.D. 196, and later rebuilt it handsomely. It was left to a later emperor, Constantine, to exploit its unique site. Like many men who have been designated "The Great", Constantine was not. Rather, he was an energetic barbarian—ruthless, mercurial and deeply superstitious. But his decisions changed the world. By Constantine's time, Rome had become too distant from the empire's strategic hub, which had slowly shifted eastwards. The emperors who preceded him had spent little time in the old capital; their court had become a wandering one, as they kept watch on the perilous frontiers of Persia and the Danube.

In May 330, Constantine, who had already turned the empire towards Christianity, formally moved his administration from pagan Rome to Byzantium, and rechristened it Constantinople. Almost overnight, the inconspicuous town became the centre of the civilized world. Rebuilt by Constantine in dazzling new stone, it spread—like Rome itself—over seven hills: senate, imperial palace, hippodrome, capitol—it had all the paraphernalia, and something of the aura, of the Eternal City.

From its oval forum rose an enormous column, surmounted by a statue of the emperor. He was depicted in the guise of the pagan god Apollo, but the orb he carried in his hand contained an alleged fragment of the True Cross of Christ's crucifixion; and at the column's foot a host of Christian relics lay enshrined. So the flavour of the new city was established. In law and government it was the daughter of Rome herself. But its language became Greek, its civilization Christian. Inhabiting a classical city dedicated to an eastern religion, its people were the medley of an empire.

For a thousand years, long after Western Europe entered the Dark Ages, Constantinople moulded the unique civilization that was called—from its former name—Byzantine. Squeezed between belligerent tribes in the north and Arab conquerors to the south, this empire alone preserved the heritage of the classical world. Its scholars knew Greek philosophy and Roman law, and ancient statues crowned the city's squares.

But the empire's soul, of course, was Christian. A strict and mystic faith permeated every aspect of its life, from the theocratic concept of a divinely appointed emperor to a penal code which could punish adultery by death. Monasteries flourished; by the 6th Century there were 83 in Constantinople alone. Even the coinage carried the portrait of Christ.

In 1453, after centuries of attrition and decline, Constantinople fell at last to the Ottoman Turks, a warrior race from central Asia. Yet the fusion of East and West continued. The Ottomans not only copied Byzantine organization and etiquette, but even appointed Christians to positions of trust. Furthermore, by the capture of Christian youths for service to the State, and by their conversion to Islam, almost the entire civil and military élite of the empire became European in blood. So, too, were the women of the imperial harem; and in time their offspring, the sultans themselves—rulers of Turkey—became scarcely Turkish at all. To a grandee of Constantinople, the word "Turk" did not apply; he referred to himself as an "Osmanli"—a descendant of Osman, founder of the Ottoman dynasty. A "Turk" to him was an Asiatic nomad, whom he despised.

So, even under Ottoman rule, the city remained a bridge between the West and the Orient. And as the empire declined under the incompetent rule of degenerate sultans, the influence of the West increased. By the 19th Century, the empire had become a pawn in the power politics of Europe; and in 1909, the whole Ottoman structure crumbled when an army group, called the Young Turks, stripped the sultan of most of his powers. For the next decade, the country's rulers belonged to a cabal of ministers ostensibly dedicated to democracy and reform. But their half-hearted measures came too late to save the country. Turkey lost the last of her European empire in the Balkan Wars of 1912-13. In the First World War, she fought beside Germany. By 1918, after losing an estimated quarter of her population, the country appeared to lie prostrate. The Allies had occupied Constantinople and had divided most of Turkey by treaty among themselves, Greece, and a newly-formed Armenian Republic.

It was at this moment of despair that a new leader—whose decisions were drastically to affect Constantinople—arose to sweep away the last trappings of Ottoman rule. Mustafa Kemal, soon to be known as Atatürk (Father of the Turks), had emerged from the war as the only Turkish general unstained by defeat. Setting himself against the dismemberment

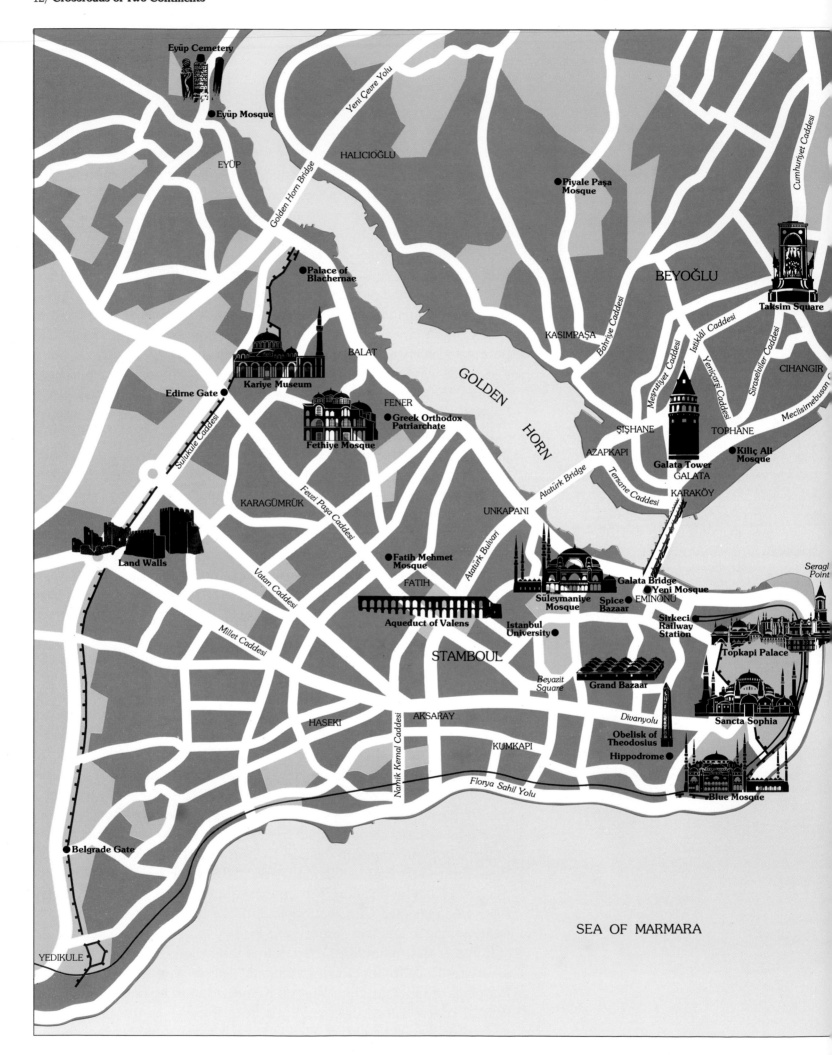

Eyüp Cemetery

Eyüp Mosque

EYÜP

HALICIOĞLU

Yeni Çevre Yolu

Golden Horn Bridge

Piyale Paşa Mosque

BEYOĞLU

Cumhuriyet Caddesi

Taksim Square

Palace of Blachernae

KASIMPAŞA

Bahriye Caddesi

BALAT

GOLDEN HORN

Mesrutiyet Caddesi

Istiklâl Caddesi

Yenicarsi Caddesi

Siraselviler Caddesi

Kariye Museum

CIHANGIR

Edirne Gate

FENER

Greek Orthodox Patriarchate

ŞİŞHANE

TOPHANE

Meclisimebusan C

Sulukule Caddesi

Fethiye Mosque

AZAPKAPI

Galata Tower

Kiliç Ali Mosque

Atatürk Bridge

GALATA

Tersane Caddesi

KARAGÜMRÜK

Feuzi Paşa Caddesi

UNKAPANI

KARAKÖY

Seragl Point

Land Walls

Vatan Caddesi

Fatih Mehmet Mosque

Atatürk Bulvarı

Süleymaniye Mosque

Galata Bridge

Yeni Mosque

FATIH

Spice Bazaar

EMINÖNÜ

Millet Caddesi

Aqueduct of Valens

Sirkeci Railway Station

Istanbul University

Topkapi Palace

STAMBOUL

Beyazit Square

Grand Bazaar

Sancta Sophia

HASEKI

Namik Kemal Caddesi

AKSARAY

Divanyolu

KUMKAPI

Obelisk of Theodosius

Hippodrome

Belgrade Gate

Florya Sahil Yolu

Blue Mosque

SEA OF MARMARA

YEDIKULE

Dolmabahçe Palace

BEŞIKTAŞ

Yıldız Park

Bosphorus Bridge

BOSPHORUS

Leander's Tower

ÜSKÜDAR

Selimiye Barracks

Karaca Ahmet Cemetery

Haydarpaşa Railway Station

KADIKÖY

## Sentinel of the Straits

Istanbul, the capital of Turkey until it was superseded by Ankara in 1923, commands a strategic position on either side of the entrance to the 20-mile-long Bosphorus—the straits that divide Asia from Europe and join the Black Sea with the Sea of Marmara (inset map, below). The straits and Golden Horn inlet cleave the metropolis into three distinct sectors: Stamboul and Beyoğlu on the European shore, and Üsküdar in Asia.

The hilly promontory of Stamboul on the south side of the Horn is the city's ancient heart. Here, according to legend, the Greek adventurer Byzas founded the original town of Byzantium in the 7th Century B.C. In A.D. 330, it was renamed Constantinople and rebuilt on lines still evident in Stamboul's groundplan; the defensive land walls constructed by the Byzantines in the 5th Century A.D. marked the western boundary of Stamboul far into this century.

The relics of the city's past include an awesome array of mosques, bazaars and palaces dating from the 450 years of Ottoman rule. And north of Beyoğlu and Üsküdar is a modern monument, the 3,118-foot-long Bosphorus Bridge, completed in 1973—the first bridge to link two continents.

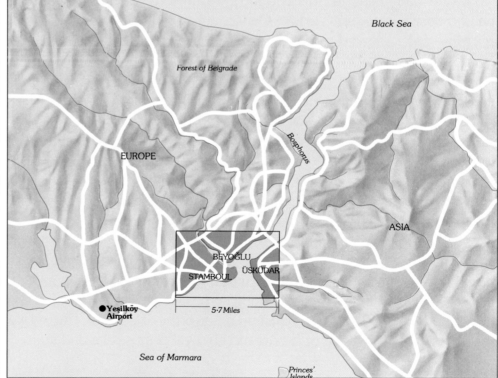

Black Sea

Forest of Belgrade

Bosphorus

EUROPE

ASIA

BEYOĞLU

STAMBOUL  ÜSKÜDAR

Yeşilköy Airport

5·7 Miles

Sea of Marmara

Princes' Islands

of his country, he now gathered an army in the highlands of Asia Minor. First he defeated the Armenians in the east, then the Greek forces invading from the west. Next he forced on the Allies a treaty guaranteeing Turkey's territorial integrity. Then, turning to internal affairs, he abolished the shadowy sultanate and founded the Turkish Republic, of which he became the first president in 1923.

For the next 15 years, until his death, this extraordinary man devoted his enormous energies to westernizing his country. His admiration for the West was naïve, but immensely fruitful. Throughout his dictatorship in the 1920s and 1930s, the eternal tension between the European and Asiatic elements in Turkish life was aggravated by massive reforms, ranging from the adoption of the Western alphabet to the abolition of religious education in schools. "We shall be civilized and proud of it," he said, and the civilization he was thinking of was that of Western technology.

Atatürk felt no affection for Constantinople. The city had been the power base of his enemies—the Allied occupation forces and the sultan. So it came as no surprise when, in 1923, he chose as his capital the little town of Ankara, 275 miles away among the bleak hills of Asia Minor. Here, where he had organized his country's wartime resistance, he began to build a spartan modern Turkey. Constantinople—the effete, the cosmopolitan—was relegated to second place. Seven years later, the city lost even its name; Atatürk ordered that "Constantinople" be replaced by a time-honoured Turkish corruption of the Greek words *eis tên polin* (to the city), traditionally inscribed on signposts. It became Istanbul.

Today, the Stamboullus—as the inhabitants of the city are called—wear European dress and use the Roman alphabet instead of their earlier Arabic script. They bear Western-style family names rather than Muslim patronymics; and they use the Gregorian calendar, and decimal weights and measures. Yet they still look to the East for much that is deepest in their culture. The Turkish race is scattered to the borders of China; and its religion is Islam—a faith profoundly different in temper from Christianity.

As I gazed across the Golden Horn at that city of ruined empire, these paradoxes swam unresolved in my mind. It is comforting, I suppose, to label things; and I found myself looking at the faces around me and asking myself: East or West? But the question is unworthy of Istanbul. The city is a magnificent alloy, a place of fusion and change. A mosaic, a bridge.

In any case, it seems unnecessary to label the Turks. They are emphatically themselves. Almost alone among Mediterranean nations, they lack the quicksilver Levantine temperament. They are a blunt people, with tough working hands and bodies. They move without the Greek or Arab narcissism. They rarely gesture or shout, and their dress is almost defiantly dowdy. Men wear dull-coloured trousers and jackets over open-necked shirts. Old women go about in headscarves and occasionally in pantaloons;

A professional belly-dancer undulates before a night-club audience at an opulent Istanbul hotel. The dance, once performed by slave girls as an erotic divertissement at the court of the Ottoman sultans, has persisted as a popular entertainment for Turks as well as tourists.

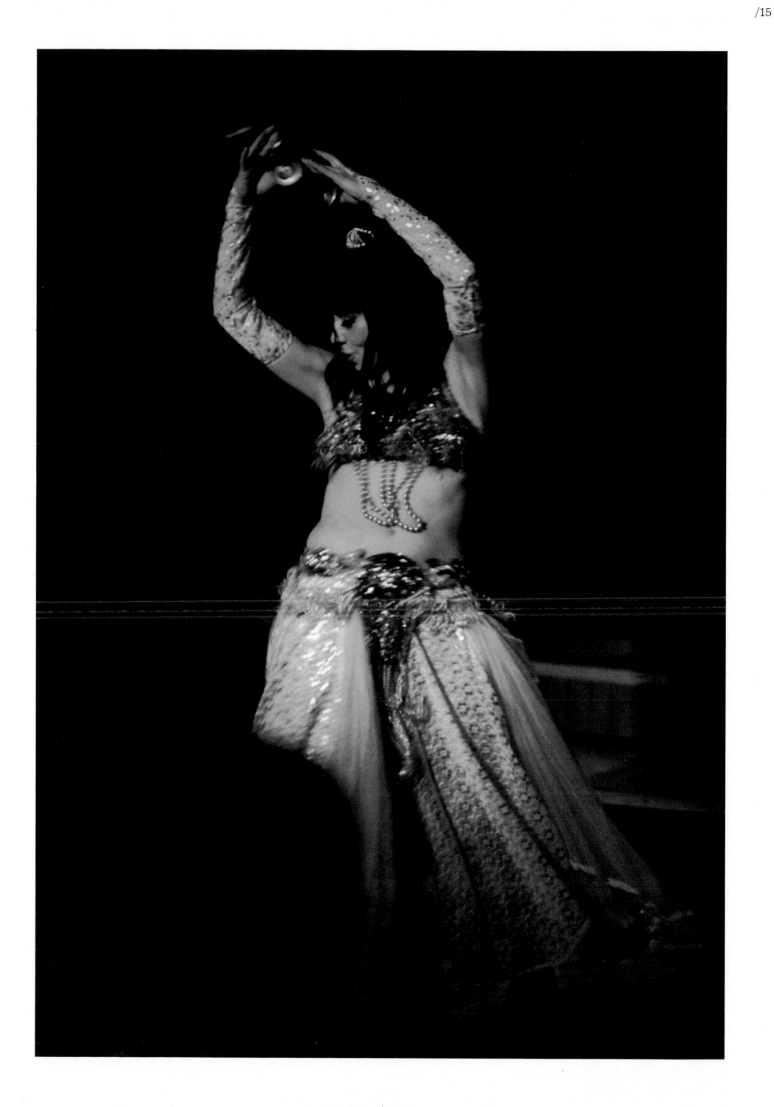

young women wear styleless versions of European fashions. No race contrives to look more utterly ordinary.

The Turk, in fact, stands apart. Europe has branded him a fanatic, and when aroused he has been capable of terrible brutality. But more typically he is passive, grave and frugal. He does not care overmuch about material things. The Greeks and Arabs see the world, and their role in it, more theatrically and more dynamically; their spirit is restless, inquisitive, anarchic. But the Turkish temper may be summarized by the national negative: *Yok!* In the mouth of a Turk, this "No" can assume an utter finality. It reflects stubbornness, endurance and a refusal to be trespassed upon. To be confronted by a *"Yok!"* is to be reminded that the Turk has never been conquered in his homeland. His qualities are those of the soldier, not of the merchant. He keeps a quiet confidence. Above all, he shows an acceptance of his own, and others', suffering.

Sometimes, it seems as if this quality alone reconciles the Stamboullu to his city. Its days of grandeur are irretrievably past. The slow decline of the Ottoman Empire plucked it piece by piece. Now Istanbul is desperately poor, its municipality bankrupt. Without the right to raise local taxes, its mayor must journey each month to Ankara and plead for money to meet the city's bills. Into its magnificent shell, hardened by two millennia of history, there no longer pour the riches of an empire, but hordes of out-of-work peasants. The city has been slow to adapt to new ways. It earns its living less by heavy industry than in a maze of small factories and work-shops, mostly dealing with metal and textiles, and as a mart for the agricultural produce of its great Asian hinterland.

Its work is done among a motley of shops and businesses slung with advertisements. The Ottomans built their homes and shops in wood, which recurring fires have purged away. So the warp and woof of the old city has gone. Instead, street after street shows concrete structures—10 or 20 years old—that must have looked decrepit almost before completion. The Turks, it has been said, enjoy constructing but hate maintaining. The result is a warren of crumbling and discoloured buildings, torn-up pavements, and sordid byways that may end miraculously at a mosque or a caravanserai, built in the grey-blue permanence of stone.

The city's activity, in fact, is that of a modern torrent flowing in ancient channels. Neither the timeless leisure of the East is here, nor the efficiency of the West. Unemployment is rife. Many Stamboullus eke out a living with part-time work. Administration, as all over Turkey, is cumbersome and sometimes corrupt; and the city's services—electricity, water, telephones—are at best intermittent. It is a beautiful, tough, congested place—a lodestar and a grave for peasant hopes—and every year its arteries thicken with more ramshackle houses, battered cars, struggling poor.

Perhaps it is this marriage of beauty and squalor that provokes such extremes in visitors. Some fall in love with Istanbul; others grow to loathe

In the district of Stamboul, a workman, unperturbed by the riot of exposed electric cables draped above his head, unloads planks from the back of a truck. Such makeshift wiring—a result of the city's explosive growth and chronic shortage of funds—produces frequent blackouts and telephone failures.

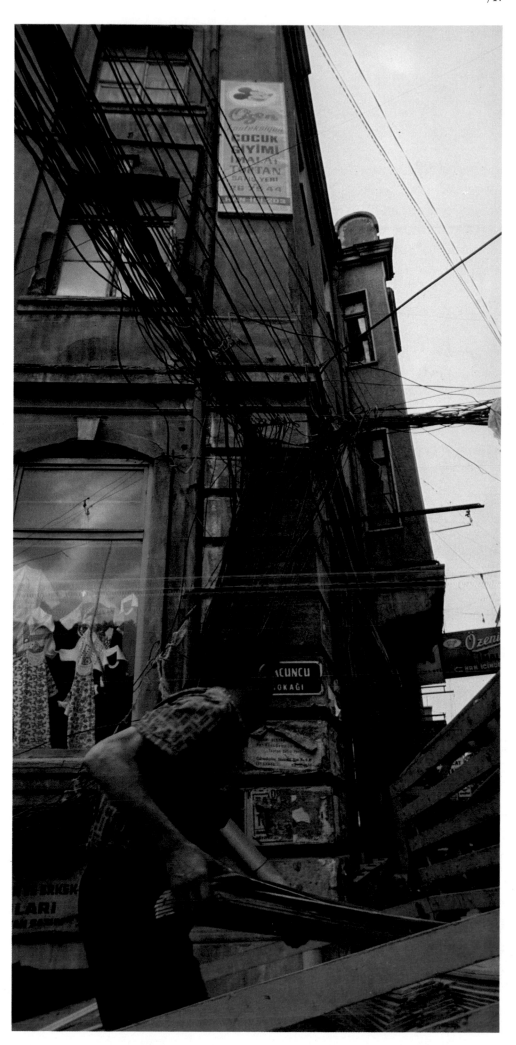

it. This is nothing new. "No other city that I have seen has so confused and distressed me," wrote a British traveller 70 years ago. "For days I could not release myself from the obsession of its angry tumult. Much of it seems to be in a perpetual rage, pushing, struggling, fighting, full of ugly determination to do—what? One does not know, one cannot even surmise what it desires, what is its aim, if, indeed, it has any aim." Even its climate provokes controversy: one visitor may describe it as mild, while the next will more accurately observe that the summers are lethargic and the winter winds bitter (because "the boysterous Tramontana," as a 17th-Century traveller put it, "that from the blacke Sea doth sweep his blacke substance, here most violently rages").

It is the juxtaposition of old splendour and present shabbiness, I think, that gives the city an extraordinary feel of decadence, of sensuous relapse into the dream of its past. From every mosque-capped hill its history haunts it. Constantinople! The gongs of Byzantium are never quite stilled in the imagination. For all the city's toil and fury, I have sometimes felt that I was walking among ruins.

Yet it continues to exert a fascination on the Turks. From all over Asia Minor they filter in, searching for the imagined riches of the capital of the sultans. In 1945, the population of the city was some 860,000. By 1965, it had risen to more than one and a half million. Since then the trickle of rural immigrants has become a storm. They come by bus or cart over the new Bosphorus Bridge, or take steamers across the straits. More than half the city's population—which reached four and a half million in the late 1970s—are now of country origins, and a hurricane of makeshift suburbs, built to accommodate the newcomers, sweeps over hill and shore.

Yet even this influx has its precedents. In Byzantine years, the numbers of immigrants from the provinces were sometimes so great that they had to be restricted. More important still was the repopulation of Constantinople after the Ottoman conquest of 1453, when communities were shifted wholesale out of Asia Minor to restock the depleted city. The district of central Stamboul, now known as Aksaray, was peopled from the town of the same name in far-off Karamania, a province of central Turkey, whose inhabitants—Muslims and Christians—were transferred *en masse* by the Ottoman conquerors. And in 1475, as many as 40,000 Genoese and Armenians were brought from the captured town of Kaffa in the Crimea.

Such movements have produced a complex and fascinating people. Walk down any street in Istanbul and among the olive complexions there will soon appear a shoe-black or a soldier with a skin of Nordic freshness, or a man with the aquiline features of a north Arabian.

Such faces send question-marks out of their past. Who were their ancestors? Were they, perhaps, a part of the great slave-family of the sultans, wrenched from a hundred subject races? Hungarian soldiers, Circassian odalisques, Venetian merchants? The people themselves rarely know.

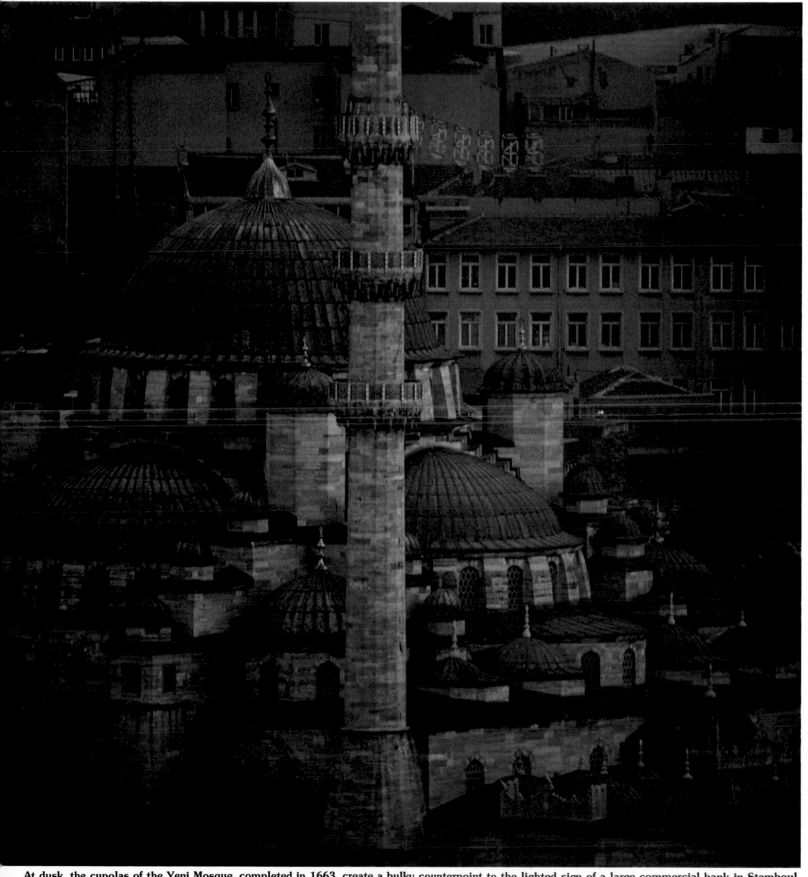

At dusk, the cupolas of the Yeni Mosque, completed in 1663, create a bulky counterpoint to the lighted sign of a large commercial bank in Stamboul.

"You can hear a dozen languages in many parts of Istanbul," a student told me. "Kurdish, French, Armenian, and a gabble of others. The city's like an enormous stew. Everything's gone into it." He pointed to his light brown hair, which was already receding. "I'm fair, but why I don't know. My father was a restaurateur from the Black Sea. My mother, I think, had Bulgarian blood. Istanbul's a great city, you see, a country in itself. It's not like Asia Minor. In fact, it's not like anywhere else on earth."

Successive bursts of immigration have also, more subtly, affected the social and physical structure of the city. The newcomers, whether brought to the city by economic hardship or by a sultan's decree, huddled together in close, self-contained communities, guarding the customs of the world they had left behind. At first, each district was centred on a mosque, church or synagogue, as many still are; and its imam, priest or rabbi was the spokesman of its people. In time, inhabitants who amassed wealth would endow the district with schools, baths, fountains, markets. A common origin, trade or religion linked its members, who preserved an individual culture and character, even distinct accents. So this extraordinary city evolved in a cosmopolitan cluster of cells that were formed from the conquered towns of Asia and Europe, then infiltrated by immigrants and finally—as the Ottoman Empire waned—by refugees. In 1871, Stamboul alone consisted of 321 such districts. Two hundred and eighty-four were Muslim; the rest were Greek, Armenian and Jewish.

Many of these village-like districts have survived to this day. To a stranger, the city looks composite and whole. But invisibly the internal boundaries continue—sometimes cut by motorways or blurred by new construction, yet circling everywhere like rings broken upon a pool. "I'm going back to my village," declares a white-whiskered seaman on the Golden Horn. And it emerges that he is not journeying across Asia Minor, but taking a tram into Stamboul. "They're cheaper in my village," asserts a housewife, passing a stall of oranges; then she turns down a street and penetrates a circle whose limits are perfectly known to those living there.

Such villages have preserved the personality of Istanbul. Today, a few avenues drive through the city's core, but stray from these and you plunge into a labyrinth where every street has a charm or squalor of its own. The closer you draw to water—the Marmara or the Horn—the quainter become the alleys. Their cobbles pave the slopes in fantastic disarray, torn up or undulating. Their stone and concrete houses, defended by iron-grilled windows and heavy doors, flake away or fracture unrepaired. Streets of wooden homes look more like theatre sets than living quarters. Their walls, patched and repatched, are at last knit together by beaten-out tins, or bunged with paper. In their bay windows the people are framed like dolls: a woman knitting, a child in tears, a man asleep. Behind lattice or lace, unseen, the eyes of old women fill the streets with a crossfire of inquisition. The smallest alley does not escape them. If you elude the lookout of Grandmother Ergin on one side of the lane, you will be spotted by Widow Sürmeli from her eyrie on the other.

In winter, the stove-flues along some of these wooden streets, protruding horizontally between first and second storeys in rows of tin pipes, pour out horror. Filled with belching smoke, whole lanes look like the converging sides of two disintegrating and fractious old galleons, cannonading one another into oblivion but still inexplicably afloat. Sometimes, from twisted vents, these broadsides are fired pacifistically into the air; more often they discharge on to the heads of passers-by. The recurrence of earthquakes, as well as the old nomadic habits of the Turk, may have created a reluctance to build more permanently. In older days the property of Ottoman officials did not survive in their families, but reverted to the sultan when they died. So even the rich did not build for posterity. Little wonder that fires have raged through such streets.

Today, new houses ape old ways, with alcove windows built in concrete. Beside them, the wooden veterans, when they die, rot to phantasmal skeletons; their walls drop away and reveal wobbly brick chimneys or a cord of clay pipes dangling inside like some indestructible intestine.

Both old and new are little furnished. The Ottomans were never much interested in furniture; they preferred carpets and cushions. Rooms provided a divan in the window, but little more. A sitting room was turned into a dining room by laying a brass tray on a low stool, and the dining room was converted for sleep by pulling rolled-up bedding from a wall-cupboard.

The houses of old-fashioned neighbourhoods still have few comforts. A tiled hall, perhaps, leads to a beetling wooden stairway. Living room walls are bare, or pinned with photographs of absent relatives. A garish new rug may show underfoot. A glass cabinet displays some precious odds and ends—souvenirs, china. Sofa and chairs, symbols of prestige, occupy the room centre. The vases hold plastic flowers.

In the poorest houses of Stamboul I have seen only bedding on the floor, a heap of kitchen utensils and a charcoal stove. Such dwellings crush together in whatever wasteland they can find. Their frail roofs are fortified against storms by hundreds of scraps of cellophane weighted down with stones. Their floors are beaten earth.

This, then, is the reality towards which the peasants come flowing with their dreams of wealth. Throughout the city's history such human floods have threatened to drown the older populace, but have generally been assimilated. Beneath its boisterous surface the ancient metropolis is constantly at work, using the newcomers' vigour. It has the absorbent complexity of so many great cities—a resilience born of a prodigious past.

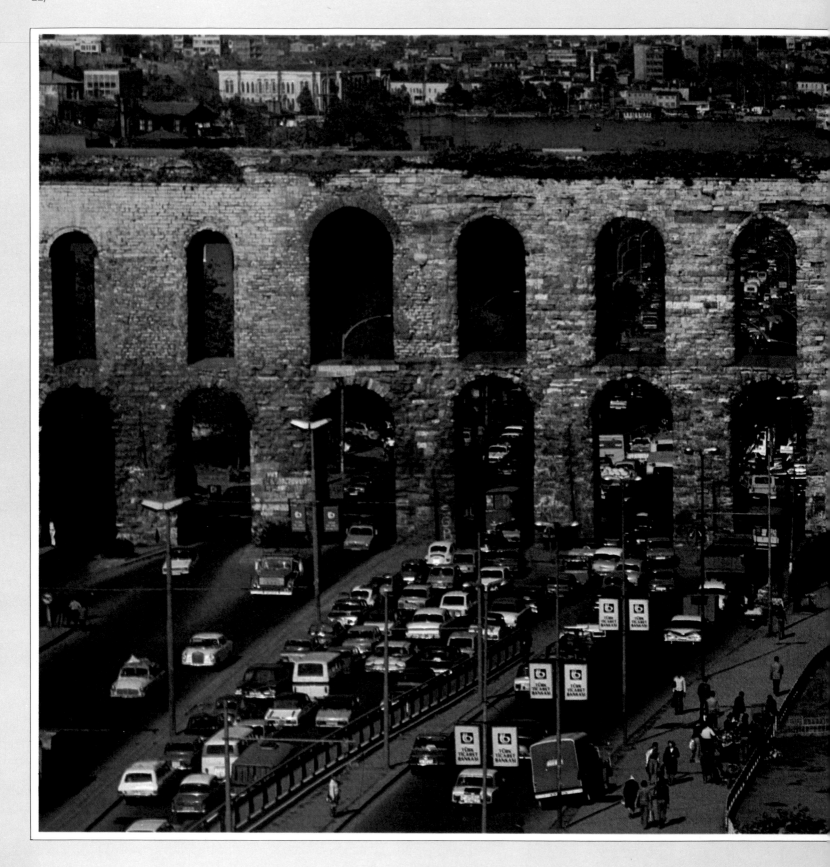

# Metropolitan Perspectives, New and Old

PHOTOGRAPHS BY MARC RIBOUD

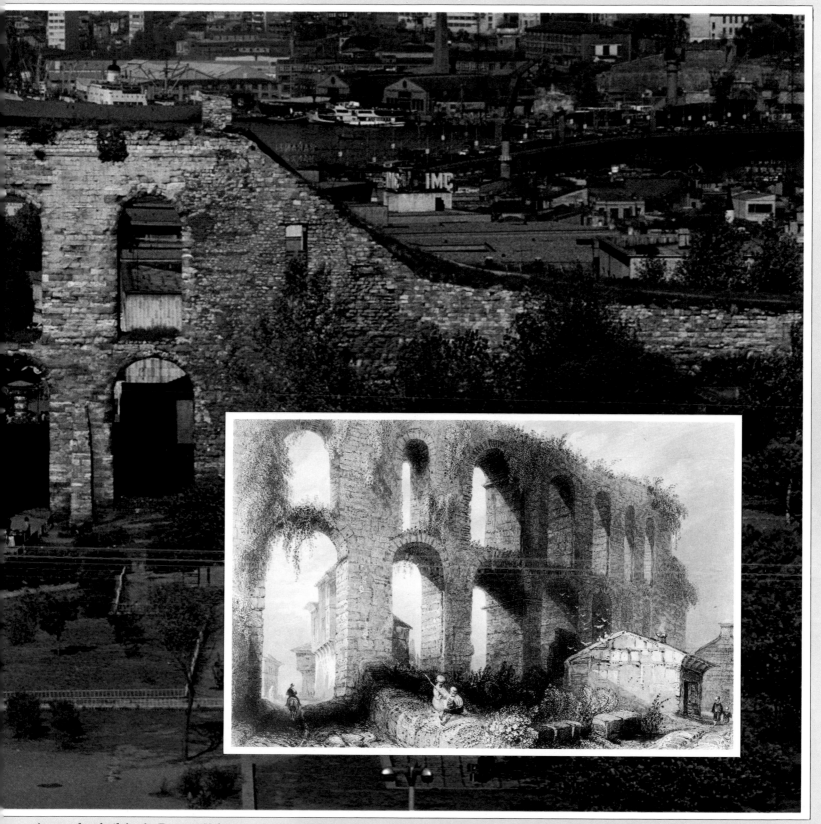

**An aqueduct built by the Emperor Valens in A.D. 378 spans a road leading to the Golden Horn—as it did in the more placid era of Bartlett's engraving (inset).**

"It seems to me that while other cities are mortal, this one will remain as long as there are men on earth." So wrote the French naturalist Petrus Gyllius when he reached Constantinople in the mid-16th Century. During the next 300 years, a succession of exotic travel books by wonder-struck pilgrims from the West added to the reputation of Constantinople as a city of ancient beauty and matchless wealth, a place mysteriously immune to passing time. Among the most enthusiastic of the literary visitors was an Englishwoman, Julia Pardoe, who collaborated with the landscape artist W. H. Bartlett to produce a detailed and evocative portrait of the city, *The Beauties of the Bosphorous*, published in 1839. Many of the scenes described by Miss Pardoe and captured in Bartlett's romantic engravings are still easily recognizable almost a century and a half later.

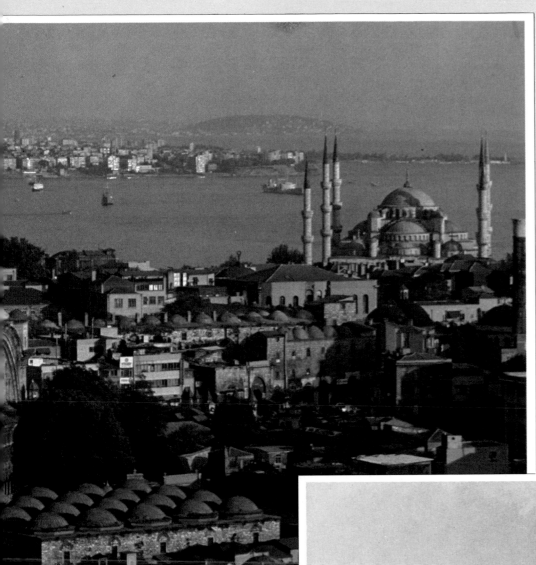

In her 19th-Century book about Constantinople, Julia Pardoe described the view westwards from a fire-watching tower in the district of Stamboul as "probably unrivalled in the world". Bartlett's inset engraving shows the scene as she knew it—with a parade ground in the foreground, flanked by soldiers' tents. In the photograph of the modern view the three buildings standing out against the Sea of Marmara are Sancta Sophia (on the left), the Nuruosmaniye Mosque (centre), and the Blue Mosque (on the right).

Makeshift workshops and small businesses
clutter the courtyard (right) of what was
formerly an impressive han—an inn where
traders from the Balkans and the eastern
provinces of the Ottoman Empire found
accommodation, storage space for merchandise,
and stabling for their horses and camels. The
fortress-like hans were still in use in the
19th Century, as seen in Bartlett's depiction
of turbaned merchants among bales of goods.

Tall, narrow houses, festooned with balconies, crowd around the fishing harbour of Arnavutköy (right), on the European side of the Bosphorus. In the 19th Century, many of the wooden houses lining the city's shores projected their upper storeys over the water in precarious inverted steps (above). But fires and decay have taken a heavy toll, and now only a few examples remain.

The cone-topped Galata Tower, here photographed against the mountainous backdrop of the Süleymaniye Mosque, has provided a pivotal feature in views of the city for more than 600 years. The 220-foot structure was built in A.D. 1348 as part of the defences for the Genoese trading colony of Galata, and later rebuilt as an observation post for the city's fire-watchers. Bartlett's scene shows the tower and the moon-blanched dome of Sancta Sophia silhouetted against the night sky.

Viewed from Üsküdar, the Asian section of
Istanbul, an evening ferry (left) crosses the
Bosphorus, passing close to Leander's Tower
—a lighthouse built on a tiny offshore island
in the 18th Century. In W. H. Bartlett's view
from the city's Asian shore (above), travellers
wait to make the crossing, upstream of the
tower, in small, high-prowed rowing boats.

Luxuriant vegetation (left) cloaks the ruins of
the massive land walls that protected the
capital of Byzantium for more than 1,000 years.
The 4-mile long barrier, built in the 5th
Century A.D. and supplemented by massive
fortifications along the shore, survived 22
sieges before it was successfully stormed by
Mehmet the Conqueror in A.D. 1453.
Subsequently, as Julia Pardoe wrote in 1839,
the main assault was from "the ever-gnawing
and corroding tooth of time"—an observation
underscored by Bartlett's pastoral scene of
shepherds grazing flocks among the same ruins.

# 2

# The Byzantine Millennium

A century after the Roman Emperor Constantine moved his administration to the shores of the Bosphorus, the barbarians were flooding south into Italy and a Dark Age began to spread over Europe. But the rich provinces and great capital of the eastern Roman world survived. For a thousand years more, the city of Constantinople, with its empire of Byzantium, was to be the keeper of Christian civilization and the crucible that fused the Orient with the West.

During this millennium of imperial rule, the frontiers of the empire ebbed and flowed over western Asia and eastern Europe. At its height, in the 6th-Century reign of the Emperor Justinian, Byzantium included almost the entire Mediterranean world, embracing North Africa, Egypt, Italy and southern Spain, and extending to the easternmost tip of the Black Sea. In its law and administration—even, at first, in its official language—this great dominion looked back to the Roman state. But as the centuries passed, the Greek legacy of its people and the influence of the East combined to reshape it into a culture of exotic distinction.

Its binding force, of course, was Christianity. Yet there has come down to us the image of a cruel, sophisticated people, whose mystical faith was matched by violently un-Christian behaviour. At the apex of this sacred empire sat the emperor, supported by a Church that at once fostered mass superstition and a rigid intellectual theology. Nevertheless, these were the people who passed the learning of the ancient world to the Slavs, whom they converted, and to the Arabs.

After the 7th Century, the empire contracted to its heartlands of Anatolia, the Balkans and Greece, with outposts in southern Italy. And in its final centuries, even this remnant was gradually gnawed away. During the 80 years before Constantinople fell to the Turks in 1453, Byzantium had dwindled to the size of a petty republic, huddled around the city that had once ruled half the world.

A stranger could walk about Istanbul today and recognize no sign of its Byzantine heritage. The sky is filled with minarets and domes, which carry not crosses, but crescents. It is as if a whole stupendous empire had been buried without memorial. Only gradually does the visitor come to notice that inside the spreading body of the Turkish city remains an alien spirit. Many mosques turn out to have been built originally as churches, but their mosaics are gone, and their porches flanked by minarets. Other Byzantine buildings have long ago decayed, slipped into the earth, but have defined the direction of a modern square or street.

In a 14th-Century mosaic expressing the fealty of the Byzantine Empire to Christianity, an imperial treasurer presents Christ with a model of the church of St. Saviour in Chora, originally built just outside the walls of Constantinople in the 6th Century. The mosaic was created over the door to the church's nave during extensive reconstruction work necessitated by collapsing foundations.

Of the city that Constantine knew, little survives; yet his plans dictated the design of the capital's heart for the rest of its history. In the city's core— a ridge near the southern tip of the Stamboul promontory—he enlarged the Hippodrome built for chariot races by the Roman Emperor Septimus Severus a century earlier, and constructed for himself the nucleus of the Sacred Palace, the home of emperors for the next 700 years. From here he laid out broad thoroughfares, increasing the city's area fivefold. It is strange to stand today in the quiet of municipal gardens, once the forecourt of the imperial palace, then to walk westwards along the road that Constantine laid to his forum and to realize that this once-great avenue— the modern Divanyolu, where traffic jams and squeals nose-to-tail—is still the straight, wide artery of the city's life.

In the vanished forum, the porphyry column on which Constantine's statue stood still rises as a fire-blackened stub, the size of a factory chimney; the base alone is five times the height of a man. The statue and upper segments of the column were blown down in a terrible gale in 1106, and the remnants have been charred by successive fires. Now its base is shored up with masonry, and the surviving segments are banded with iron rings to hold them together. The Turks call it the Hooped Column, and it has given that name, Çemberlitaş, to the surrounding district.

Half a mile beyond, the street opens into the chaotic Beyazit Square, which is still a centre of Stamboul's life. Some 60 years after Constantine died, Emperor Theodosius I spread his own massive forum here, adorning it with a triumphal arch whose decorative columns now lie in broken chunks by the roadside. These fragments, as big as boulders, seem to belong to a world of vanished Titans. Some are carved with a strange design, like tears, or like the eyes of peacock feathers. One is sculpted with the fingers of a giant hand; it lies, enigmatic and disturbing, among the refuse of the street, grasping at nothing. Embedded in the base of a nearby Turkish bath are fragments of sculptured soldiers gathered up and used as foundation material. Dislocated heads, arms, shields are all that remain of a column commemorating Theodosius' victories.

By the time of Byzantium's most powerful emperor, Justinian, who reigned from 527 to 565, the long street had become vastly embellished. Called the Mese, or Middle Street, it was one of the great thoroughfares of the world. On either side shone marble porticoes that formed an arcade of shops below and a terraced promenade above. The promenade was lined with statues of emperors, pagan divinities and popular actresses; to ensure that imperial dignity was not infringed, it was made illegal to replace an emperor by an actress.

Certainly there was a tinge of vulgarity about this new Rome. We learn of a nobleman's palace being converted into a luxury hotel and filled with priceless antiques: masterworks of classical Greek statuary that included several figures by Lysippus; the Venus of Cnidus by Praxiteles, the finest

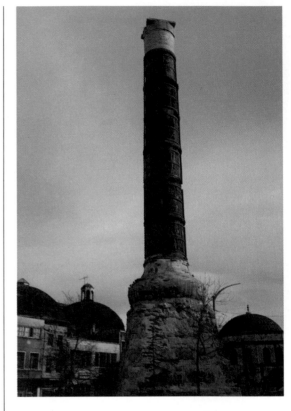

Damaged by storm and fire, the so-called Hooped Column in Stamboul bore a statue of the Emperor Constantine on its top when it was erected in A.D. 330. To promote unity among a populace that then subscribed to pagan beliefs as well as Christianity, the effigy represented Constantine as the god Apollo but holding an orb containing an alleged fragment of the Cross.

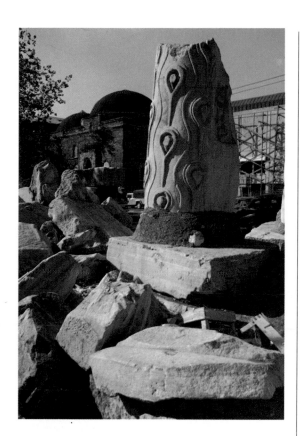

Carved peacock feather eyes adorn the remnants of columns that once supported a triumphal arch in the Forum of Theodosius—site of modern Beyazit Square in the heart of Stamboul. Built by the sixth Byzantine emperor in A.D. 393, the arch was pulled down by an Ottoman sultan a thousand years later and its stones used to build a nearby public bath.

statue of its age; and the ivory and gold Zeus of Olympia by Phidias, one of the Seven Wonders of the ancient world.

In Justinian's day, the magnificent and heterogeneous street was matched by its people—600,000 inhabitants whose temper and culture were Greek, but who called themselves Romans. Their ancestors might be Goths, Illyrians, Slavs, Greeks, Syrians, Copts or peoples of 20 other races; but their character was already their own: an unlovable blend of turbulence, cynicism and family virtue; of intellectual vigour within a deep conservatism; of religious mysticism but a love of the world's vain things.

Already their passion for theology was at its height—a passion that for 500 years, between A.D. 325 and 843, hammered out the dogmas of the Christian world: the nature of the Trinity, the worship of icons, and the status of Christ. The meanest streets and markets were filled with such disputes. "If you inquire about the price of a loaf," wrote a visiting divine, "you are told by way of reply that the Father is greater and the Son inferior; if you ask 'Is my bath ready?' the attendant answers that the Son was made out of nothing."

Through the city's marts poured the spices, ivory and porcelain of the East; gold from the south; slaves, furs and honey from the barbarian lands north of the Black Sea. Nor was this wealth ephemeral. As late as the 12th Century, when the empire was declining, a visitor to Constantinople wrote that "the Greek inhabitants are very rich in gold and precious stones, and they go clothed in garments of silk with gold embroidery, and they ride horses, and look like princes."

The history of Byzantine times (as of most others) is the record of the few. Almost nothing is heard of the welter of lower classes. The marble thoroughfares of Constantinople were carved through a maze of slums and alleys. Slaves were common until at least the 10th Century—the Church itself owned many—and there was chronic unemployment. But there are records, too, of state-supported orphanages, poor-houses, old people's homes and even a free health service.

Under Justinian, Byzantium knew a Golden Age. As heir to Rome and Christianity, he charged the empire with the sense of mission that gives to all its history a dimension of tragedy. Its emperor was deemed to be the regent of God on earth and his dominion the reflection, however pale, of the Kingdom of Heaven. Justinian's dream was to reconquer the western provinces of the Roman world from the barbarians and thus to unite the empire once more. He never fully realized it; Gaul and most of Spain remained beyond his reach. But, by the brilliance of his generals, his rule was extended to Africa, to Milan, even to Rome itself.

Government, like all else, stood at the service of religion. Even the imperial court became a living hymn to the god-emperor, and its riches the symbol of Heaven. The crowns of the emperor's family dripped pendants of pearls and jewels on to their shoulders. Their gloves and slippers were studded with gems, and the necks and ears of the royal women glistened with precious stones dangling from gold chains. In slow and gorgeous ceremonies, every gesture was dictated by ritual, as if the whole entourage had been bewitched into some majestic and timeless ballet.

As for Constantinople itself, Justinian constructed squares, harbours, baths, parks and—in the greatest profusion of all—churches and monasteries. Byzantine chroniclers called their capital the "God-guarded city", and its mystique lingered long after the reality was gone. Countless legends grew up among the Ottomans after they had captured it. In the emperor's palace, they believed, a sea-creature breathed out fire to blast enemy fleets sailing in the Marmara. And once a year, wrote the wonder-telling historian Evliya Çelebi, a brazen ship, filled with the city's witches, put out into the White Sea (the Marmara) to defend it, while another, filled with sorcerers, sailed into the Black Sea. They believed, too, that the memorial columns scattered about the city had been topped by live talismans. On one, it was said, a brazen cockerel had crowed every morning and awakened all the roosters of Constantinople; on another, four cherubim clapped their wings in warning of disaster.

Some of these columns have survived to the present day. Two of the most remarkable of them stand in the centre of the Hippodrome—an immense stadium, now almost vanished, that once seated 60,000 spectators. The best-preserved of the columns is the most ancient: an Egyptian obelisk 3,500 years old, shipped from Luxor and raised with infinite difficulty during the reign of Theodosius I. The base on which it is set bears a frieze of the emperor and his family sitting in their box at the Hippodrome. But their faces are blurred now, their eyes worn to dimples. All staring in the same direction, they seem hypnotized by some monstrous event, while above, the razor-sharp obelisk announces in hieroglyphs that the Pharaoh Tuthmose III has crossed the Euphrates and slaughtered his enemies.

The other column, in greenish-black bronze, is shaped as the twined bodies of three serpents. Brought from Delphi by Constantine, it had originally been dedicated to Apollo by the Greek cities that defeated Persia at the Battle of Plataea in 479 B.C., and was cast, it is said, from the shields of the fallen. Now a twist of metal shorn of its serpent heads, it comes down from 25 centuries still redolent of ancient heroism and beautiful with the patina of time.

Seated on stone tiers around the central columns, the citizenry roared applause, shouted abuse or broke into riots in support of their chosen chariots. Each chariot in a race was sponsored by a militia-like faction, dating from Roman times, that had its own hierarchy of officials and employees. Originally there were four such factions, known simply as the Reds, Whites, Blues and Greens—but the Blues and Greens soon absorbed the others, and their race-track antagonism became dyed with religious and political rivalry. In 532, in an empire worn down by

## A Cavalcade of Emperors and Sultans

| | |
|---|---|
| c. 660 B.C. | A party of Greek adventurers founds a colony on the site of present-day Stamboul. They give it the name of Byzantium after their leader, Byzas |
| 340 | The Greek warrior-king Philip II of Macedon lays siege to Byzantium. A surprise night assault by his troops fails when the moon emerges unexpectedly from behind clouds, and Philip's army eventually withdraws. The crescent moon is subsequently adopted as the emblem of the city |
| A.D. 73 | Byzantium is incorporated into the Roman Empire |
| 196 | The city is sacked by Emperor Septimus Severus for abetting a pretender to the imperial throne |
| 203 | Severus rebuilds and enlarges the city. The Hippodrome is laid out |
| 324 | Emperor Constantine the Great chooses Byzantium to be the eastern capital of the Roman Empire. The city is transformed over the next six years by a hasty building programme that enlarges its area five times. The nucleus of the Sacred Palace of the Byzantine emperors is constructed, and the Hippodrome is expanded and decorated with columns |
| 330 | The new capital is dedicated; it becomes known as Constantinople |
| 378 | The Aqueduct of Valens is built at the command of the emperor of that name, to bring water to the city |
| 413 | Emperor Theodosius II builds a four-mile barrier of fortifications from the Golden Horn to the Sea of Marmara to protect the city from landward attack |
| 476 | The fall of Rome to Ostrogoth invaders puts Western Europe in the hands of barbarian tribes, leaving the Byzantine rulers of Constantinople as the principal guardians of Christian civilization |
| 527 | Justinian, greatest of the Byzantine emperors, accedes to the throne. In his reign, Rome and many of the dominions of the Roman Empire are temporarily regained |
| 532 | Much of the city is destroyed during the riots caused by the heavy taxation needed to finance Justinian's campaigns. The rioting is put down at the cost of tens of thousands of lives. In the course of the ensuing reconstruction of the city centre, the church of Sancta Sophia is built in its present form |
| c. 550 | Constantinople's population reaches half a million |
| 640 | By decree of the Emperor Heraclius I, the Greek language—spoken by most of the city's inhabitants—replaces Latin as the official language of the empire |
| 1054 | The schism between the Catholic and Orthodox branches of Christianity is formally confirmed when the Pope and the Patriarch of Constantinople excommunicate each other |
| c. 1150 | Blachernae Palace in north-west Stamboul replaces the Sacred Palace as principal home of the emperors |
| 1204 | Troops of the Fourth Crusade, diverted against Constantinople by their leaders, storm the city, decimating its population and pillaging many of its treasures. The city's Greek rulers escape to Anatolia. A dynasty of crusader emperors is established in their place |
| 1261 | The Byzantines under Emperor Michael VIII Palaeologus recapture the city. After more than half a century of crusader rule, Constantinople is economically impoverished and its population has fallen to roughly 100,000 |
| 1348 | Galata Tower is built by the Genoese as part of the defences of the semi-autonomous trading-post they occupy on the north bank of the Golden Horn |

Justinian's taxes, the two factions united briefly in an attempt to force the election of a new emperor. The ensuing riots shook the city, and fires swept away the Senate and half the palace.

The crucial figure in this crisis was not Justinian but his empress, Theodora. One may see this extraordinary woman—ex-actress, ex-prostitute—portrayed in a church mosaic at Ravenna in Italy, reconquered by Justinian's armies from the Ostrogoths. Pale and delicate, she stands among her retinue wearing a pearl-encrusted crown beneath which the huge, sad eyes presage, perhaps, her approaching death from throat cancer. Her insight and decisiveness were far superior to those of her husband. Justinian, wrote the historian H.A.L. Fisher, searched in the gutter for a wife, and picked out a diamond.

At the height of the riots, her husband contemplated flight and his council trembled. But this diminutive woman shamed them. "Death is the condition of our birth," she said, "but they who have reigned should never survive the loss of dignity . . . I adhere to the maxim of antiquity, that the throne is a glorious sepulchre." Justinian was braced; the Blue faction returned to loyalty; the imperial general Belisarius slaughtered 30,000 Greens in the Hippodrome; and the emperor was left with a devastated city.

One of the buildings destroyed in the riots was the 5th-Century church of Sancta Sophia, which stood near the Sacred Palace. Justinian now set about rebuilding it to a stupendous design. Contemporary accounts of how it towered in an almost unearthly majesty might inspire scepticism if the building did not stand, in the bones of its glory, to this day.

There had been no church like it before. Infinitely more ambitious than its predecessor, it solved with precocious daring the old architectural problem of how to raise a dome on a rectangle. By the use of immense pendentives—curved triangles that convert the rectangle to the hemisphere—its architects, Anthemius of Tralles and Isidorus of Miletus, created one of the largest spaces in the world to be covered by a single roof. The dome, wrote the historian Procopius, "seems not to rest on solid masonry, but to cover the space beneath as though suspended from Heaven". So shallow and delicately poised was it, that towards the end of Justinian's reign it came crashing down in an earthquake. But the aged emperor lived to see it rebuilt more steeply, using light, porous bricks bound by a cement mixed (runs a legend) with the spittle of holy men.

It is said that Sancta Sophia's embellishment so impoverished the city that its schools and universities were forced to close and their teachers were dying of starvation. Five years' tax revenue from Egypt was reputedly spent on the pulpit alone. The altar was a slab of solid gold, studded with gems. Before it hung a curtain sewn with half a million pearls; above it rose a silver-pillared canopy with a gold globe that weighed 118 pounds and was crowned by a jewel-encrusted cross. During the celebration of the liturgy, 300 musicians, brilliant in crimson silk, played harps, dulcimers and mandolins, above whose chiming the chant of a hundred eunuchs, a hundred women and 200 boys rose in unearthly praise.

I cannot remember what I expected to see when I first approached the church's entrance. But a man standing nearby said: "There's nothing to see in there. Everything's gone."

I entered the narthex over a wasteland of cracked marble paving. Its size was awesome. Tourists' voices dwindled to lonely echoes and the ceiling soared. I was dimly aware of a mosaic far above: a Christ not of love but of justice, his robes violent in their folds, his brow contracted. Nine brass-sheathed doors led into the nave, but I noticed, for some reason, more intimate things: thresholds worn shallow by the tread of centuries; ancient curtain-hooks still above the doors; and, in the floor on either side of the Imperial Gate into the nave, deep, shining indentations where generations of court chamberlains had stood, shuffling their feet.

I passed through the Gate and looked up with a heartleap. The mosaics, the glittering church paraphernalia, are almost gone—scattered by the Turks—and I saw instead a pure geometry. The nave is formed by arcades that carry deep galleries. For a moment I felt as if I were standing less in a building than in a landscape, for these colonnades give a feeling not of enclosure, but of endless extension into other light and other darkness.

From four piers rise huge pendentives, where mosaic seraphim hover in a whirl of feathers. Supported by these pendentives and by two half-domes, the giant cupola lifts in muted black and gold, ringed at the base by 40 windows, but so vast as to be barely touched by the light. It is almost as broad as that of St. Peter's but stands less than half as high and is thus immeasurably more impressive. The effect is one of floating immensity, suggesting, as was intended, the infinitude of God. It is recorded that on December 26th, 537, when Sancta Sophia was dedicated, Justinian entered the nave alone and cried out, remembering the Temple in Jerusalem: "Ho, Solomon, I have surpassed thee!"

I tried to study details. But even these were mesmerizing. Monolithic columns thicken in the aisles, while marble panels, multi-veined and many-coloured, cover its walls. My eye travelled over capitals carved like fretted baskets, and over the lace-like decoration in the spandrels above nave and gallery. High in the conch of the apse sit a mosaic Virgin and Child, flanked now by only one superb but broken archangel. His plumage dripping to the ground, he cradles a crystal orb; his haloed face, like that of some converted classical god, stares wide-eyed across the apse. Opposite, a second archangel has disappeared, leaving behind only a few feathers.

The mosaics of Justinian's time were simple decoration, and those left are not, in their dulled state, impressive. But others were added in later centuries and their loss is irredeemable. The Byzantines were fascinated by the science of optics and by flame. Every mosaic was related to the play of light from a lantern or a window, and its tiny glass tesserae were

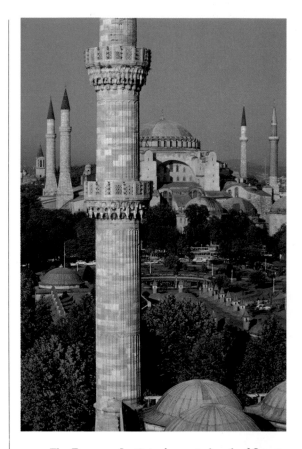

The Emperor Justinian's great church of Sancta Sophia—flanked today by minarets (above) that were added after its transformation into a mosque in the 15th Century—was built by the labours of 10,000 craftsmen between A.D. 532 and 537. In spite of inscriptions on each brick that read, "It is God who founded this, and God will provide for it", an earth tremor soon brought down its original dome; a taller one (right), rising 184 feet above the floor, was constructed within Justinian's lifetime.

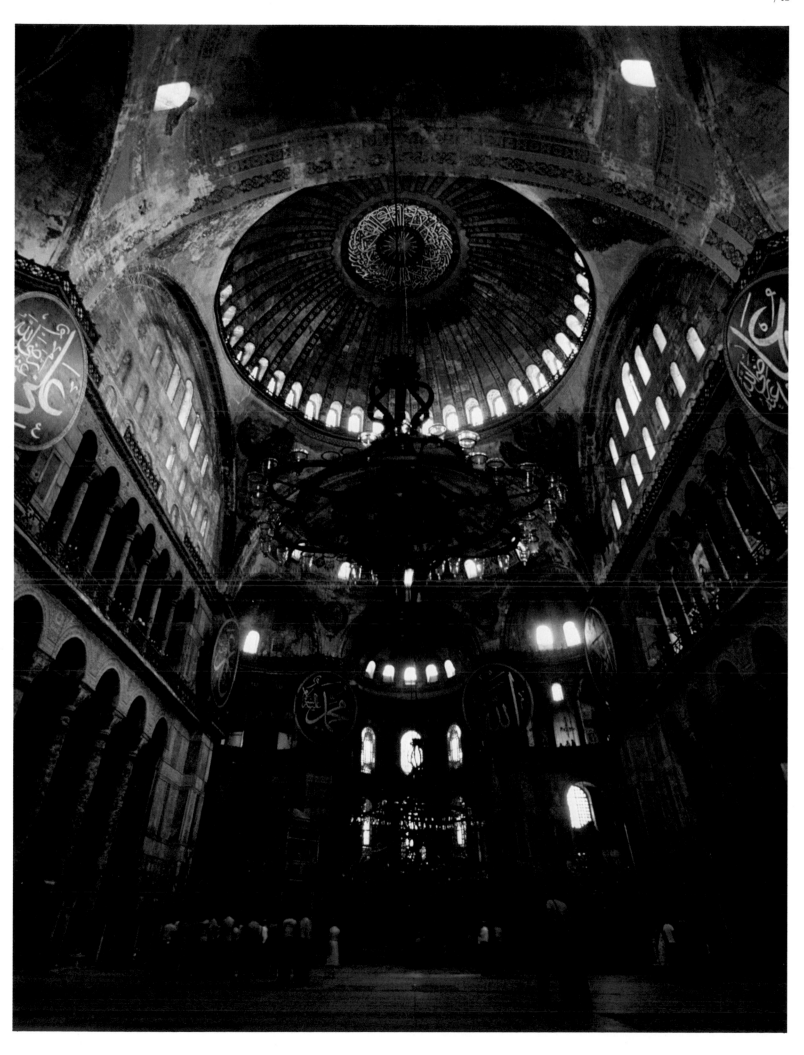

fractionally tilted to transmit a shimmering life. Out of the darkness of Constantinople's nights or winters, men entered the cathedral as into some hushed powerhouse of sanctity, in which the celestial army of saints and martyrs gazed from their walls in zones of flickering fire.

Along the galleries on either side of the nave, a few of these later mosaics remain. Most are portraits of emperors or empresses who ruled between the 9th and 12th Centuries. Wedged in the narrowness of a pier, fantastic in his scarlet and jewel-chequered robes, we see the Emperor Alexander, an alcoholic madman who died of apoplexy while playing polo. In the gallery opposite is the much-married Empress Zoë, with her third husband, Constantine IX. Nearby stands the red-haired Empress Irene; with her rouged cheeks and pleated hair, she looks like a playing-card queen. Beside her is her sickly son, who died before he could succeed to the throne; nearby, the Virgin receives imperial tribute from the Emperor John II—a bluff, capable man, cradling his money-bag like a merchant banker.

But these portraits pale beside the largest and most beautiful mosaic in the church, in which the Virgin and John the Baptist petition Christ for the pardon of mankind. Composed during the later years of the empire, when its greatness was foundering but a new humanity had touched its art, the figures are almost twice life-size. Their bodies are half obliterated, but their faces survive, full of gentleness and a kind of exalted reverie. The huge Christ, haloed in blue and gold, lifts his hand in a tentative blessing. His face is ringed with a softness of hair and beard, and the long, thin Byzantine nose and bud-like mouth are lit above by eyes of uncertain majesty. The expression is sad, fallible; salvation does not lie in His power.

This, surely, is one of the greatest works of Byzantium. Each of the three figures is exquisite, and the rippling splendour of the mosaic wall, lapping upward like the scales of a goldfish, gives fluidity and brilliance to the space which they inhabit.

Yet for all this, I found myself returning to the centre of the church, to the ultimate miracle, the dome. Again came the feeling of a clearing in some immense forest, fringed with the darkness of trees, but overspread by infinity. All noise—a voice, a handclap—resounds here in far recesses, taken up, repeated and remembered in the light-filled galleries, as if the forest echoed, dimly, later. One receives the extraordinary impression that it is indeed the air, so gloriously enshrined, that is truly holy—the illumined emptiness itself, sanctified by the invisible presence of God.

There was never such building again. Later Byzantine churches were intimate and modest by comparison. Those left in Istanbul—about 30 in all —have mostly been converted into mosques, but are betrayed by their rosy brick, their projecting apses and quiet, wavy domes. A hall in Fethiye Mosque, where 14th-Century mosaics were discovered under whitewash, has even been restored; and while the central building resounds to Islamic

Approximately twice life-size, a mosaic that portrays a gentle, sad-eyed Christ dominates one of the galleries of Sancta Sophia. The mosaic was created in the early 14th Century, when Byzantine art enjoyed a last flowering even as the Ottomans were swallowing almost all of the once-vast Christian empire.

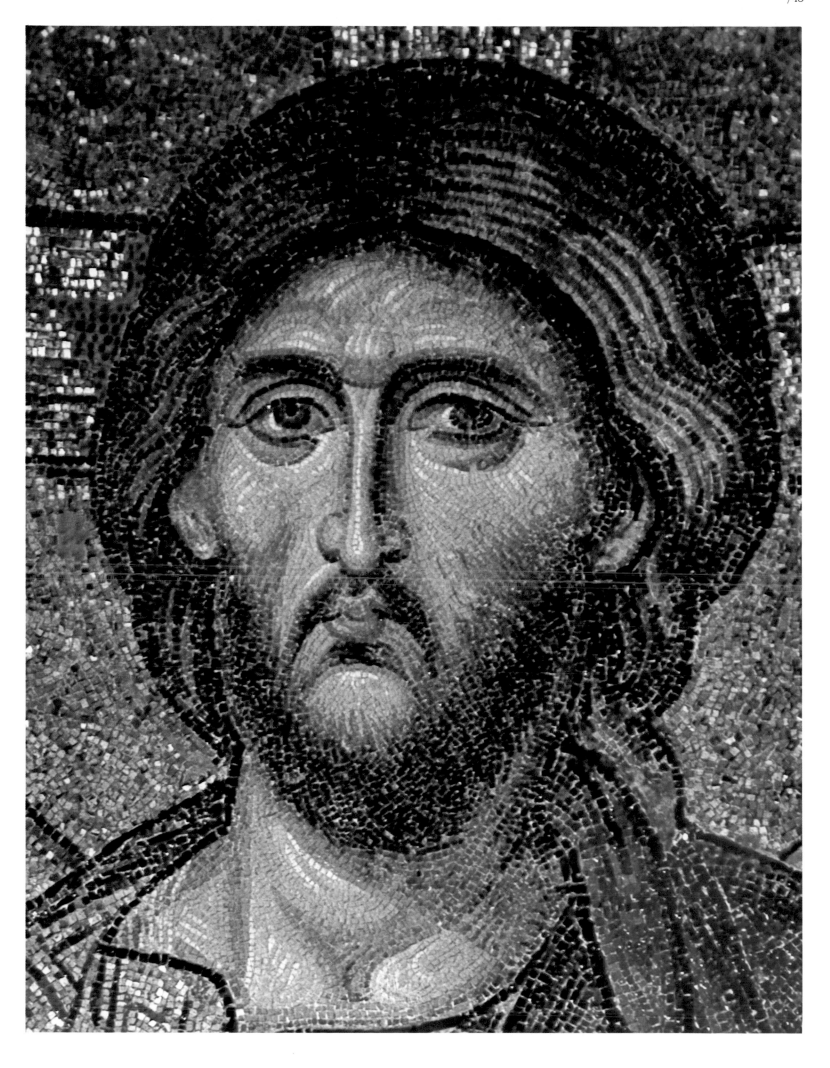

prayer, this jewel-like chamber glistens in silence with Christian prophets.

Other churches have been less fortunate. Over the venerable mosaic floors that survive in St. John of Studius, local youths play soccer. The church of St. Saviour Philanthropos, where the great 11th-Century Emperor Alexius Comnenus is said to have been entombed, is used by a wholesaler to store soft drinks. The little church of Saints Karpos and Papylos is a carpenter's shop; while the monastery-church of Pantocrator —mausoleum of Byzantium's last emperors—is falling to pieces, thick with pigeons' dung and invaded by squatters.

Even the Byzantine cisterns—immense feats of engineering—have not escaped decay. From Roman times, fresh water was channelled along aqueducts into the city. The Byzantines conserved it in three giant open reservoirs that once contained a million cubic yards of water; and at least 24 underground cisterns supplemented them. Now two of the reservoirs, long since dried up, shelter whole tumbledown villages, while the third accommodates a football stadium. The underground networks fell into disrepair as the Byzantine population declined. Today there are parts of the city where the entire earth underfoot seems riddled by corridors, vaults, tanks, stairways, most of them choked with debris or inaccessible.

The cistern that supplied the Sacred Palace is weirdly beautiful. Deep underground, more than 300 columns stand in its waters, holding up vaults as firm as a church's. No light penetrates to their end. The columns seem to move, like quieter echoes of one another, back into their reflected shadows, crossing and recrossing in dimming multitudes. Far in the vaults water drips with a faint metallic distinctness, or is seen as silver splinters that glisten in the air and vanish. Little wonder the Ottomans called this cistern the Sunken Palace; the long arcades, rising from quiet shallows, are indeed like the courts of some silence-loving king.

By the 9th Century the Sacred Palace itself had grown into a labyrinth of chambers, gardens and summer pavilions on many levels. Here ambassadors would be led into the throne-room, where the emperor sat in state surrounded by mechanical devices that filled barbarians with wonder. Long since vanished, these marvels are known from the amazed account of an Italian bishop who visited the court in 949. At the foot of the dais a golden tree was crowded with birds that burst into song, each singing its own melody—and celebrated by Yeats in his poem *Byzantium*:

> *Such a form as Grecian goldsmiths make*
> *Of hammered gold and gold enamelling*
> *To keep a drowsy Emperor awake:*
> *Or set upon a golden bough to sing*
> *To lords and ladies of Byzantium*
> *Of what is past, or passing, or to come.*

On each side of the emperor's throne, lions of gold roared and thrashed their tails. A golden organ played. And as the prostrate bishop lifted his

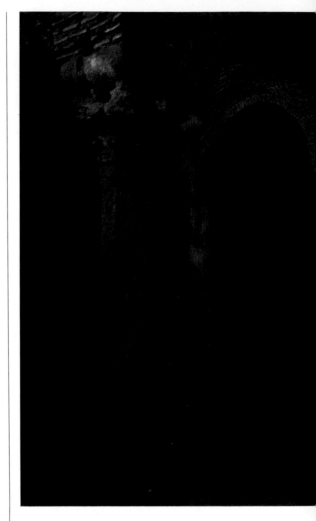

Dark water rises a third of the way up the ornate pillars of the Byzantine cistern known as the Yerebatan Saray, or "Sunken Palace". The underground reservoir, covering 2½ acres, was built by the Emperor Justinian to supply the ever-flowing fountains of his palace. Later, it provided water for the gardens of the Ottoman sultans' Topkapi Palace.

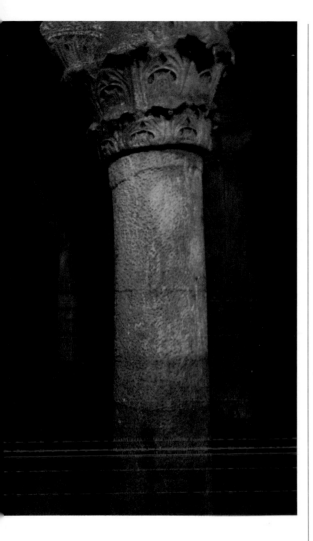

eyes, he saw with amazement that the emperor's throne, driven by an unseen mechanism, was rising into the air.

The ruler Theophilus, who commissioned these fanciful toys, was no pampered aesthete. A veteran of campaigns against the Arabs, he rebuilt the sea walls of Constantinople along their whole length. The long procession of his bastions still stretches in blistered defiance along the Marmara. Their towers have been half pecked away by winds, their crenellations are thin as paper, their stones rotting and askew. Caves have been dug out of their foundations and are inhabited by destitute families. Mile after mile the ramparts go, turning down the Golden Horn, weakening, vanishing, reappearing. Some look as if they might crumble at a touch.

As for the Sacred Palace, little is left of it but torn floor mosaics, excavated 40 years ago. Instead of victories or pious legends, they mostly portray country pursuits: a man feeding a donkey, children herding geese, a boy leading a camel. Did these quiet occupations, I wonder, so tedious for those shackled to them, hold some rustic glamour for the palace's inhabitants, racked by worldly cares?

By the time of the Ottoman conquest the palace had fallen into decay. So desolate was it that, on conquering the city, Sultan Mehmet II, gazing at its ruins and moved by the impermanence of all earthly things, momentarily forgot his triumph and murmured a verse of the Persian poet Sa'adi about vanished kings:

> The spider is curtain-bearer in the palace of Chosroes,
> The owl sounds the relief in the castle of Afrasiyab.

The last emperors, finding the complex too vast for their court, had long before moved to the palace of Blachernae against the north-west city wall. But this palace too has all but vanished. On the empty terraces where it stood, lashed by the wind from the Golden Horn, I found broken towers in the ramparts, and a derelict passage that disappeared underground. As I groped into it, my hands touched the rough damp of stone-built walls and I heard animals scuffling ahead. I twisted a newspaper into a torch, lit it, and saw that I stood at the entrance to a wide stairway.

As I descended, I assumed I was penetrating the substructures of the palace, built into the battlements where they plunge into the valley abutting them. My footsteps made no echo. The air was fetid, the place filled with cats. Soon my makeshift torch burnt to ashes in my hand. But below me, where daylight fell through slit windows, I saw vaulted chambers. I clambered along a twilit glade of piers, built in alternating brick and stone. Holes showed in them where floor-beams had been slotted in, but these had long ago rotted away and the ceiling now hung far above me.

I followed a narrow ramp into other chambers, but became lost in the darkness again. I suddenly realized I was in the prison tower of Anemas, named for a Cypriot conspirator incarcerated here in 1107. In these dungeons the Emperor Isaac Angelus was blinded by his usurping brother in 1195, restored sightless to the throne by the nobles, then imprisoned here again and strangled at the command of a second usurper. From a palace bedroom above, his son, the Emperor Alexius IV, was tricked into flight down a secret stairway, believing that the palace had been invaded by rebels; but the stairway led to this subterranean warren, where he was murdered. The chronicles of Byzantium are filled with such things.

I felt my way back along the walls, which were dank and cold to the touch, and stumbled up to the light.

As for the rest of the Blachernae Palace, only a three-storeyed hall survives. For what purpose this hall was built is unknown, but after the Ottoman conquest it became, at various times, a brothel, a pottery, a Jewish poorhouse, and a zoo. A traveller in 1597 was astonished to see a giraffe displayed there. "A beaste newly brought out of Affricke, (the Mother of Monsters)," he wrote, "which beaste is altogether unknowne in our parts: he many times put his nose in my necke, when I thought my selfe furthest distant from him, which familiarity I liked not; and howsoever his keepers assured me he would not hurt me, yet I avoided those his familiar kisses as much as I could."

By the end of the 11th Century Byzantium was tipping into its protracted decline. In the East a new wave of invaders, the Seljuk Turks, had gobbled up most of Asia Minor; in the West the Normans drove the Byzantines from their last foothold in Italy and were crippling sea trade.

The loss of Asia Minor cost the empire dearly in grain and manpower, and it never fully recovered. The emperor was forced to buy foreign aid against the Normans by granting dangerous commercial privileges to Venice; and soon the Italian maritime powers—Venice, Genoa, Pisa—were making inroads into Constantinople's foreign trade. In the 11th Century, for the first time in its history, Byzantium devalued its currency by adding base metals to gold.

But Constantinople itself was still rich enough to attract the avarice of the West. In 1204, the soldiers of the Fourth Crusade, originally bound for the Holy Land, were deflected against the city by the Venetians, to whom they were heavily in debt. For the first time in Byzantine history, Constantinople fell; and never had a city offered such loot. The soldiers of the Cross raged through its streets, raping, murdering, plundering the treasures of a thousand years. In Sancta Sophia the great silver screen was hacked into pieces, while the soldiers drank themselves maudlin from the vessels of the Eucharist, and a harlot lolled on the Patriarch's throne singing a bawdy song. "Even the Saracens would have been more merciful," wrote a contemporary.

As for sacred relics, never was there such a scattering of holy limbs and heads. The cathedral of Soissons in France received the Veil of the Virgin

Two boys and a pet bird appear to over-burden a diminutive camel in one of a series of 6th-Century mosaic floors excavated near Sancta Sophia in recent decades. These decorative floors, consisting of idealized views of rural life, are almost the only relics of the vanished Sacred Palace, home of the Byzantine emperors for more than 700 years.

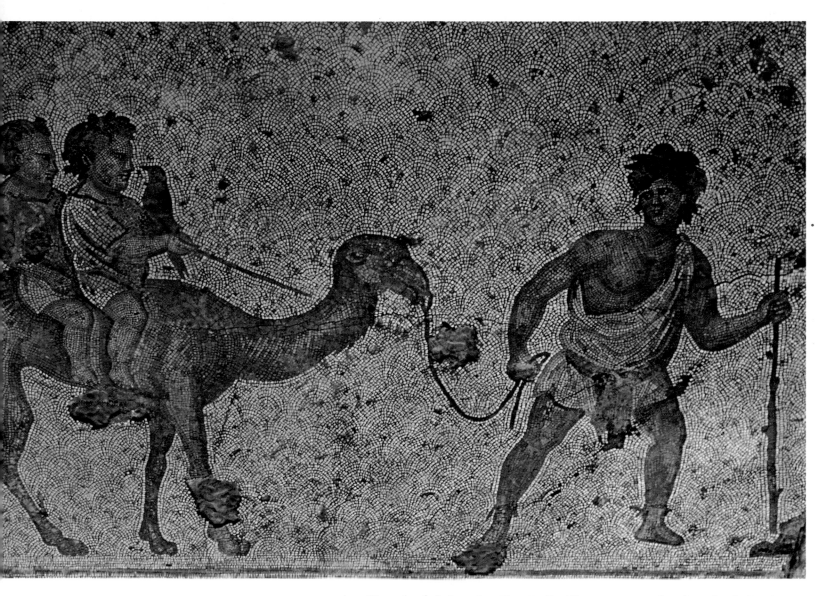

and a "head of John the Baptist". Chartres got the head of St. Anne. A piece of the True Cross came to England.

Secular treasures suffered even more cruelly. French and Flemish soldiers indulged in wholesale destruction. Entire libraries went up in flames, and the priceless statues of ancient Greece were melted down or chopped to bits. Only the Venetian contingents preserved what they could plunder; they took away the bronze horses of Lysippus and placed them upon the façade of St. Mark's.

After 57 years of Crusader rule, the Byzantines, attacking from the provinces, recaptured an enfeebled city. Plague and civil war dogged their shrunken dominions, while the power of the Ottomans, successors to the Seljuk Turks, was swelling ominously in the East and at last overlapped into Europe. Constantinople began to shrink within its walls; its churches and monasteries decayed. Before its fall in 1453 the Byzantine Empire, ringed by enemies, consisted of little more than the city and its suburbs. So poor were the emperors that as a trading privilege they ceded to the Genoese the town of Galata across the Golden Horn. They kept only a semblance of ceremony now: the imperial jewels were made merely of glass.

Yet in these last years, inexplicably, the city's culture burst again into splendour. Defiantly, it almost seemed, scholars and artists found a new pride in their classical past and in the humanism that had been the hall-mark of the ancients. A little church, St. Saviour in Chora, bears witness to this fragile and stupendous moment. The man who commissioned its decoration—an imperial treasurer called Theodore Metochites—was symptomatic of his age: a philosopher-statesman who was scholarly and rather incompetent. Wearing an outlandish oriental sunhat, he kneels in mosaic over a doorway of his church, nervously offering it to Christ.

The double narthex of this church, finely restored, is covered with mosaics portraying the lives of Christ and the Virgin. They form a kind of celestial comic-strip, filled with anxious humans and sudden miracles. In every arch and bay this graphic, shimmering life is going on. In one cupola stand the "ancestors of Christ", a spiral of haggard patriarchs elongated into the narrow ribs of the dome. In the other hang the ancestors of the Virgin, better-fed kings of the House of David.

But it is a side-chapel that holds the treasure of the place: one of the most moving of all frescoes. Composed at a time when Giotto was painting his murals in Padua, it yet has no sovereign. Its theme is one familiar to Byzantine thought: the descent of Christ into Hell. Bathed in a mandorla of stars, this Christ is a figure of superhuman strength and grace. Hell's locks and bars are shattered under his feet. His white robes are so subtly highlighted that they seem to glow in an unearthly sheen. With one hand, effortlessly, he grasps the wrist of the aged Adam, whom he pulls like a hurricane from his tomb. With the other he resurrects a crimson-clad Eve. The picture has a kind of holy and magnificent violence.

Such a work was to be the last of its kind. By the middle of the 15th Century the full weight of Ottoman arms, under a vigorous new sultan, was to crash against Constantinople's walls. Mehmet II, who succeeded to the sultanate in 1451, was a blend of much that was best and worst in his people: soldier-statesman, poet, voluptuary and tyrant. His preparations for conquest were lavish and careful. A Hungarian military engineer, Urban, whom the Byzantine emperor had been too poor to employ, offered his services to the sultan and was set to work casting a battery of cannons, including a monster capable of throwing a 1,300-pound stone ball for a mile. A fleet of 125 Turkish boats assembled in the Marmara and a hundred thousand troops were mustered on the European side of the Bosphorus.

The walls that faced these forces were surely the most magnificent defences of any city in the world. On the Marmara side alone they were studded with 188 towers. On the vital landward side, they presented an almost unassailable triple barrier. Built by the Emperor Theodosius II in the 5th Century, they were raised against the threat of attack by the barbarians who had sacked Rome. Behind a 60-foot-wide moat stood two lines of walls: a 27-foot-high outer rampart and—looming on a terrace behind it—a 40-foot inner wall. The lines were strengthened by 192 square, polygonal and crescent-shaped towers.

The ruins of these defences still stretch across the Thracian slopes between the Marmara and the Golden Horn. The moat is filled with

In the oldest surviving map of Constantinople, drawn by an Italian visitor in 1420, the Byzantine capital seems impregnable within its massive ring of fortifications. In fact, Ottoman pressure had already reduced the city's population to a few thousand from a peak of perhaps a million; and just 33 years after this overview was sketched, the besieging Turks finally breached the walls.

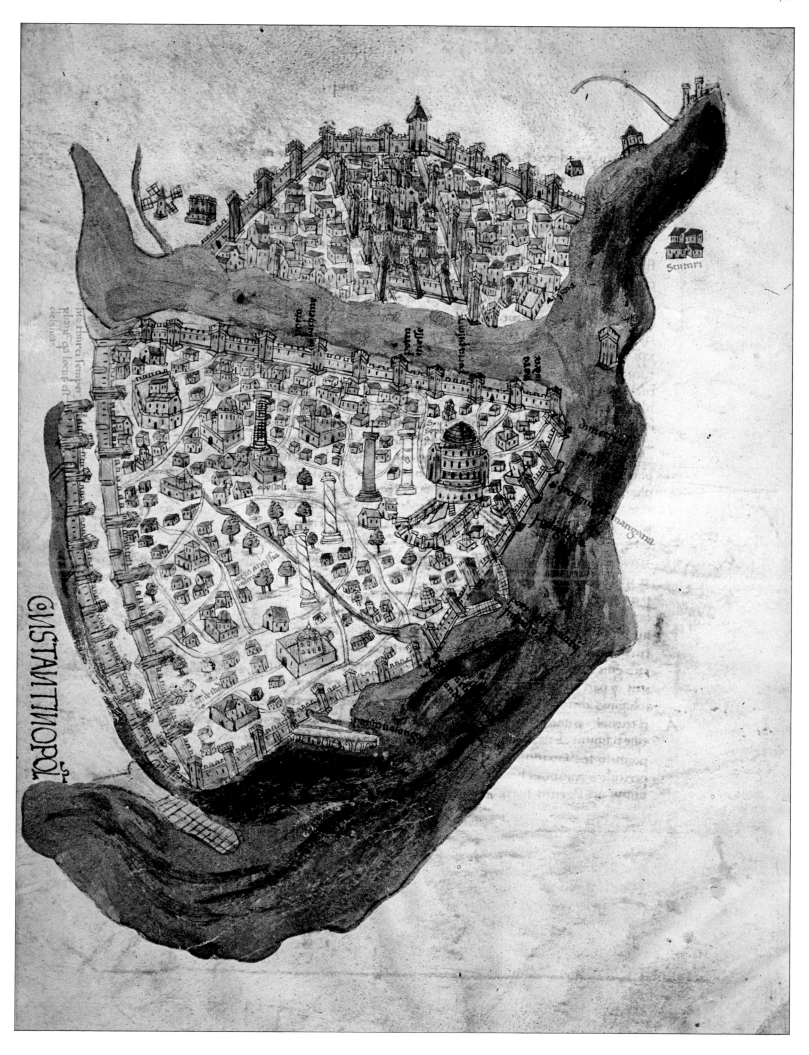

@VSTANTINOPOL

Scutari

vegetable gardens. The outer rampart is scaled by undergrowth and enfiladed with hovels, scrap-yards and refuse. But behind them, the pale-stoned towers of the inner wall stretch for four miles in unbroken ranks. When they fall, they don't crumble stone by stone, but split apart in massy chunks—such is the cohesion of ancient cement—to teeter in threatening plinths above the shacks of the poor. Huge rents slash them from top to bottom. Some have burst outwards. Others are cleft in two.

Inside the towers I found only emptied floor-sockets, the moan of the wind and the tossing of shrubs high up in the open sky. Although they failed at the last, they had previously sustained 22 sieges unpierced. Persians, Avars, Bulgarians, Slavs, Russians—all had been repulsed. Attila, the Scourge of God, looked at the walls in despair and departed to ravage the West. And for more than a century they were all that stood between an immature Europe and the risen power of the Arabs, who fell back from them in 718 with terrible losses.

It was behind these walls, in 1453, that the last of the emperors, Constantine XI, gathered what resources he could against the Ottomans. The pitiful state of the empire had obliged him to seek help from the West at the price of communion with the Church of Rome and alienation from his own people. But his forces amounted to no more than 7,000 men of whom the best were Italian and Spanish. Shortly before the siege, a Genoese defence expert, Giustiniani, landed with 700 picked men and was placed in command of the besieged.

On April 2, 1453, the sultan pitched his crimson-and-gold tent outside the city walls, and nine days later the new cannons began a bombardment that was to continue without ceasing for more than six weeks. The thrust and counter-thrust of this momentous siege occupied all fronts. The Turks soon cleared the first defences, bridging a section of the moat with rubble and brushwood. Although the cannons of Urban were so unwieldy that they could only fire seven times a day, their stones exploded against the walls like an earthquake and within a week had levelled a breach in the outer ramparts. Yet Giustiniani filled the gap with a stockade of wood and earth so powerful that the repeated attacks of the Turkish heavy infantry failed. When the sultan's sappers tried to undermine the ramparts, counter-mines were dug against them and they were buried or smoked out, and their galleries flooded. By sea, a great iron chain was stretched across the Golden Horn to halt the enemy's vessels. The Turkish squadrons were repulsed and their blockade broken by Genoese galleys. Undeterred, the sultan hauled many of his ships on greased planks over the hills, to float them in the Golden Horn at the rear of the Christians and bombard the Blachernae Palace.

Within the city, food and powder were growing scarce. A Byzantine vessel, after scouring the seas, returned to say that no Christian help was coming. Men now remembered a prophecy that Constantinople would

The luminous eyes of Theodora, the brilliant courtesan who became wife and adviser of the Emperor Justinian, vie with her opulent jewels in this 6th-Century mosaic in Ravenna, Italy —then part of the Byzantine Empire. A contemporary poet rhapsodized: "To picture Theodora you need one skill and one alone—the power to paint the sun."

5

stand so long as the moon waxed in the sky. On the night of May 24 there was an eclipse and three hours of darkness. Thereafter, the moon waned. A revered icon of the Mother of God was carried round the streets in solemn procession, but it slipped from the shoulders of its bearers and fell to the ground. Next day the city lay in dense fog, a phenomenon unknown in May. The Divine Presence was clouding itself, men said, and abandoning them. That night weird lights, which have never been explained, were seen by both armies, playing about the surrounding hills and hovering around the dome of Sancta Sophia.

On the nights of May 26 and 27 the Turks were seen, by the light of their flares, preparing for an immense assault. The next morning, the emperor assembled his commanders and nerved them for battle by reminding them of the glories of their classical heritage. Then he asked each of them to forgive him if he had ever caused offence, and in the shadow of death they embraced one another. The crowds began moving to Sancta Sophia. Towards nightfall the emperor himself rode there to pray. Then he returned to the Blachernae Palace to say farewell to his household and took up his post on the walls. In the small hours of the morning of May 29 the assault began.

It came in wave after wave against the tired defenders, beating against the outer wall, where the cannons of Urban had blasted the towers to stubs. The first assaults were repulsed and it seemed for a time as if the city might be saved. Then the Ottomans' elite corps of Janissaries— 12,000 men—advanced at the double. Giustiniani was shot through the breastplate as he defended the stockaded breach. His Genoese soldiers lost heart and carried him, wounded, to the harbour, leaving the Greeks to defend the battlements alone. In the north, someone returning from a sortie left open a little sally-port in the inner wall and a small body of Turks rushed it. Here, and from the breach nearby, the Christians were at last pressed back and caught in the defence ditches between their own ramparts, where many died. The emperor, with three followers, tried to rally the defenders and for a few moments held the gate in the inner wall opposite the breach. But it was jammed with Christian soldiers, fleeing now. Constantine then flung off his imperial insignia, hurled himself into the oncoming hordes and was never seen again.

# 3

# The Hold of Tradition

It is barely possible for a Western visitor to feel lukewarm about Istanbul; more likely he will be fascinated or repelled by it. The modern bustle that bewilders newly arrived Anatolian peasants strikes the Westerner as crazily oriental. The city's daily life—the secret, labyrinthine world of tenement and alley—puzzles and amazes him. How do they spend their time, he wonders—these fleeting faces at the smeared house windows, the thronging heads in the tea-shops?

The very streets seem, in their purpose, different from his own: they are less a channel for movement than an arena for living, and each kind of thoroughfare, from boulevards to alleyways, presents problems of its own.

Avenues called *cadde* cut across whole districts. Lined with banks and restaurants, ornamented by traffic lights that rarely work and monitored by policemen fruitlessly blowing whistles, these roads are so heavy with traffic that you may wait an hour to advance a mile. Trolleys, buses and taxis stuff them from end to end. Some of the buses—long single-deckers encrusted with grime—are run by the municipality. ("Fellow countrymen, let us not be ticketless," the conductors implore with archaic politeness. "Let us move along, gentlemen.") A ragbag of other vehicles includes the *Halk Otobüsler* or "People's Buses". Run by free enterprise, they may be converted trucks or vans as well as coaches; but all are hung with strings of blue beads—charms to avert accidents and the Evil Eye. Taxis—old, bruised American monsters that seem continually on the point of breaking down—are distinguished by a chequered line painted in black and yellow along their sides. Similar in shape and size, but marked with a continuous yellow line, is the *dolmuş*—meaning "stuffed" taxi—which carries several different fares at once. Grinding along close to the curb, and honking to attract would-be passengers, these communal cabs are barely more expensive than buses.

An ordinary Istanbul street—or *sokak*—inflicts miseries of another kind. Constricted by markets, stranded lorries, heaps of uprooted cobblestones, it forces the motorist to take unintended directions, or simply peters out. Its natural traffic is the horse and the pedestrian, and its name may be vigorously romantic: the Street of the Sweating Whiskers, Dwarf's Fountain Street, the Street of Ibrahim of Black Hell.

Finally there are the *yokuş* and the *çikmaz*—the true impenetrables. The *yokuş* is narrow and violently steep (life, the Turks say, is a *yokuş*); and the *çikmaz* is a dead end. Both are the playgrounds of children: tatter-demalions with black-currant eyes and insolent expressions. Up the *yokuş*

Wearing a corsage of bank notes that have been pinned to her gown by relatives, a bride attends a reception with her husband after a brief wedding ceremony at Istanbul's City Hall. Since 1926, when Atatürk introduced a secular legal code, only civil marriages have been officially recognized in Turkey.

and around the *çikmaz* they go—skipping, firing plastic pistols, battering one another with pieces of wood, whispering secrets, and kicking the irresistible football, for soccer is the city's passion.

But the streets do not lend themselves to loitering. Istanbul is probably the dirtiest city in Europe. Winds lift the rubbish from place to place; the litter includes dead pigeons, excrement, rotting fish, plastic dolls' limbs. Packs of dogs sleep in the clefts of the huge piles of garbage scattered across the city; and Stamboullu cats—long-bodied and of many dirty colours—roll, gallop, spit, howl, copulate and die in every corner.

This is the aspect that Istanbul presents to the newcomer. It is teeming, squalid and incomprehensible. Yet gradually the visitor may detect a pattern behind the chaos. Of course, this is not the superimposed logic of urban planners. Rather, it is a way of life transposed into the city from Asiatic villages, keeping its ancient structures and habits.

The three pillars of the old society are the family, the sense of community, and the mosque. The mosque's influence is pervasive but it is the aura of family and community that is most felt in the city's streets.

The hold of the family is still immensely strong. In the older and poorer quarters, it is normal for several generations to live together in one cramped house or flat. Even in daily work, a nepotistic network of friendships and alliances underpins both business and bureaucracy.

Within the family, the woman comes into her own. The home is the domain around which her life revolves; it is the theatre of her hopes and ambitions, her place of work. In theory, the equality of women before the law has been established since the time of Atatürk; today there are women in parliament, in the judiciary, in all the arts. But such emancipation remains typical of only a tiny, educated minority. Few peoples are more patriarchal than the Turks. An ingrained idea of man's superiority often reduces women to the status of objects; even today, man and wife are seldom seen together in the traditional quarters of Istanbul.

So the city's public pleasures—food, drink, sport—are the preserve of the male. Tea-houses, cinemas (which emphasize sex films and banal adventures), and cheap restaurants are filled almost exclusively by men.

The tea-house is the neighbourhood club and to enter one is to recognize immediately a national style. You hear no feverish arguments, few political discussions, little self-assertion at all. Friendships are warm but sober. Nothing could be farther from the mercurial Levantine spirit. Seated under trellises in summer, but more often crammed at evening into a smoke-filled, harshly lit room, the tea-house clients play backgammon, called *tavla*, or whist. In their square, workmen's hands they cradle little tumbler-shaped glasses on saucers. The tea may be drunk with sugar, but is never defiled with milk.

Tea has long been grown on the Black Sea coast, but it only became popular in Turkey after the coffee-growing area of Arabia—a former

A dolmuş, or shared taxi, carries a full load of passengers through Beyoğlu. Such taxis — usually roomy, old-model American cars — follow a fixed route and charge customers fares which are slightly higher than buses but much cheaper than ordinary taxis.

Ottoman province—was lost from the empire in the First World War. The tea-house is the descendant of the coffee house, which was itself introduced from Syria in 1555, then passed from Turkey to Vienna, and later became the "café" of France. In Constantinople, coffee became so popular that puritans fulminated against it. In 1600, with the introduction of tobacco—inhaled through the hookah, or water-pipe—the coffee-house became a double haunt of addiction. As in Europe, it was the rendezvous of literati and pamphleteers. "Puff-puffing in each other's faces and eyes," wrote a disgusted contemporary historian, "they made the streets and markets stink. In tobacco's honour they composed silly verses, and declaimed them without occasion."

The habit of smoking soon caused terrible fires in the city, and coffee-houses were condemned as centres of debauch and insurrection. Tobacco and coffee, said the religious, were two of the Four Ministers of the Devil (the others being opium and wine). In 1633 the ruthless Sultan Murat IV, himself a drunkard, destroyed all the coffee-houses he could locate. Men caught smoking or drinking coffee were hanged or impaled.

Today coffee-drinking is a decorous luxury, to be enjoyed in a restaurant or at home with friends. The art of roasting and grinding the coffee-berry is carefully observed; and the obligatory surface foam is produced by studious boiling. Turkish taste in coffee has changed not at all since the days of the Ottoman Empire, when the ideal cup was described as "sweet as love, hot as Hell, with a foam so thick you can stride across it in jackboots".

Draped in a small towel, a client at the 18th-Century Cağaloğlu Hamam in Stamboul lathers himself thoroughly, using water from an elaborate marble basin.

## Palaces of Heat and Steam

One of Istanbul's most venerable institutions is the *hamam*, or Turkish bath, where patrons can experience a new world of physical well-being for the equivalent of perhaps 25 U.S. cents. Derived from Roman baths, these establishments found special favour under the Ottomans because of the emphasis put upon cleanliness by Islam.

Although the spread of modern plumbing to private homes has reduced the number of hamams to 85—a quarter of the number that flourished during Ottoman times—they still hold a powerful attraction for Stamboullus. Strict segregation of the sexes is preserved by the provision of separate quarters or different bathing times for men and women.

Illuminated by a shaft of steamy sunlight, a bather submits to the sybaritic warmth of the "navel stone"—a marble slab heated from below.

As for smoking, the hookah has almost vanished. Instead, men puff their cigarettes of mild Black Sea tobacco. But occasionally a group of old-world philosophers will gather in a circle around the traditional pipes. In these, the tobacco called *tömbeki*—flavoured with jasmine—burns on a porcelain grille. The smoke is inhaled through a filter of scented water by means of a long, snaking plastic tube. Connoisseurs have their special amber mouthpieces—amber, they believe, is sovereign against germs. Their lips mumble in delectation. They suck and gurgle, and the smoke vanishes into their lungs in a cool fragrance, to be exhaled invisibly during drowsy conversation. A good bowl lasts half an hour and at its end the addicts have often fallen quiet altogether, calmed into an aromatic dream.

Another disappearing pleasure is the Turkish bath, which is enjoyed by both men and women, strictly segregated. Until 50 years ago, the bath rivalled the coffee-house as a meeting-place, and every district had one. The advent of running water in houses has brought about their decline, and the few that remain are now frequented mainly by the working classes —a luxury they can ill afford, even though entry is cheap.

In their arrangement the baths resemble those of ancient Rome, whose bathing system was inherited by the Byzantines and later adapted by the Ottomans. Each bath has three rooms. The first is the *camekan*, or dressing room. Here the bather disrobes, and here—when clean and possibly tender from massage—he will return to recline in a cushioned recess and sip tea. Next comes the *soğukluk*, a room that is now almost redundant; the bather merely passes through it, lingering for a moment to allow its warmth to prepare him for the heat to come. For in the *hararet* —a steam room equipped with marble basins and hot and cold taps for washing—the temperature may rise to 125°F.

The finest bath I entered was more than 200 years old. Wearing a towel and high clogs, I clattered into the *soğukluk*, where an attendant lay fast asleep among stacks of towels. It was here, in Ottoman times, that all body hair was removed by slaves, who applied a paste of quicklime, then scraped it away with the sharp edge of a mussel shell. In the women's baths, such services were often performed by a friend. "It is common knowledge," wrote an Italian early in the 16th Century, "that as a result of this familiarity in washing and massaging women fall very much in love with each other. . . . And I have known Greek and Turkish women, on seeing a lovely girl, seek occasion to wash with her just to see her naked and handle her." This no longer happens; but women still go naked, while men retain their towels.

When I entered the third chamber, I found myself in a domed hall, filled with steamy light, where men lay sprawled on marble slabs in postures of grotesque indolence. Columns, floors, side-chambers—all were of grey-veined marble. The place could have been a vestibule to Dante's Inferno. It shone with a weird, lustreless glow. Every noise echoed.

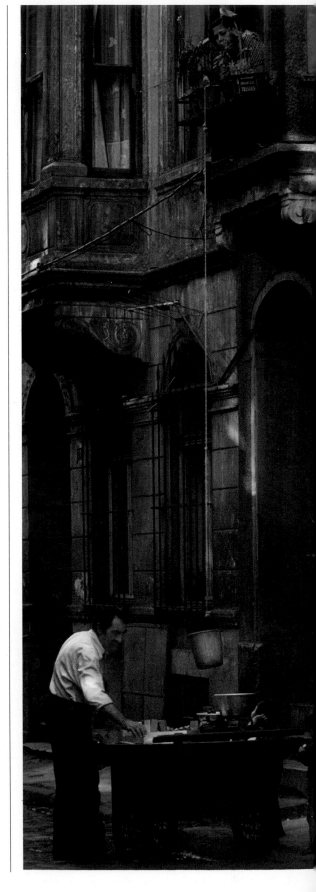

Shopping efficiently for groceries in a fashion widely practised in Istanbul, a Beyoğlu resident lowers a plastic bucket down to a street vendor. Many such merchants sell vegetables and fresh fruit directly to their customers at home.

I squatted at a magnificent baroque basin and washed myself, pouring water over my head from a plated bowl. In the vapour, phantom bathers came and went, clopping on wooden shoes. Others were being massaged by attendants wearing coarse cloth gloves, then dowsed in hot water and soaped—a sybaritic Ottoman leftover.

Such steam-halls are like a palatial prelude to oblivion. My body started to sweat, then to pour. And as I lay on the navel-stone—a huge, hexagonal slab heated from beneath by an unseen furnace—I gazed up at a dome filled with tiny round and star-shaped windows, so that in the haze I imagined I was staring up at the firmament.

The languid pleasures of the bath seem at odds with the temper of modern Istanbul. But the Turk's history has created a double image— puritanical peasant and helpless voluptuary—and he echoes this contra- diction even now. Who, for instance, would have thought that this hardy people could produce one of the classic cuisines of the world?

Yet the Stamboul working-man's restaurant is frugal. Its meals are served on fastidious little plates in an atmosphere of reticence. The waiters, like the customers, are always men. The restaurant furniture never varies: bare tables; unupholstered chairs; and a glass-fronted cabinet, heated from below, in which beans, chick-peas and assorted stews lurk in gravy. The walls are decorated with a weird disarray of pictures: the obliga- tory portrait of Atatürk, a text from the Koran, a nude woman—or all three.

Meat and fish are expensive. Rice and vegetables are not. So the worker's basic diet has changed little since Byzantine times, when he lived on bread, vegetables, and the cheapest fish in season. But nowadays a small piece of *karaman*—the strong-tasting, fat-tailed sheep of Asia Minor—occasionally relieves this regimen, along with a good lentil or spiced vegetable soup; there are also tomatoes or sweet peppers stuffed with flavoured rice and meat, or rice rolled in vine leaves to become a *dolma*. And the worker's meal may end with yoghurt or cold ground-rice pudding called *mahallebi*—flavoured with cinnamon, but sweet—which he loves. The only food he eats hugely is bread, piled automatically in front of him by the waiters, in quartered white loaves.

Many restaurants specialize minutely. Some devote themselves ex- clusively to rice puddings, others to meat-balls. Eating-places called *ciğer- ciler* produce tiny helpings of sliced sheep's liver, as if they were diamonds; while others called *işkembeciler* serve pieces of tripe skulking at the bottom of a cloudy soup. But the most common of the specialist restau- rants is the *kebab* salon, serving lamb or mutton. In its window, as like as not, a stuffed sheep accuses you with rheumy eyes as you enter. Inside, a charcoal grill is covered by morsels of mutton and by the meat-balls called *köfte*, which are served with a bowl of salad and beans. The lamb itself comes in many forms. *Pideli kebab* is enclosed in flat, oval bread.

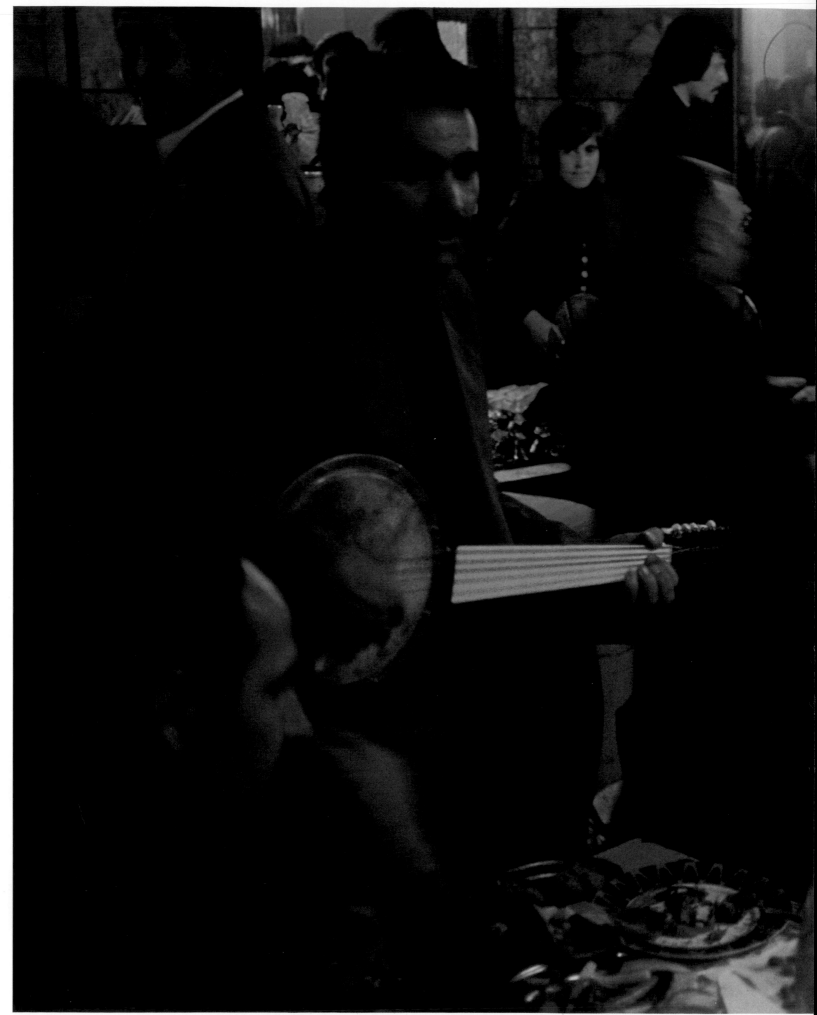

Strumming on a banjo, a singer accompanies himself in a Beyoğlu tavern which—in accordance with near-universal Turkish custom—is frequented by men only.

*Döner kebab* is shaved off a vertical spit of tightly packed meat turning against a charcoal fire. And in more expensive *kebab* salons, *şiş kebab* arrives on skewers, interlarded with tomatoes, onions and peppers.

The expensive restaurants, of course, are less common than those frequented by the working class. Many of them are in Beyoğlu; a few, in Stamboul. But the true Eden of gastronomes is in the dilapidated and convivial restaurants that line the Bosphorus almost to the Black Sea. Some are smart and exclusive; but most have a raffish charm. They overhang the water on rickety stilts, and their décor is a styleless pandemonium of chandeliers and fish-nets. In summer, sitting out under the moonlight, you may watch the great ships pass like moving Christmas trees, while you taste fried sea-bream or red mullet, and think gratefully of the tough Stamboullu fishermen asleep, perhaps, on the black waters of the Marmara.

In such restaurants a stupendous *meze*—officially an appetizer—may encircle you in 10 or 20 dishes of bewildering variety: artichoke hearts, fried gobbets of liver, sheeps' brains, two or three different salads, anchovies, *tarama* fish eggs, white beans, varieties of *dolma*, asparagus (called *kuşkonmaz*, literally "birds cannot settle on it"), and little hot pastry *börekler* stuffed with meat or cheese.

These, for the gourmand, will be followed by a main course: fish perhaps, or braised aubergines called *imam bayildi*, "the imam swooned" (because they were so good), or turkey stuffed with rice, liver, currants and pine kernels. The meal will be rounded off with fruit—perhaps the sweet red apples of the south—or by some of those syrup-drenched Turkish sweetmeats that dissolve beatifically in the mouth. You may see otherwise sober businessmen cramming these outrageous tidbits behind their teeth with expressions of almost pained delectation. Slobbering and smacking, they will devour a plate of *bülbül yuvasi*, "nightingale's nests", then seize a "lady's navel" or nibble at a cluster of mouth-shaped "beauty's lips"—lubricious pastries rolled in sugar syrup. Finally, with near-satiety, comes coffee and *baklava*—pastry layered with walnuts and syrup—or *helva*, a ground-up compression of sesame, butter, honey and nuts; and the meal ends, as did those of the sultans, with the jellied sweets the Turks call *rahat lokum*, "giving rest to the throat", and known to the West as Turkish Delight.

Such a meal will probably be washed down with alcohol. The Koran forbids wine; but, by a delicate casuistry, many a Muslim consumes other alcoholic drinks invented after the time of Muhammad. The Stamboullu loves his *raki*, a beverage of grape alcohol flavoured with aniseed. He can barely contemplate *meze* without it, and he swills it down with water—and a clear conscience. Other spirits, masquerading under distantly familiar names, turn out to be old friends, or enemies. Gin becomes *cin*; brandy is *kanyak*; and among several good liqueurs *Beyendik*—which in Turkish coyly means "We liked it"—is close to Benedictine in taste.

Customers at Markiz, a café in Beyoğlu that opened in 1902, take tea beneath a tile mural inspired by the art nouveau posters of the Czech artist, Alphonse Mucha. The combination of turn-of-the-century European décor and excellent Turkish pastry has established for the café an enthusiastic following among prosperous Stamboullus.

The Stamboullu has also taken to beer, which is sold everywhere. In particular, Beyoğlu's Passage of Flowers—a pedestrian alley lined with taverns—roars and riots its way into the night. Its tough, bawdy clientele, sprawled at beer barrels topped with marble slabs to form tables, can drink as heavily as the Turks of tradition—"not believing they have so much as tasted drink," according to a 17th-Century traveller, "unless they can feel the effects of it in their heads or their stomachs three days after".

Nor has the Koran's taboo on wine been rigidly obeyed. The bibulous Ottoman sultans revelled in the vintages of Cyprus, Samos and Tenedos, and even in the heyday of the empire the side-streets of the capital were littered with drunken Turks. Now Turkish wines are freely drunk. Most of them are unreliable—a pleasant wine one year may be undrinkable the next—but red or white Doluca and Kavaklidere are more constant.

Yet for the average Stamboullu no drink has quite replaced water. The meanest restaurant will set before him a bottle of cold mineral water, as much for his pleasure as for his health (tap water being suspect). Many springs are credited with healing powers; and their waters are sedulously stored, labelled, and sold from grocers' shops. One, it may be rumoured, cures gout; another relieves rheumatism, or boils, or headaches. *Taşdelen*, "rock-piercing" water, is full of minerals; *Memba* is a fine restorative; *Terkoz*, "wild hazel sweat", comes from the Black Sea hills; *Hamidiye* is a hard water from springs north-west of Istanbul.

In Ottoman times much ingenuity was devoted to the city's water supply. Almost every sultan, and countless lesser dignitaries, built fountains in the streets. So numerous are these lovely benefactions, carved with marble geometry or flowers, that they generally go half-noticed. Some are simple wall fountains: jets of water falling into stone basins. Others are elegant pavilions, their waterspouts enshrined by marble panels that are decorated with inscriptions as florid as the carved plants that surround them.

Still finer—and rarer—is the enclosed *sebil*, a type of kiosk from which water was once served free to passers-by. These happy foundations (whose waters have long since run dry) continue their usefulness today as tiny shops. The owners pass their wares—newspapers, toothpaste, ball-point pens—through exquisite iron grilles; and they are so oblivious of the borrowed glamour of their booths that they rarely know who built them. Sometimes the benefactor's grave lies nearby; and one Ottoman soldier, whose *sebil* in Beyoğlu has become a tea-house kitchen, is buried unhygienically beneath the fountain kiosk itself.

The tea-houses, the public baths—such pleasures are those of the city's old communities. But in the past 20 years there have grown up whole districts that have been wrenched from such traditions. Beyond Beyoğlu, in particular, high-rise apartment blocks lumber for miles into the distance. Here the old Ottoman society, based on religion and blood, has been reassembled into patterns shaped instead by wealth and education.

The styleless apartments of these suburbs are mainly the homes of upper-working-class and *petit bourgeois* citizens, who are beginning to acquire the superficialities of Western culture: a radio, a settee, a motor scooter. The father of the household, who may own a small shop or have a minor clerical job, lives very modestly; probably, in his leisure, he enjoys chess or bezique as well as backgammon; and perhaps he has a television.

Amidst this new, demi-educated populace—but living in flats a little grander or more central—is a growing middle class that reaches up through infinite gradations to an élite of lawyers, doctors, industrialists, bankers, and the poorly paid but prestigious civil servants. This new bourgeoisie speaks English as a second language and has largely replaced the old Stamboullu *haut monde*, which spoke French or Greek and lived in dignified mansions in the older sections of Beyoğlu.

The new suburbs, in fact, are the symbols of a new Istanbul, half-Westernized, consumer-oriented, less individual than the old. In its feature-less streets, the influence of two of the pillars of traditional society—the mosque and the local community—are slowly fading. Modern voices have arisen to challenge the old certainties. News is passed by radio, television or the press (some 27 newspapers are published in the city), rather than by word of mouth; and the power of the media is growing all the time.

Yet the modern radios play traditional Turkish songs. New appearances disguise old realities. Even in the Beyoğlu suburbs, time-honoured habits linger. The influence of the family—the clannish cohesion of the Anatolian village—remains as strong as ever. Respect is still paid to age, and visits among relatives are carried out with conscientious ritual. A few middle-class boys and girls now daringly go out together; but most do not, except in the company of relatives or friends; and as in Ottoman times, many marriages are arranged, still, by the parents.

Looking at the outskirts of Beyoğlu through half-closed eyes, you might imagine yourself in some placeless urban wilderness. But you are not. "Our high-rise apartments", as one resident remarked to me, "are really just vertical villages."

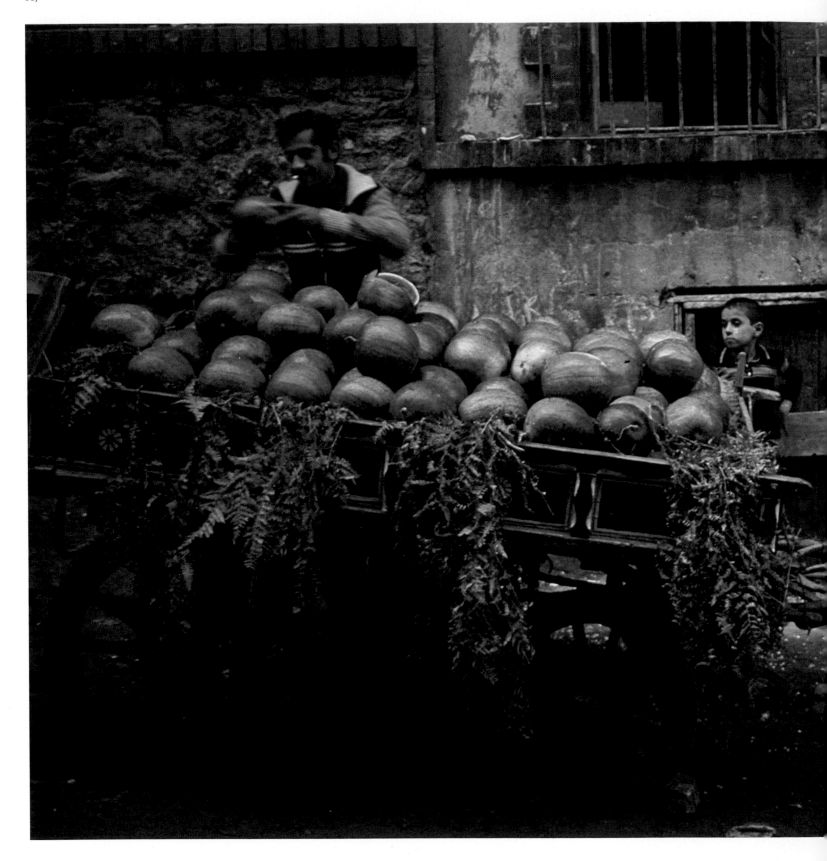

# Country Touches amid the Urban Tumult

PHOTOGRAPHS BY MARC RIBOUD

A water-melon vendor tests the ripeness of a fruit for a Stamboullu family. Horse-and-cart delivery of food is still commonplace in Istanbul's neighbourhoods.

In an alliterative phrase that is perhaps his best-loved legacy, Kemal Atatürk, the founder of modern Turkey, once told his people: "*Biz bize benzeriz* (We resemble ourselves)", which implies a disdainful refusal to imitate others. This spirit is reflected in Istanbul's division into scores of small communities whose inhabitants are little attuned to the mixing and mobility typical of most great cities. The neighbourhoods, many of them surviving from Ottoman times, have few amenities: houses are ramshackle, the lanes crooked and untidy, and the centre of local society is often no more elaborate than a cluster of shops or a fountain. But in compensation, these communities foster an easy-paced intimacy that seems the antithesis of urban existence; indeed, it resembles nothing so much as life in the Anatolian villages where most Stamboullus were born.

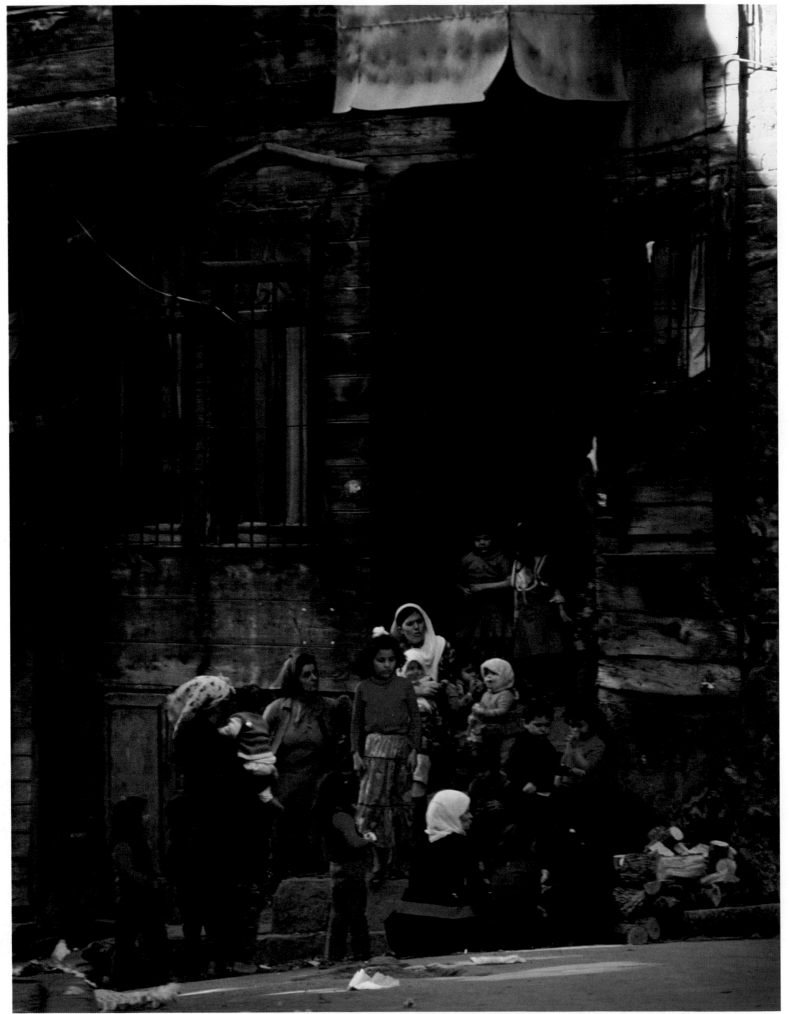

With their families in attendance, housewives gossip in front of a decaying home. Such casual gatherings are virtually the sole diversion for the city's women.

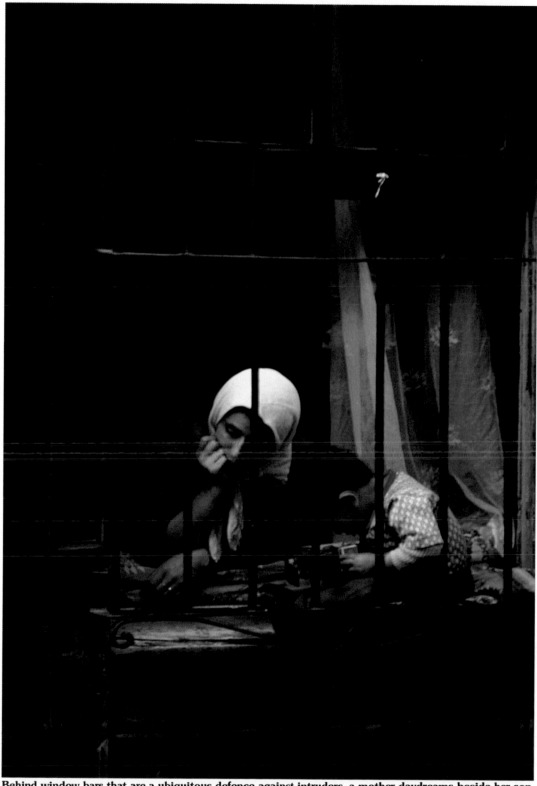

Behind window bars that are a ubiquitous defence against intruders, a mother daydreams beside her son.

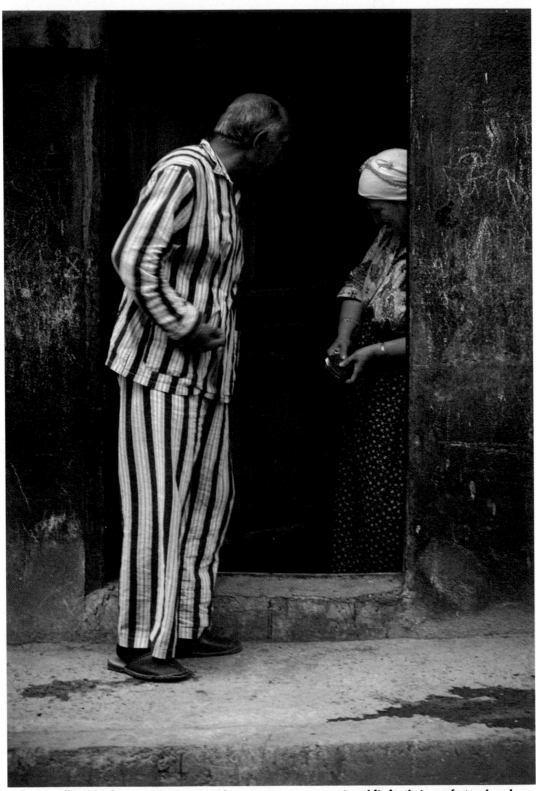

A Stamboullu embarks on a shopping errand in pyjamas—worn even in public for their comfort and coolness.

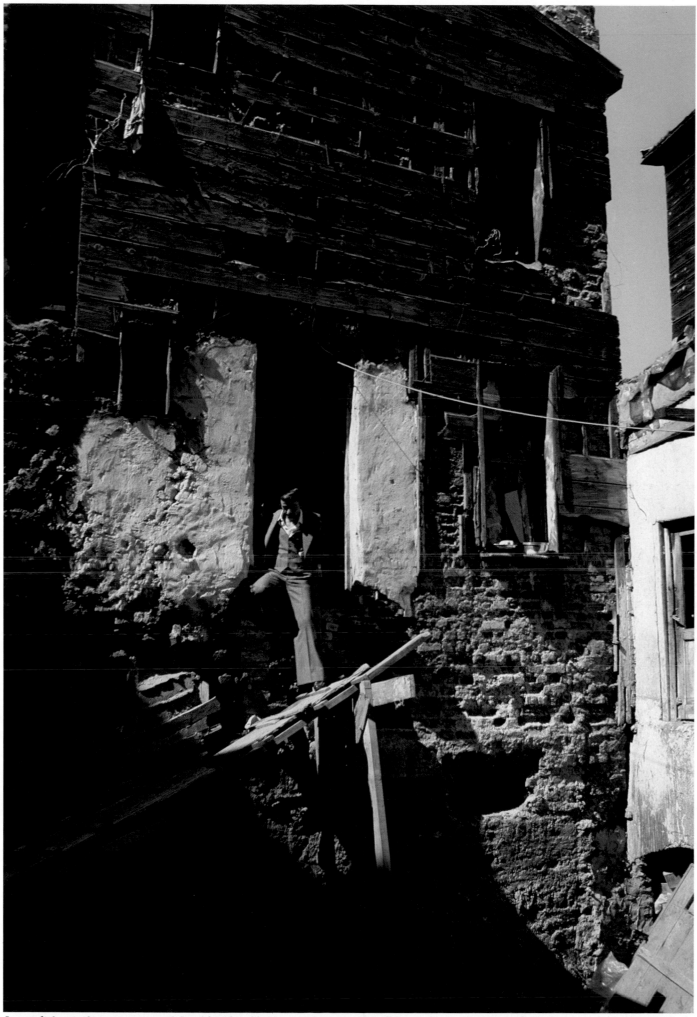

In a stylish suit that contrasts with his dilapidated home, a young man sets off for work, stepping gingerly down an improvised gangplank.

Seated outside an unprepossessing tea-house, a customer sips his drink and watches vacantly as a vegetable cart jolts its way along a roughly cobbled lane.

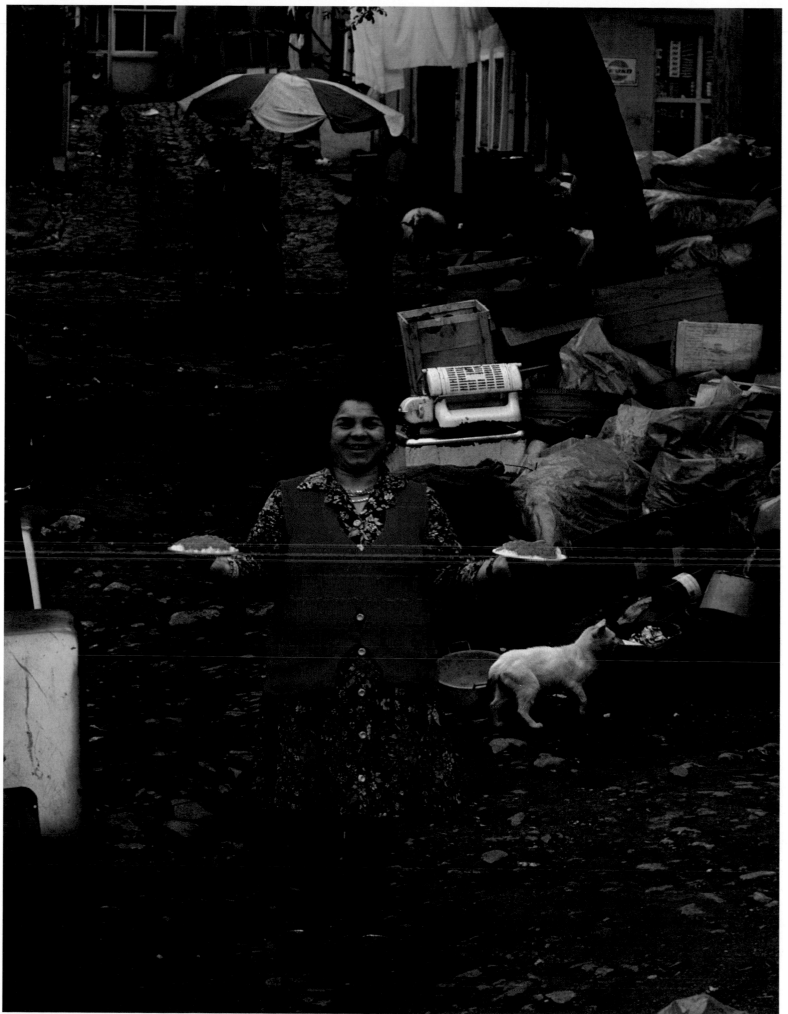

With a pile of rubbish as a backdrop, a housewife displays a favourite cheap meal—servings of chick-peas and rice obtained from a passing push-cart.

# 4

# Sanctum of the Sultans

In all the congested peninsula of old Stamboul—among the anarchic lanes, the labyrinthine markets, the traffic-laden roads—one area is silent. The tumult dies at the long, secretive point of the headland itself, where the sultans' Topkapi Palace spreads. Overlooking three waters—the Marmara, the Golden Horn and the Bosphorus—it lies like a self-contained city within an ever-deepening maze of walls and courts.

Dim-lit by night, veiled in trees during the day, Topkapi is amputated from the modern city like a poisoned limb. On the landward side its sombre fortifications, studded with square towers, move in a crooked line from shore to shore. Seen from the sea, it emerges above the foliage only as a range of conical chimneys and eerie battlements.

Yet here, for almost 400 years, was the heart of the Ottoman Empire. Named Topkapi, "Cannon Gate", for a heavily armed entrance in its sea walls, the palace was founded during the reign of Mehmet, the conqueror of Constantinople, and was expanded and embellished by later sultans until its buildings and courtyards stretched over more than 30 acres. By the 16th Century it had grown to house the school where the empire's high officials were trained, the vaults of its Treasury, the seat of its councillors, the harem—and the sultan himself. Five thousand highly trained and rigidly stratified personnel served and inhabited it: a slave-family that was masculine, feminine and, pathetically, neuter.

Few buildings remain from Mehmet's time, but much of the ground-plan has survived: four successive courts, each one smaller than the last, all fringed by parklands falling to the sea. In later centuries other sultans added to the palace, while fires swept many parts away. So today the four courtyards display a jumble of different styles and fancies: state rooms, pavilions, gardens, arcades, kitchens.

Each courtyard, in Ottoman times, was more private and more difficult of access than the last. Few foreigners ever penetrated beyond the second court; those who attempted to do so risked their lives. And the rooms of the Harem they never saw at all.

Today, the parklands have been turned into municipal gardens containing a giant archaeological museum and a zoo. The chambers of state and of the Harem are open to the public, and the sultans' treasures are displayed in a dazzling series of rooms in the second and third courts. Yet even now I entered the palace with a sense of penetrating the forbidden.

The vaulted Bab-i-Hümayun, "the Gate of the Majestic One", loomed over me as I passed into the first court. Long and irregular, more like a park,

The Ottoman Sultan Mehmet II pensively sniffs at a sprig of roses in a portrait by the court artist Sinan Bey. A sensitive patron of the arts, Mehmet earned renown as "the Conqueror" whose forces captured Constantinople from the Byzantines in 1453 and established the city as capital of the Ottoman Empire.

this outermost enclosure is flanked by walls of indeterminate age, ruins. Once they protected the arsenal, mint, bakery and other palace services— buildings that have disappeared. I noticed tourists strolling beneath plane trees; in the distance a line of buses waited. Nothing suggested the hushed fear that in past times always filled the yard, however crowded, with an awesome silence. (Even the officials' horses, thought an early traveller, had been trained to tread softly here.)

Some call this outer enclosure the Courtyard of the Janissaries (the Turkish *Yeni Çeri*, or New Soldiers), who may have kept a small guard here. Founded in the late 14th Century, long before any modern standing army in Europe, this élite corps developed into the most formidable fighting force on earth. It was recruited exclusively from captive Christian children who had been torn from their families. Hardy, celibate, their ties of family and nation forgotten, they were brought up in the Islamic faith and the use of arms. Their discipline, equipment and physique were alike superb. They owed allegiance only to the sultan, and so became his creatures, more than his own people were.

Even their appearance was larger than life. They wore boots coloured according to their rank—black, yellow and red in ascending order—and ornate and varied head-dresses: the plumes of the veterans cascaded in bird-of-paradise feathers almost to their knees. Their regimental insignia evolved from the cooking utensils around which they gathered on campaign. Their standard was a cauldron. The corps itself was called "The Hearth". A battalion officer was "Chief Soup-Maker"; and beneath him came a "Head Cook" and a "Head Water-Carrier"—homely names that came to breathe out terror.

Walking beneath the plane trees of the outer court, I found it difficult to resurrect these ghosts. Their wooden barracks have gone. The place is peaceful and rather drab. But it was at an innocent-looking fountain at the court's northern end that the imperial executioner used to wash the blood of beheaded victims from his hands and sword. On a marble block nearby—the "example stone"—the severed head was first displayed. The heads of officials were then exhibited, according to their rank, on the spikes or in the niches of the palace gates. If there was no room left, severed noses and ears were substituted. Since royal blood could not be shed, erring members of the imperial family were strangled with a silken bowstring.

Beyond this first court looms the Middle Gate. Flanked by octagonal turrets with conical spires, it looks both fey and sinister. Only officials and ambassadors ever penetrated beyond it into the second court. Each of the palace gateways marked a deepening and more perilous advance towards the sanctuary of the sultan.

Through the dark of the Middle Gate, I emerged into an imposing, cloistered garden. Five avenues radiated over its lawns to gates and buildings more than a hundred yards away. The grass was covered by wild-

**The 18th-Century Sultan Ahmet III scatters gold coins across the terrace of Topkapi Palace's Baghdad Kiosk in celebration of the circumcision of his four sons—shown in their beds in the pavilion at right. The painting comes from a volume cataloguing events of the 15-day festival surrounding the religious rite.**

flowers; and through tall cypress trees the sun spread dappled pools and rivers of light. The gazelles that once pastured here have gone; in their place grow rose bushes, and urns spill out an all-concealing ivy that turns them into enigmatic hillocks of green-white leaves.

The court is lined with buildings, all of them low. Its feeling is of business done not in council-halls, but in narrow chambers where the splash of a fountain foils eavesdroppers, in crooked passageways, in the silence of gardens and kiosks—or not at all. Everywhere the intertwined oases of rooms and courts invite murmured confabulations, intimacies, treacheries. The buildings, in fact, echo the structure of the Ottoman city: the life of the latticed window, the cul-de-sac.

The Divan, council-chamber of the imperial ministers, shares in this intimacy. Under elaborate eaves it abuts unobtrusively into the court—a domed room lined on three sides with low, cushioned seats. Here, from Saturday to Tuesday in the heyday of the empire, the sultan or his chief minister, the grand vizier, presided over the assembly of councillors. And even if the ruler was absent, nobody could be sure that he was not still there. For high in the wall, behind a grilled opening, was a chamber called the "Eye of the Sultan", where he sometimes lingered.

On days of council and on state occasions—the reception of ambassadors, the circumcision of a prince, the marriage of a princess—this second courtyard became a theatre of solemn, lavish ceremony, acted out in utter silence. Thousands of officials attended, their ranks identified by the shape of turbans, the fall of sleeves, the cut of beards. Viziers wore green, court chamberlains scarlet, teachers blue, lawyers violet. Their head-gear jostled in a fantastic sea: sugar-loaf cylinders two feet high with red bobbles; black or crimson fezzes plumed and bound in muslin; turbans heaped on the head like coils of whipped cream; butterfly-shaped structures dropping a veil behind; pointed black gnomes' hats—all massed together like a field of fabulous mushrooms above ceremonial robes fringed in sable and black fox.

Official duties were at all times minutely allotted; and palace life was portentous with the comings and goings of such imperial servants as the "Chief Nail-Parer", the "Great Turban-Winder", the "Custodian of the Heron's Plume" (which adorned the imperial turban), and the "Chief Keeper of the Nightingales" (which were treasured for their singing). Many Ottoman offices and customs descended directly from Byzantine ones; and just as in the Byzantine capital the cosy title of the "Great Domestic" concealed a state councillor who was the most powerful official in the empire, so in Topkapi the apparently menial "Head Gardener" controlled half the palace administration, including the guards, the harbour police, the executioners, porters, bargemen and a flotsam of minor offices.

Like the Janissaries, these high officials had been born Christian but reared as Muslims. In the select Palace School, supervised by the Chief White Eunuch, the pick of captured boys underwent a rigorous training for the imperial civil service. They might rise to become provincial governors, lords of the Treasury, members of the Divan, grand viziers. Even the harem was drawn exclusively from foreign races, so that within a few generations the sultans themselves had scarcely a drop of Turkish blood in their veins and the entire Ottoman Empire was administered in all its civil and military hierarchy by a slave-élite that was originally Christian.

For all its inhumanity, this regimen, which moulded the sons of peasants into statesmen and generals, created a court of pure merit. An astonished and admiring Habsburg envoy, Ogier de Busbecq, wrote in the 1550s that the Turks bred men with a care that Europeans lavished only on horses, hawks and hounds; and he remarked on his audience with Süleyman the Magnificent that "there was not in all that great assembly a single man who owed his position to aught save his valor and his merit".

In the golden reign of Süleyman, between 1520 and 1566, the transition of the Ottomans from warrior-tribe to cultivated nation was superficially completed. Surrounded by his Christian-born court, succeeding to the aura of the Caesars, he had inherited by conquest the leadership of Islam, and so assumed, like the emperors of Byzantium before him, a sacred majesty. The Europe of his day was dominated by great rulers—Charles V of Spain and Austria, Pope Leo X, Francis I of France, Henry VIII of England—but Süleyman was more powerful than any of them, unsurpassed not only as a warrior, but as an enlightened statesman and legislator. At a time when Europe was steeped in bigotry, he tempered a stern and pious disposition with tolerance. Still known to Turks as "the Lawgiver", he codified and simplified the statutes of his empire. Eastwards, his dominions stretched beyond the borders of Persia; westwards, to Morocco; southwards, to Yemen. His fleets probed the Atlantic and Indian oceans; he conquered Hungary and Rhodes, and in 1529 he came close to capturing Vienna.

A rigid protocol grew up about the sultan's person, as it had around that of the Byzantine emperors. His silken robes were worn once and then discarded. He ate off porcelain, alone. And every night, to avoid assassination, he slept in a different chamber of the palace, lit by giant tapers and watched by four bodyguards, who extinguished the tapers facing him whenever he turned in his sleep.

"He is 32 years old," wrote a Venetian envoy in 1526, "deadly pale, slender, with an acquiline nose and a long neck; of no great apparent strength, but his hand is very strong, as I observed when I kissed it, and he is said to be able to bend a stiffer bow than anyone else. He is by nature melancholy, much addicted to women,"—this was untrue; he was faithful to a single wife—"liberal, proud, hasty and yet sometimes very gentle."

In his day Istanbul was probably better policed and freer from crime than any city in the world. The bulk of its people lived simply, in wooden houses, sleeping on rugs. Their diet was mainly black bread, rice and fruit, which they ate off wooden plates with three fingers (the Moors used five, said a Turkish proverb, and the Devil two). Their only glimpse of their ruler was on Fridays, when he moved in procession to Sancta Sophia, which had been converted into a mosque. Four thousand Janissaries and cavalrymen led the way, followed by jewelled and caparisoned horses, and the high dignitaries of the imperial household. Then, accompanied by the officers of his privy chamber—the Masters of the Keys and of the Stirrup, the Bearers of the Turban and the Sword—the sultan appeared in scented robes on a white horse. But he was almost invisible to the gaze of the vulgar, because around him the helmets of his bodyguard threw out a bizarre cascade of plumes whose effect, wrote the Venetian, was of "a muslin canopy through which you could catch only the occasional glimpse of the Sultan's grave, stern face".

By the middle of the century the years were beginning to tell on Süleyman's physique. When anxious to impress ambassadors as to the state of his health, wrote Busbecq, "he conceals the bad complexion of his face under a coat of rouge. I detected unmistakable signs of this practice of his, for I observed his face when he gave me a farewell audience, and found it was much altered."

He died in 1566 during his seventh campaign in Hungary. For nearly eight weeks the grand vizier concealed his death from the army, which continued to fight battles and sack cities in his name. The covered litter of the sultan marched among the soldiery with the honours due to a living monarch, but it contained an embalmed corpse, at whose death the zenith of the empire had passed.

In the armoury of the palace, something of this fierce splendour remains. I wandered among cabinets of weapons: curved and damascened swords, like patterned snakes; gilded head-armour of horses; inlaid helmets and chain armour; Turkish bows with their slim arrows, which look as if they would have stung and pestered rather than killed; and last the crazily decorated blunderbusses of the 19th-Century Janissaries. Here, too, are the swords of Mehmet the Conqueror, their edges bitten and chipped; the evil and beautiful sabres of Süleyman himself; and the arms of subject peoples: Tartar bows from the Asian steppes, Mamluk battle-axes from Egypt, Persian scimitars.

But the most impressive amenities that remain from Süleyman's time are the kitchens, under whose 10 domed halls 150 cooks sweated. On an ordinary day the palace consumed 200 sheep, 100 lambs, 60 geese, 200 guinea-fowl, 400 chickens and much else. A state banquet might comprise as many as 50 dishes, served at a table of solid silver.

Yet the prodigality and order of the palace and of the empire depended on one man—the sultan—and he alone entered its hierarchy through the chance of birth, not merit. After Süleyman's death, for more than a hundred years, the sultans were nonentities. The seat of power lay not in the throne-room nor in the Divan, but through a small door, heavy with iron, in this second courtyard. It leads to the Harem—a maze of rooms, built from the 16th Century onwards and straddling the western sides of the court and of the third court beyond it. The Turks call this era "the reign of the favoured women"; and Süleyman himself precipitated it by moving the imperial harem into Topkapi from a palace in the city that had been distant from the everyday business of state. Then, in a rare and terrible lapse of humanity and sense, Süleyman executed his talented eldest son and heir on a groundless suspicion of treason. So he was succeeded instead by the indolent drunkard known as Selim the Sot; and for decades thereafter, as if congenitally unable to recover, the sultans were dominated by their women, whose experience did not extend beyond this iron door.

I approached the door with fascination. Outside, it used to be guarded by a picked corps—the Halberdiers-with-Tresses—from whose caps dangled two false curls to blinker their view of the women. Inside, in obscure antechambers, lived several hundred black eunuchs who watched and controlled the Harem. Their tiny, marble-paved rooms, with barred windows, rise in tiers off a dim-lit central passage—pathetically cramped.

Reliance on eunuchs was ancient in the East—it is recorded in Assyria in the 2nd millennium B.C.—and had been revived by the later Roman emperors. In the Byzantine court several of the most powerful officials and generals were eunuchs. The Ottomans inherited the custom; but because

A Topkapi tableau records the reception of a dignitary by Sultan Selim III at the palace's Gate of Felicity. Selim occupied the throne from 1789 to 1807.

performing castration was forbidden under Islamic law, it was carried out by Christians, from whom the eunuchs passed as gifts to the sultan. At first, white eunuchs from the Caucasus predominated; but by the 17th Century, the sultans had begun to favour black eunuchs from central Africa, sent by the Governor of Egypt. Castration produced extremes of character: cruelty and petulance, fawning subtlety and child-like credulousness. The eunuchs were prey to obesity, baldness, insomnia and loss of memory. Their love was given to children, pets—and sometimes, cruelly, to women. For impotence might not eradicate longing.

The eunuchs might be compensated by power. As the status of the Chief White Eunuch—the Master of Ceremonies—declined, that of the Chief Black Eunuch increased. He became not only manager of the Harem, but a member of the Divan and personal confidant of the sultan—the most feared, and bribed, official in the empire. Yet passing his chamber in the Harem, I realized that this resplendent figure—outlandish in his flowered silks and sashes, his pelisse with its ground-sweeping sleeves—retired at night to little more than a cell.

Beyond, I entered the quarters of the women themselves. A phantasmal strangeness pervades them. Dim corridors twist through a labyrinth of tiny rooms—more than 300 in all—linked by staircases and little courtyards where the sun scarcely falls. Here and there a wall shines with blue or sea-green tiles. I caught glimpses through barred windows of the meagre dormitories of the concubines, of dusty lanterns and baroque mirrors, and of passages winding through an empty twilight. The whole Harem, ironically, resembles nothing so much as a convent, whose nuns must have lived like shadows—hundreds of them, mostly ungratified and forgotten.

The overseer of these girls, in concert with the Chief Black Eunuch, was the sultan's mother, the Valide Sultan, whose rooms adjoined theirs. Her apartments, too, are modest, but intimate and civilized in a blend of Western baroque and classic Ottoman styles. Above wall-tiles and inlaid cupboards appear mural landscapes of the world the women would never inhabit—elysian hills and pale, watered valleys.

The sultan himself had rooms beside the Harem, where he would sometimes invite the women to join him during entertainments. Several of these apartments are bewitching. In the largest of them, the blending of East and West has produced a spacious chamber whose tilework is framed in plum- and gold-coloured friezes, pure baroque. Here musicians played on a delicate-looking balcony while slave-girls danced before their ruler. The furniture is gone, but the doors are still painted with swags of pastel fruit, and the ceiling with arabesques.

Other rooms, private to the sultans, are more lovely, more purely Turkish. Their walls shine with the stark, impenetrable beauty of tiles— flower-patterns almost overblown, but never quite. In the summer heat such chambers resemble shady orchards; in winter, immortal gardens.

On the headland of Stamboul, the 30-acre complex of Topkapi Palace, rising above a municipal park, overlooks the Sea of Marmara (background) and the Sirkeci Railway Station abutting the Golden Horn (foreground). Founded in 1459 by Sultan Mehmet II, the conqueror of Constantinople, the palace was greatly expanded during the next 400 years of Ottoman rule. It ceased being the sultan's residence in 1854, and today its restored pavilions and kiosks are open to the public as a museum.

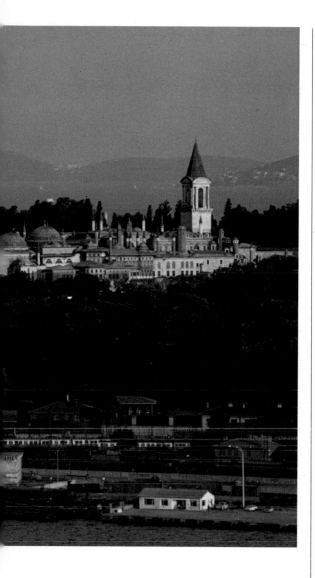

Their stained-glass windows wash them in blue light. Emptied of furniture, they are like caskets for some unimaginable treasure, now vanished.

But the concubines were generally excluded from such rooms. They were, after all, slaves. Captured, purchased or sent as gifts, and mostly Christian-born, they spent their days in idleness, in the gardens and the perfumed baths. Some took to jam-making or music; and they were, of course, schooled in the arts of pleasing and of love. Velvet caps, embroidered in gold and tilted at an angle, gave them a saucily seductive look, and their hair fell over one shoulder in long, jewelled tresses. Silken waistcoats and pelisses barely concealed their breasts, and even their curled-up slippers were spangled with pearls and precious stones.

Thomas Dallam, an English organ-maker sent in 1599 by Queen Elizabeth I to present one of his works to the sultan, was one of the few outsiders who ever glimpsed them. While installing the organ in the seraglio, he noticed a grille in a courtyard wall. Peering through, he saw several girls playing with a ball. They were, he said, extremely pretty: "No bands about their necks, nor anything but fair chains of pearls and a jewel hanging on their breast, and jewels in their ears. They wore britches of scamatie, and fine cloth made of cotton wool, as white as snow and as fine as lawn; for I could discern the skin of their thighs through it."

Their relations with the sultan were governed by a gracious ritual. When he came to visit them, wrote a Genoese early in the 16th Century, the girls were assembled in the courtyard by the Chief Black Eunuch, and the sultan would "pass along the line saluting them courteously, and if there be one who pleases him, he places on her shoulder in the presence of the rest a handkerchief, and walks on with the eunuch to the garden to look at the ostriches and peacocks, and many other birds which are kept there; and he afterwards returns to the ladies' apartments to sup and sleep; and being in bed he asks who had his handkerchief, and desires that she bring it."

The girl, meanwhile, had been the centre of frenzied attention. She had been massaged and scrubbed by slave-women with a mudpack of oil and rice-flour, all her body hair had been removed, her skin pomaded with henna to prevent sweating, her hair perfumed, her nails dyed, her eyes rimmed with kohl. The next morning, when the sultan went for his bath, she would examine the pockets of his clothes for money, which became hers by right. Then, after her name and the date were entered in a register, she returned to the Harem.

Few among the odalisques could have been so favoured. In the reign of the sensual Sultan Murat III—son of Selim the Sot—their number rose from the average 300 to 1,200 (among whom he sired 103 children). Those who aroused the sultan's interest were called *gözde*, "in the eye", and were immediately segregated and pampered; women whom he bedded became *ikbal*, "among the fortunate"; while the most favoured —never more than four—who bore him sons, took the title of *kadin*.

Such formality was important in a system that could crumble into licentiousness. Sometimes, of course, it did crumble. In the 1640s the maniacal Sultan Ibrahim, stuffed with aphrodisiacs, charged naked about the Harem like a bullock and eventually, either bored or suspicious of his concubines, had all 280 of them sewn into weighted sacks and thrown into the Bosphorus—a common execution for women. A few years later a diver, searching for a wreck off Seraglio Point, found these ghastly sacks still upright on the sea bed, swaying to an invisible current.

But the Harem was generally a place neither of horror nor of simple happiness. A twilight world of emasculated men and fretting women, its days were filled with petty feuds and jealousies. In their loneliness the odalisques fell in love with one another, with the eunuchs or with the castrated page-boys, who went by such flower-names as Carnation, Narcissus, Hyacinth. So frustrated were the women, wrote a Venetian envoy, that even cucumbers were given to them sliced, "to deprive them of the means of playing the wantons".

This pathetic waste continued to the grave. For, with a sultan's death, the whole of his harem was compulsorily retired, to end its days in an imperial residence in the city, which the Turks called the Palace of Tears.

Yet to many women the Harem was preferable to the drudgery of life outside. Peasant girls from the Caucasus even offered themselves voluntarily. As for the native Turkish women, neglected because of the Ottomans' preference for foreign slave-girls, it is hardly surprising that they became, as a traveller wrote, "lascivious within doores, and pleasing in matters of incontinency". Voluminously shrouded, they enjoyed total liberty of movement, and such was the uniformity of their white-cloaked shapes that their own husbands would not recognize them in the street. So they intrigued with little danger of discovery; even their lovers had no means of discovering their names.

Lady Mary Wortley Montagu, wife of an English ambassador to Constantinople in the 18th Century, saw these women in the public baths and thought them beautiful, with figures like Titian goddesses. But other visitors considered that the baths prematurely aged them, and deplored their smoke-blackened teeth and stooping shoulders. "For the most part they are fat," wrote an Italian, "because they eat a lot of rice with bullocks' meat and butter, much more than the men do."

By contrast, the beautiful odalisques of Topkapi could dream of succeeding the Valide Sultan—the woman who might rule the empire through her son—or at least of becoming *gözde*. This select group occupied luxury suites, whose terrace still overlooks a garden to the sea. Ever since 1909, when the last odalisque left, the rooms have been locked and deserted. The shutters of the windows are falling now. Inside, under cobwebs and rotted sheets, only the forms of a mirror or an old canopy are dimly visible, like memories discarded in the darkness.

In a miniature from an album chronicling the achievements of his reign, Sultan Süleyman the Magnificent holds audience from a throne set up beyond the walls of the Hungarian capital of Buda after its surrender in 1526. Süleyman's advances against Christian Europe were not halted until his armies were thrown back from Vienna after an 18-day siege in 1529.

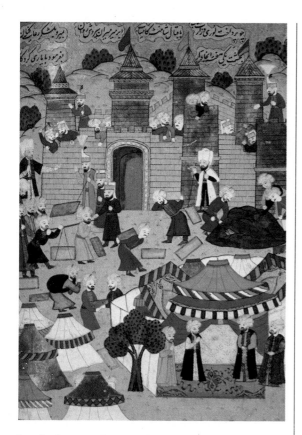

In a lively scene from a volume commemorating the deeds of Murat III, Turkish workers repair a castle captured by the sultan during his invasion of Georgia, a Christian vassal state of Persia in the late 16th Century. The Ottoman Empire reached its greatest extent under Murat's rule, encompassing almost eight million square miles of territory.

Among the taboos and preserves of Topkapi, the third court defined yet another depth of privacy. Those wishing to enter it passed to the end of the second court, ignoring the Harem entrance, and approached the Gate of Felicity that led to the sanctum of the sultans and the Palace School. Here, under the jealous scrutiny of the White Eunuchs who guarded it, they would kiss the gate's threshold and penetrate, if they were privileged, into the deathly silence of the third court.

It is intimate still, soft with chestnut and medlar trees, and with cypresses half mummified in ivy. The imperial throne room stands opposite the gateway; inside, the jewel-studded covers of the sultan's seat still exhale a barbaric splendour. All around the court the old state reception rooms and chambers of the Palace School have been converted to house the treasures of half a millennium. One building is devoted to the clocks that European rulers sent as gifts and that so fascinated the sultans; another contains illuminated manuscripts and miniatures; still another displays the imperial costumes.

The Treasury itself occupies half the court's eastern flank. Its halls are filled with diamond-mounted aigrettes and jewellery that must have turned the sultan into a walking sea of light. Here is another Ottoman throne, used until the sultanate's end—a pale blaze of gold and chrysolites; and here, in a gold sheath crusted with diamonds, hangs the Topkapi dagger, commissioned as a gift for an 18th-Century ruler of Persia, who was killed before he could receive it. Its hilt burns with three giant emeralds; a fourth, at the top, opens on a spring mechanism to reveal a watch.

I wandered through these rooms in alternating stupefaction and recoil. There is no implement of everyday life, it seems, that was not tortured into opulence. I passed cases full of jewelled spoons, a glinting gold cradle, quivers fat with pearls. And then there are the gems: sumptuous emeralds; rubies like huge wine-gums, uncut, meaningless; a whole mesmeric, dazing universe, so profusely set that wrought gold at last looked like mere copper, diamonds became glass.

Among the Ottomans, it seems, a lingering uncouthness mistook richness for beauty. Even gifts of rare porcelain from the Chinese emperors were given a hideous encrustation of gems by Turkish goldsmiths. Perhaps the greatest palace treasure of all is the collection of dusky green Sung and Yüan celadons, now displayed in the kitchens; it was discovered after the fall of the sultanate, still unused in its packing-cases from China, where it had lain for more than a century.

These are the wealth of Topkapi—these and the relics enclosed at the end of the third court in the Pavilion of the Holy Mantle. But here a different sort of treasure is enshrined. The pavilion's gaunt halls hold only a few exhibits, and they attract a hushed awe. Those who linger longest are not tourists, but Turks. A wisp of hair in a crystal reliquary, a plain bow, a footprint traced in broken stone—reputed relics of the Prophet

Two women play an African bead game.

A concubine dances to castanet rhythms.

## Glimpses of Harem Life

Although no foreigner ever saw how the sultan's concubines passed their lives, an indirect exposé of sorts was provided by a series of engravings published in France in 1715. They were based on paintings by Jean Baptiste Vanmour, a Flemish artist who lived in Constantinople. Well-acquainted with the Ottoman élite, Vanmour apparently gained access to the harem of a lesser official and sketched vignettes of enforced indolence that undoubtedly had parallels within the recesses of Topkapi itself.

A long-stemmed pipe helps pass the hours.

An attendant plaits a girl's hair.

After bathing, an odalisque relaxes.

A zither provides a pleasant pastime.

Coffee and sweets are served.

Muhammad, brought back by Sultan Selim I from his conquest of Egypt in 1517. Beyond them you may peer through a grille into a last chamber. Here a golden coffer encloses the rough goat-hair mantle of the Prophet; and in the casket beside it rests his banner, which the Ottomans, in times of crisis, unfurled against the infidel.

This hall is the bridge into the fourth and last court of the palace. It is less a court than a series of gardens and pavilions raised high above the headland. Emerging on to a marble terrace where a pool shines between kiosks, I found myself gazing along the length of the Golden Horn. The city lay below in sudden, shocking modernity. Traffic crawled and glinted. Ships prowled the inlet.

I walked to the kiosk that hangs at the terrace edge. It stands wide-eaved, like an elaborate cottage. Shutters and cupboards inlaid in tortoise-shell and mother-of-pearl, ceiling ablaze with decorative paintwork, it is the quintessence and paragon of all pleasure-domes. Sitting inside this radiant and very private creation, circled by sky-blue tiles, I could imagine its builder to have been a man of leisure and quiet refinement. But in fact a ruthless bull of a sultan, Murat IV, raised this near-perfect loveliness to commemorate his capture of Baghdad in 1638, in which thousands of innocent people were slaughtered.

The works of kindlier men have decayed. Weeds choke the pond on which an earlier sultan enjoyed sailing in a tiny boat filled with court buffoons; and beyond the Baghdad Kiosk the tulip gardens of Ahmet III are remembered only in terraces whose wrought-iron balustrades, rusting and dripping with plants, overlook a spreading desolation.

Ahmet, who came to the throne in 1703, was one of those gentle voluptuaries beloved of art historians. He inaugurated the Ottoman "Tulip Age" —one of the most hedonistic and irresponsible of times. The life of the court in those years seems to have been passed in an aesthetic dream of flowers, fêtes and poetry, so that the building of kiosks and the purchase of tulips from Persia or Holland became a mania that threatened to drain the treasury. In April, when the moon was full, the sultan would surround his tulip gardens with an amphitheatre of lanterns, cages filled with singing birds, and globes of coloured liquids that shone as if with their own light. Even his guests dressed in costumes of pre-ordained colours. On other nights, to entertain his harem, he had his slave-girls dance there, throwing golden balls to one another, while in and out among the flowers meandered tortoises with lighted candles on their backs.

This refinement, and this humanity, were short-lived. Like so much else, they depended on one man. The causes of the slow decline that eroded the Ottoman Empire from the 17th Century onwards were complex and many, but the degeneration of the sultanate was a vital factor. "A fish starts to rot at the head," as the Turks say. And decadence was now precipitated by a fatal practice. In previous centuries, on a sultan's accession, his

Portrayed as a 19th-Century artist imagined her, the Russian-born concubine Roxelana exerted a fateful influence on the Ottoman dynasty by so captivating Süleyman the Magnificent that he moved the imperial harem into Topkapi Palace in 1541. From a position close to the throne, Roxelana schemed to ensure that her drunkard son Selim would succeed Süleyman. The sultanate was weakened by harem intrigues for generations afterwards.

brothers were strangled to eliminate rivalry. But with the reign of Sultan Ahmet I in 1603, the custom changed. For the next two centuries, brothers of the sultan were instead confined above the Harem in a suite of rooms known as "the Cage". There, with only deaf-mutes and sterile concubines for company, they might remain for decades, yet would mount the throne if the reigning monarch died childless. The debauched Sultan Ibrahim had been immured in the Cage since the age of two, until his elder brother, the ferocious Murat IV, died unexpectedly. Mustafa I, who spent 14 years there, was totally demented by the time he emerged in 1617. After three months he was deposed to make way for his nephew Osman II, who was reputed to use prisoners of war as living archery targets, and became the first sultan—but not the last—whom the Janissaries killed.

Slowly the authority of the sultans declined. Throughout the 18th Century many provincial lords and officials pursued their vendettas and taxed their peasants without check from Constantinople; and the growth of inherited power in the more distant provinces loosened the whole fabric of the empire. At the same time a long series of wars with Russia sapped the Ottomans' resources. By the turn of the 19th Century, their armies were antiquated, though stubborn, and the Janissaries had become a force only of reaction and chaos.

At length, in 1826, the city's Janissaries were themselves exterminated by troops loyal to Mahmut II—a sultan who succeeded, a century after the tentative enlightenment of the Tulip Age, in starting his country on its long transformation from a medieval feudalism to a modernized state. Yet this goal was never achieved under the sultanate. The rulers who succeeded Mahmut were either ineffective, corrupt, or mad. Their empire splintered around them. They all but abandoned Topkapi for grandiose baroque palaces on the Bosphorus and their way of life became an unhappy *mélange* of Occident and Orient.

But from Mahmut's time onwards, a restless middle class had been growing, educated in schools of military and higher education based on European models. These men, trained for the sultan's service, came instead to dream of the political freedoms of Europe and America. Once again, in the timeless ebb and flow between East and West, Istanbul was becoming the recipient and the bridge of another culture.

# An Opulent and Secret World

PHOTOGRAPHS BY STEVE HERR

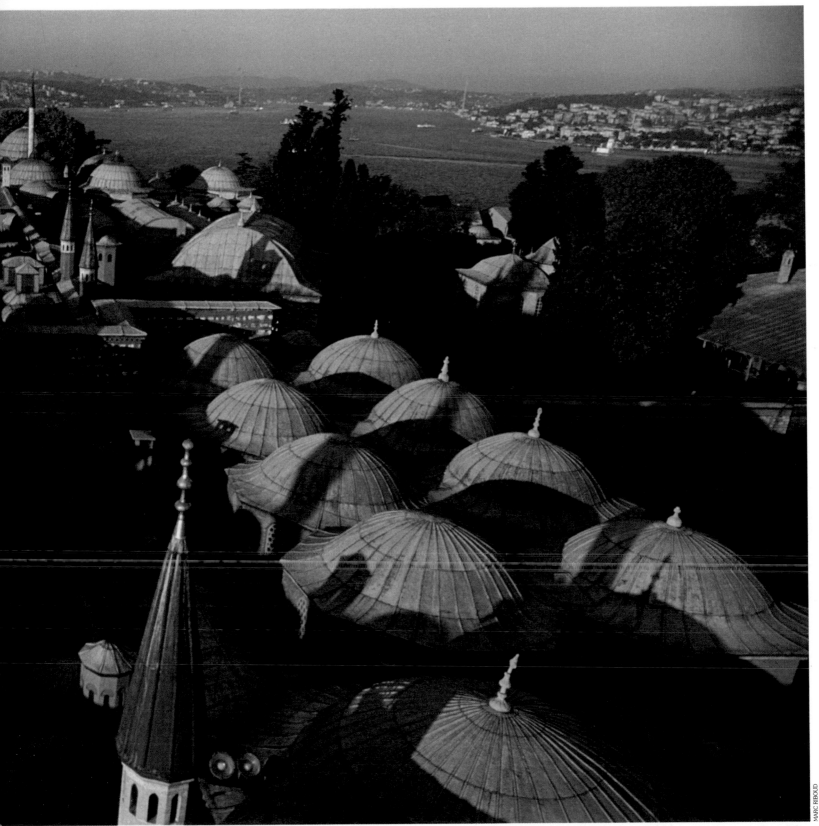

On a headland that juts into the Bosphorus, a forest of turrets and domes conceals Topkapi's Harem, uninhabited since 1909 but now open to the public.

Of all the buildings that make up Topkapi Palace—seat of the Ottoman sultanate for almost 400 years—none titillated the imagination of foreigners more than the imperial Harem. Here, within a maze of chambers never viewed by outsiders, lived the sultan's concubines, a cossetted battalion whose numbers reputedly reached 1,200 under one insatiable sultan of the 17th Century. The odalisques were guarded by black eunuchs and supervised by the Valide Sultan—the monarch's mother, herself a former concubine—who occupied apartments almost as generously decorated as those of the eunuchs were bleak. But the ultimate focus of this secret portion of Topkapi was the sultan's rooms, where the décor sometimes attained such a pitch of gleaming intricacy that it alone might have justified the Ottoman term for all of Topkapi: "Palace of the Shadow of God".

In a stage-like corner of the Valide Sultan's apartments, low couches ranged against the walls surround a four-legged tray on which meals were served.

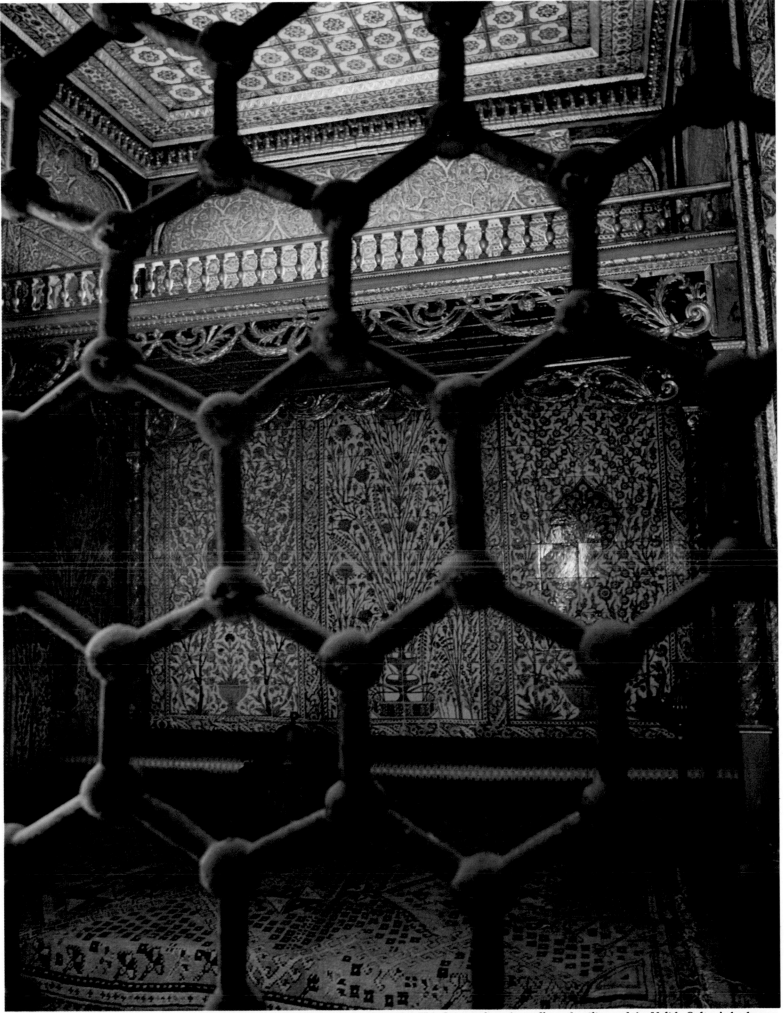

Seen through a corridor grille, gleaming blue-and-white floral tiles dating from the 17th Century line the walls and ceilings of the Valide Sultan's bedroom.

In a section of the Valide Sultan's rooms apotheosizing 18th-Century European taste, a window opens on to a trompe l'oeil view across a passageway.

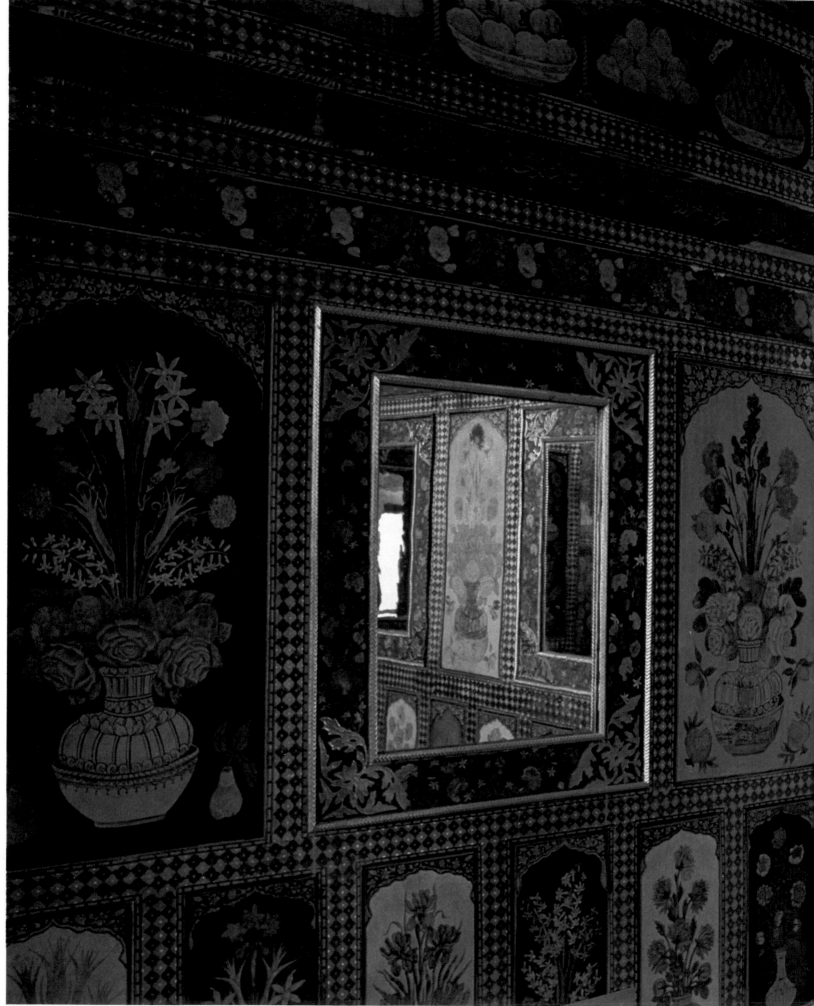

Paintings of floral displays and bowls of quinces, pomegranates and apples adorn the "Fruit Room", a sanctum of the 18th-Century sultan, Ahmet III.

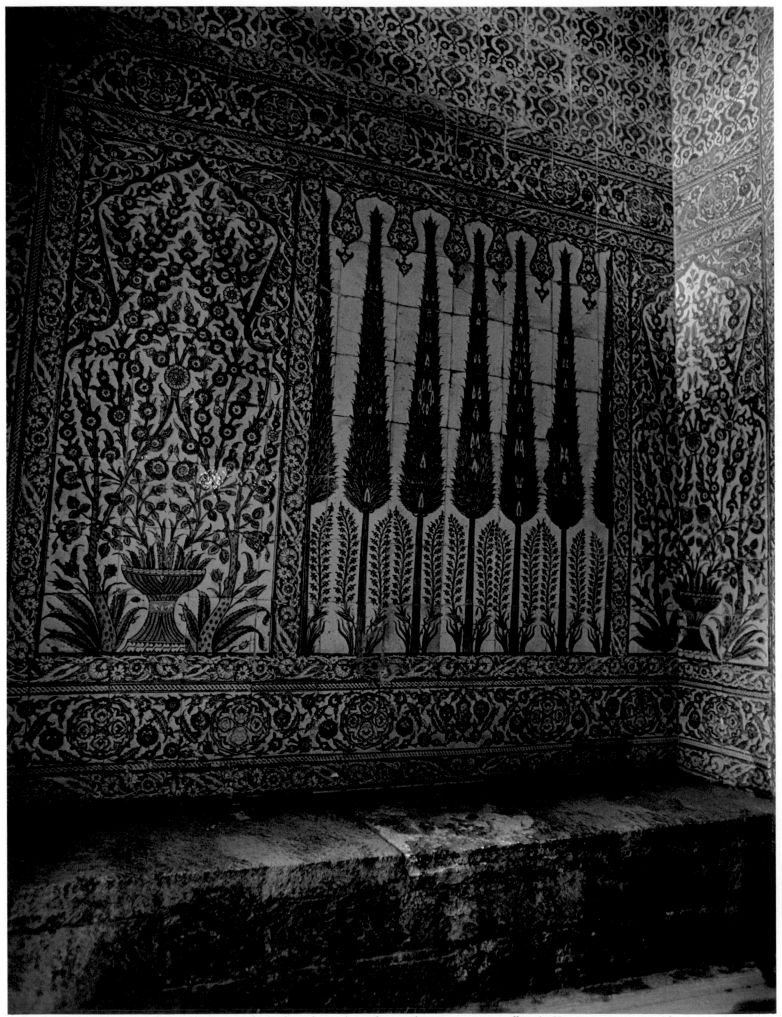

Stylized cypress trees, a popular motif among Turkish tile-makers, elegantly complement a soaring wall in the Harem rooms reserved for the black eunuchs.

Triple-tier dormitories for the palace eunuchs flank a corridor leading to a hooded fireplace. Quarters for the highest-ranking slaves were on the ground level.

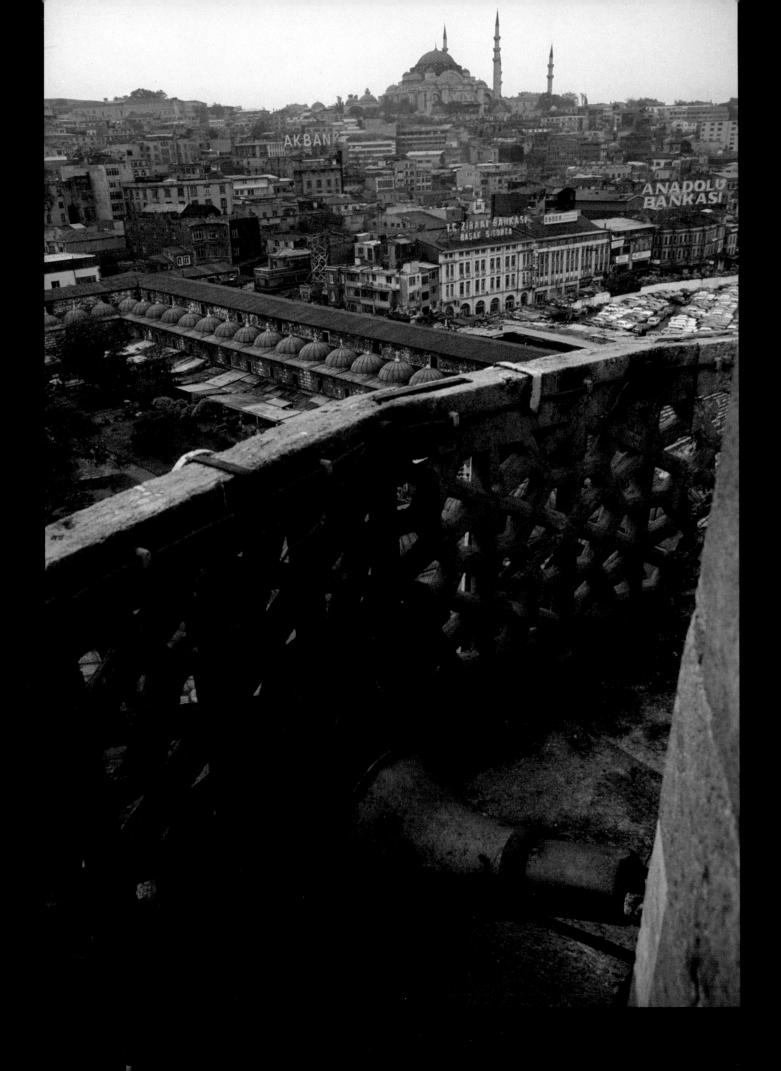

# 5

# The Pervasive Spirit of Islam

Istanbul has long been Turkey's religious heart. After Sultan Selim I won the title of Caliph—leader of Islam—by conquering the Mamluk rulers of Egypt in 1517, the Ottoman sultans became the acknowledged defenders of the Muslim faith, and the city partook a little of the magic of Mecca. Its most precious possessions were the mantle and banner of the Prophet Muhammad, brought back by Selim from Cairo; and the Ottoman Empire's struggle against the Christian powers in the north took on the passion of a *jihad*—a holy war against the infidels.

So, when Atatürk moved the capital of Turkey to Ankara in 1923, he tacitly repudiated not only the decadence of the older city, but a whole religious tradition. Religion, indeed, was Atatürk's chief concern. He saw that, in a nation whose whole life was dominated by the laws of God, the laws of reason could have no place. Wherever Islam barred the way to Western civilization—and this was almost everywhere—he determined to push it aside. For the next 16 years, until his death, he carried out an astonishing policy of secularization. Arabic script—the script of the Holy Koran—was replaced by Roman; and the brimless fez, so convenient for touching the head to the ground in prayer, was ousted by the Western cap. He disbanded the dervish orders—mystical Islamic sects that had grown powerful; he replaced Koranic law with the legal codes of European countries; he erased all reference to Islam in the constitution; and he forbade religious education in schools.

Yet, since Atatürk's death in 1938, the influence of Islam has again grown formidable. Colleges for imams—prayer-leaders—have been resurrected and produce a stream of graduates immersed only in a narrow Muslim culture. Schools for teaching the scriptures have multiplied by the hundred. Officially, Atatürk is almost worshipped—in ubiquitous statues, in texts pinned up on the walls of every municipal office—but the desires of the Muslim faithful are pulling fiercely in another direction.

It is remarkable now that the young Stamboullu is often more religious than his father. Older men, who were brought up under the reforms of Atatürk, may be indifferent to faith, even atheistic. It is the young, and those in early middle age, who crowd the houses of prayer. Often I have seen 60 or 70 men crammed into tiny mosques that would have been almost empty 15 years ago. Their worship is like a vigorous salutation—bowing, kneeling, standing together—impressive in simplicity and brotherhood.

The scriptural pillars of the Islamic faith are the Koran—the word of God given to Muhammad; the Traditions—a compendium of the Prophet's

Serving in lieu of a muezzin—the Islamic official who calls the community to prayer five times a day—a loudspeaker aims its messages outwards from a balcony of one of the Yeni Mosque's minarets. The traditional call must be electrically amplified because of the rising noise of the city.

sayings; and the Holy Law—a jurisprudence based on both. Muhammad, who was born in Arabia in A.D. 570, proclaimed himself the last of the great teachers in the Jewish and Christian tradition. He did not wish to annihilate the past but to crown it. So the Koran reveres the Biblical patriarchs; Christ is a prophet second only to Muhammad.

But Islam is less idealistic than Christianity. A Muslim sees himself as a servant of God, not as a son. God to him is unknowable; and the Koran, unlike the Bible, gives little insight into His nature. It only records His laws. Sin, in Islam, is no cataclysmic fall from grace; it is rather a breach of law. And a Muslim's consciousness of God's all-pervading power makes remote the possibility of His personal love. The God of the Koran is both compassionate and merciless; the fatalism in Islam derives from an acceptance of this omnipotence and is the logical outcome of a deeply believing temper.

The Muslim's approach to God is very simple. Five times a day, if he is pious, he enacts a solemn ritual of worship—laying out his prayer-mat, often in the fields or by the roadside, wherever he happens to be, and reciting prayers and passages from the Koran. Every Friday he will join the noon worship in a mosque. And once a year, in the month of Ramadan, he fasts so strenuously that nothing—not even a cigarette or a sip of water—may pass his lips from dawn to dusk. At its end the Turks celebrate the Şeker Bayram, or "Feast of Sugar", a time of eating sweets and giving gifts. And two months later comes Kurban, when thousands of families, even in the city, slaughter a sheep or goat in memory of Abraham's sacrifice.

Simple, too, is the average mosque. In its courtyard stands an ablutions fountain, above it a minaret. Around it lies a small cemetery—a sacred enclosure whose dead may never be disturbed. Inside, it is less the house of God than the lobby of His servants. Its focus is the *mihrab*, a niche oriented to Mecca. Its furniture may be only a high pulpit and a dais where the imam sometimes reads the Koran. The little hall is clean, functional. An amplifier, perhaps, sits on a shelf, ready to transmit a prayer-summons to a loudspeaker atop the minaret. A glass chandelier holds electric bulbs.

But almost all the worshippers will be male. Islam is a very masculine faith. Many women never go to mosques at all, and if they do, they are segregated, usually on a balcony. The Koran is written for men and stresses their dominance; and so inbred is the sense of female inferiority before both God and man that all but a small middle class assume that women constitute a lower order of being.

I remember once sitting in the courtyard of a Koranic school in Istanbul surrounded by some 50 tense and silent men, while a woman friend of mine asked the imam about the revival of Islam. It was distressing to see how the charity and dignity of this religion, so admirable in its directness, evaporated in the presence of a woman. The imam made me sit between himself and her, lest her closeness corrupt him. We occupied three stools around a mosque fountain and I thought for a moment that he would make

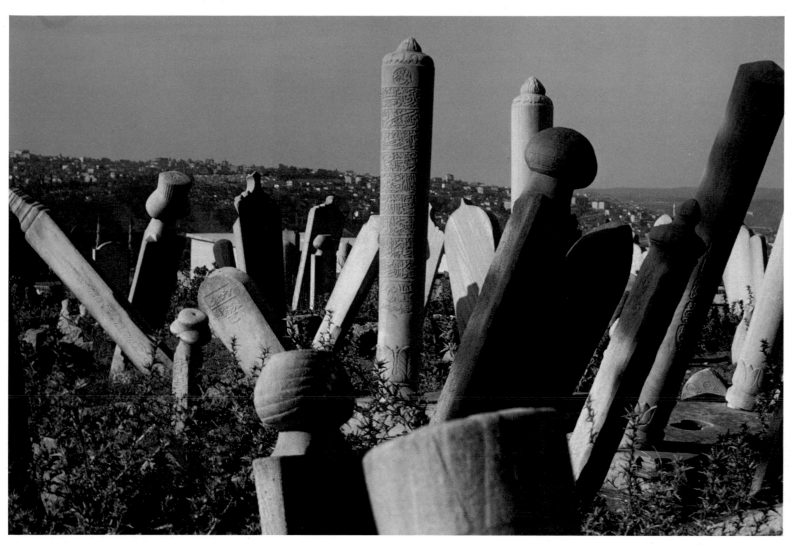

At a hilltop cemetery in north-west Stamboul, old Turkish gravestones have been thrown into lopsided confusion by the slow settling of the soil. Stone turbans, carved above the two monuments in the foreground, identify the rank of the men interred, while most of the women's memorials are capped by floral designs.

her wash. Instead, he said: "Islam is growing and will continue to grow. Nothing will stop it. These questions you ask me are all very well, but there are more important things. First, who made you? Who made the world?"

She said: "We've come to ask you."

"Who made you?" he asked again. "God," he answered. "Repeat."

She did.

"Who made the water, the sky, my clothes? God made everything and we are his slaves. The water is his slave. The rocks are his slaves." All the time he spoke he excluded her from his vision, sitting with eyes closed behind spectacles, as if he were concentrating upon the heavenly spheres.

"You heard about the Taksim massacres?" he asked. (Two days before, 34 factory workers in Istanbul had been killed in an attack by unknown terrorists.) "Why do you think such a thing happened? Why? Because none of those people had Islam. They were without religion."

"But you said everything was commanded by God," she answered, growing irritated. "Wasn't God responsible for this too?"

His soft-lipped mouth opened very small in a greying beard, while his round face and smooth skin gave the impression of some childlike oracle. "God creates men's being," he said, "but it is man who acts it out."

She murmured: "So that's how you see it."

"That is how it is."

Such certitude, which for centuries laid its dead hand on the Ottoman Empire, has again become a force in politics; and Istanbul, as the age-old centre of religion, is a spearhead in its return. Its most extreme embodiment has been the National Salvation Party, whose programme, which includes the restoration of Arabic script and of Koranic law, would reverse all that Atatürk accomplished.

I watched a belligerent demonstration of this party as it moved down the Divanyolu, the spine of old Stamboul, towards Sancta Sophia. Atatürk converted the great monument from a mosque to a museum, and now the Salvation Party wanted to convert it back into a mosque. The party leader had proclaimed that he would pray in it that day, and his followers, some 10,000 of them, moved towards the building in a vigorous, ordered march. Some were students, wearing clean white shirts and faintly pampered expressions. ("You wait," said a smartly dressed Turk beside me. "As soon as supper time comes, they'll be going back to their mothers and saying what a jolly day they had.") But most had the hardened faces of low-paid factory workers or the tan of recently arrived peasants. A kind of concentrated bitterness possessed them. As the march grew in purpose and in harshness the smartly dressed Turk fell silent. The men came on and on, shouting slogans in unison and striking upwards with their arms.

But the great Orea Porta, the "Beautiful Door" of Sancta Sophia, was closed against them. Some 400 police and heavily armed troops stood in front of it. The procession halted and built up around the shrine until it filled the open spaces and jammed the street. For hours its leaders harangued the seething army. Sometimes it seemed less like a crowd than a waking monster that might sweep away troops, police and gates by a casual pawing. But slowly, as the hours went by, the anger and the people drained away. Some caught buses home. Others, I noticed, went into mosques, there to become again the impersonal servants of God.

Yet their power—the power of reawakened religion—cannot be dismissed. Secularism may gild the Turk's mind; but his heart is old in piety.

Although Sancta Sophia is lost to Islam, the great imperial mosques, built by Mehmet and his successors, remain centres of devotion and pride. The wheeling sun—shining on their multitudes of domes, semi-domes, buttresses and turrets—turns them, like the shaking of a great kaleidoscope, into ever-changing patterns of brightness and shadow. From east to west they dominate the Stamboul skyline: the Blue Mosque; the Beyazit among tombs and trees; the Süleymaniye crowning them all; the elaborate Şehzade; the rebuilt Fatih, "Mosque of the Conqueror"; the colossal simplicity of the Selimiye.

All these were built to a classic pattern: domed prayer halls, generally broadened by semi-cupolas and preceded by arcaded courtyards of a stern simplicity. This formula was first tentatively approached in the Fatih, completed in 1470, soon after the Ottoman conquest; but the mosque was destroyed by earthquake 300 years later, and rebuilt in a dull pastiche. So the oldest of the imperial foundations today is the Beyazit, started in

## A Celestial Emblem

The national emblem—a five-pointed star set beside the horns of a crescent—is omnipresent in Turkey's largest city. On the Turkish flag (above), the celestial signs fly in tandem against a red background, a design adopted by Sultan Selim III in the early 19th Century. But the origins of the two symbols date to more distant times and are befogged by legend. The crescent, according to one story, was adopted by the citizens of Byzantium in 340 B.C., after a waxing moon had emerged from the cover of clouds in time to expose and foil an attack on the city by King Philip of Macedon. The star is said to have been added in 1459 by the astrologically minded Sultan Mehmet II.

In modern Istanbul, the motif shows itself in countless ways. It appears outlined in light bulbs on a fence in Beyoğlu (top row, left); it decorates the funnel of a Bosphorus ferry (centre row, right); and it is even imprinted on Turkish playing cards (bottom row, left), the sale of which is a government monopoly. Today, the composition of the insigne is strictly prescribed by law. But in earlier times the elements were used in multiple arrangements, or one or the other was sometimes dropped: for example, an old drinking fountain in the Grand Bazaar in Stamboul is topped only by a burnished crescent, embracing cobwebs rather than a star (centre row, centre).

1501, whose domes and wide-spaced minarets still crowd the skyline.

But the greatest of the mosques date from the mid-16th Century, when the city was blessed by a rare conjunction of patronage and talent. The patron was Süleyman the Magnificent, "Lord of his Age". The talent was that of the architect Sinan, a captured Christian, probably Greek, who became Imperial Architect when already in his late forties and who for the next 50 years adorned the empire with his works. European comparisons—Bernini, Wren, Fischer von Erlach—pale before the stupendous output of Sinan. He recreated Constantinople in the image of imperial splendour. Even today, more than 80 of his buildings remain—mosques, hospitals, public baths, schools, shops, fountains, tombs.

From the beginning he was haunted by Sancta Sophia. This one building, it might be claimed, inspired a whole architecture and passed, wraithlike, into the definitive form of the Ottoman mosque. But Sinan did not merely copy. From the start he pursued techniques of his own. His first great achievement in the city, the Selimiye, is extraordinary for its simplicity, balancing a shallow dome on a square chamber, without galleries or arcades. By the 1540s, he aspired to the complexity of the Şehzade with its lavish ornament and ribbed domes. And finally, in the 1550s, he enshrined the memory of his patron, and the glory of a whole era, in one of the classic sacred complexes of the world: the Süleymaniye.

The approach to this monument is almost casual. A crooked climb, the last twist of a street, and suddenly its terrace hangs above. Yet all is on a titanic scale. For half a mile, insect-like, you follow a perimeter wall perforated by the barred windows the Ottomans loved. Nowhere better can you see and touch the reticent, grey-white beauty of the city's stone.

Inside this wall the outer courtyard, more than 200 feet long, is merely a socket from which the soaring bulk of the mosque lifts in a sombre counterpoint of dome and buttress. It dominates the whole complex by the sheer height and volume of its stone. The massing of dome and semi-dome, the rings and arcs of windows, round or pointed, all mount in giant steps to the calm of the cupola that crowns them without vanity. In all this sculptural mountain, only the gold finials of the domes throw a gleam of colour. Nothing evokes better the grandeur and austerity of Süleyman.

Approaching it across the courtyard I felt this grandeur intensify. I entered a second, smaller forecourt that gives access to the mosque itself. From its corners, four minarets flowered high up into lace-like balconies. Porphyry and granite arcades surrounded it; and beyond them, to the east, the mosque's domes surged and multiplied so high that the pigeons fluttering there looked like grey butterflies.

I pushed aside the leather flaps covering the doorway and entered a hall 150 feet high. Like Sancta Sophia, which Sinan hoped to surpass, it balances a giant dome between two semi-domes. But the darkened vistas of the older church are here replaced by a crystalline order. The

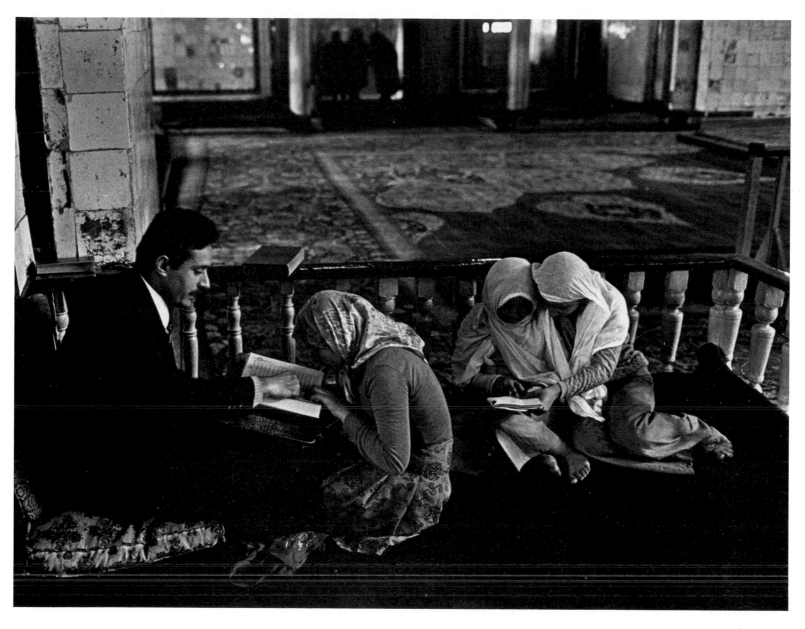

In a corner of an Istanbul mosque, a young girl learns to read the Koran in Arabic under the guidance of an imam, while two other youngsters pore over an exercise book. Memorizing the Koran in its original language is regarded as a central element of Muslim education, but only males are encouraged to interpret or argue over the meaning of the holy book.

arcades are narrow and high. There are no galleries. The whole interior is washed by a clear light.

To a Christian, this austerity may seem empty. But a mosque is not a shrine. It does not lure the worshipper up and forward, as a church may, to some half-defined point of mystery. Rather, it is a theatre for the quiet of Muslim worship. In particular, the domes and arches of the Süley-maniye do not hover and coalesce as do those of Sancta Sophia. They stand bright, defined, whole.

I began to walk. My feet fell silently over a scarlet blaze of carpets. High up, the stained-glass windows lacked any medieval richness; but their flower-like patterns hung in beads of bright, congested colour.

I wandered out into the sun, among other buildings grouped about the courtyard. The imperial mosques were always attended by a host of charitable foundations. Those of Süleyman were unrivalled, and included six religious schools, a soup kitchen for the poor, a primary school, a hospital, a medical college, baths and shops. Such complexes were like self-contained towns. Food, lodging, hygiene, education, worship—a religious man could spend his life here, like a snail in an all-sufficient shell.

Of Süleyman's foundations the religious schools to the north of the mosque, flowing down a steep slope on five different levels, are particularly

Pigeons thronging the courtyard of the Yeni Mosque are showered with maize by a member of its staff. Local Islamic tradition treats the birds as semi-sacred.

charming and original; but they are starting to decay and have been occupied by gypsy squatters. The schools on the south side have been converted into libraries, centred on pretty formal gardens; the primary school is now a reading-room for children. The baths have become a workshop, the medical college a maternity clinic, and the hospital a printing house for the Army. Finally, the domed and chimneyed galleries of the soup kitchen serve as an Islamic museum, filled with carpets, Turkish and Persian miniatures, and furnishings in wood and ivory, as if an atelier of ants had been weaving, painting, carving for a millennium.

This mighty but strangely cold complex of Süleymaniye softens into delicacy in one other place. By a marble fountain that no longer flows, an exquisitely fretted wall encloses the garden where, in a little domed tomb, Sinan himself lies buried.

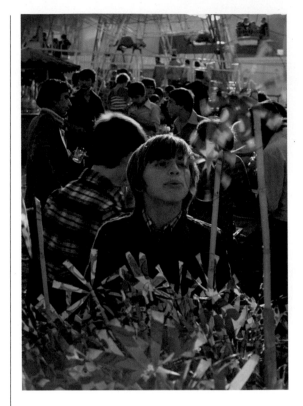

Many such complexes—whether founded by a sultan, a vizier or a wealthy official—are woven into the city's fabric. Some continue their old service; but more often the buildings have been turned into hostels or offices or, in ruin, have become the homes of rag-pickers. From the window of the lodgings where I used to stay, in a street called Alemdar Caddesi, I could look down into the courtyard of a theological school built by the great Sinan for the Chief Black Eunuch in the service of Süleyman. Its arcades were walled up by wooden boxes, forming an enclosed corridor in which a poor family lived. Boys kicked footballs between the pillars and the fountain had decayed into a tumbledown flower-bed. Beside it, seated pleasantly in the sun, old women knitted together while history disintegrated about them.

All over the city such schools, ranged about open courtyards, are distinctive for their clouds of little cupolas and goblin chimneys turbaned in stone—each one covering a student's cell. Many now are havens of silence: domed libraries set in gardens, inhabited by a few scholars. Of the schools designed by Sinan, some seduce by the charm of disorder or surprise; others fulfil their purpose with an inspired architectural economy. His Rüstem Paşa school, for instance, is an octagon within a square—cells around a courtyard, baths filling out the corners, fountain in the centre.

Ottoman architecture and its decoration, perhaps by mutual stimulus, reached their zenith together. As the great mosques were rising on their hills, the faience tiles which were to be their loveliest feature were approaching perfection. By the second half of the 16th Century, the empire's great tile works at Iznik, 50 miles south-east of Constantinople, were producing designs in new, rich colours. To dark blue, turquoise, mauve and leaf-green was added coral-tinted clay—a beautiful colour—that stood in low relief under its glaze. These shades, on a matt white background, were used to portray flowers in schemes of ravishing intricacy.

Only a handful of buildings were ever clothed in such tiles in their

Immediately after the month-long fast of Ramadan, a Muslim family reward themselves for their abstinence by celebrating the Şeker Bayram, or "Feast of Sugar"—a three-day festival when sweets are distributed to the children. At left, a youngster tests a plastic windmill on sale at one of the many fairs that open in the city during the Feast.

perfection. Their walls shine with a jungle of vegetation at once cool and sensuous. Tulips, carnations and wild hyacinths mingle and twine minutely among fantastical, pollen-laden peonies, bifurcating across window-shaped panels as if espaliered there.

Within 50 years, the Iznik factories were in decline. The secret of the coral colour seems to have died with its discoverer. The great age of Ottoman architecture was itself coming to an end, and its decay is mirrored in the last great imperial mosque to be founded in the capital: the Blue Mosque of Sultan Ahmet I, finished in 1617.

Its construction, in a time of disaster abroad and unease at home, was an act of imperial piety and bravura. "Three whole years were employed in laying the foundations," wrote the historian Evliya Çelebi. "The workmen penetrated so far into the earth that the sound of their pickaxes was heard by the bull that bears up the world. . . ." After its completion, he added, its six minarets, lit up by 12,000 lamps, resembled fiery cypresses.

Viewed through the chestnut trees and gardens that separate it from Sancta Sophia, the froth of its domes and the rise of its pencil-fine minarets create a feel of ethereal graciousness, almost of unreality. Inside, the enormous hall, lit through stained-glass windows, is open yet mysterious, a world of submarine colours. The only noise is that of two grandfather clocks given by Queen Victoria during the Crimean War, which strike the hour with a mellow dinging at the wrong time. The twilit feeling of the building stems from the shine of its tiles, in which blue and sea-green predominate, and from the blue paintwork that covers arch

A cluster of girls, dressed in scarves and long coats identifying them as students at a Muslim school, wait at a Stamboul bus stop. Muslim private schools, banned by Atatürk in 1924, were again made legal in 1947, and religious education is now compulsory even in state-run institutions.

and dome. The dome itself is upheld not by subtly integrated piers, but by four intrusive, elephantine pillars.

By the 18th Century, fascination with things European—especially French—was affecting Turkish taste, even in mosque design. The results were at best stylish and buoyant; the curvacious arcades and kiosks of the Nusretiye Mosque in Beyoğlu, for instance, seem a place for a banquet rather than a prayer. From then on, the West began to mesmerize the East. Already there were being planted the seeds of today's schizophrenia—the conflicting claims of Islam and modernism, of Asia and Europe.

The graveyards of Istanbul are as ubiquitous, and often as beautiful, as its mosques. From the huge cemeteries of Karaca Ahmet on the far side of the Bosphorus to the fields of tombs along the walls of Stamboul, the city is locked in its dead. Even in Istanbul's heart, cemeteries are inescapable. Whichever way you approach the city, wrote a 19th-Century English traveller, "it is through a burial-ground; you cannot pass from one quarter to another but through a burial-ground; you look out of a window on a burial-ground; your only promenades are in the burial-grounds".

The consciousness of death pervades many Turkish attitudes. It leads to sayings about the uselessness of hurry and of too-strenuous endeavour. The dead, in fact, are not viewed with Western apprehension, but with a philosophic equanimity that turns a graveyard into a parable on mortality.

A few of the dead are even elevated to the status of folk-saints. In life, these holy men were probably dervishes, preachers, or even madmen

On a traffic island in Istanbul, two flocks of sheep, their backs still showing the dye applied by shepherds in order to mark them for eventual slaughter, wait to be auctioned off to Istanbul families during the festival of Kurban—a commemoration of the sacrifice offered up by Abraham. At right, Stamboullus bundle their purchase into a car; after the sacrifice of the sheep, its meat will be distributed to the poor.

(lunacy was thought to be a visitation from God). But in death a legendary sanctity accumulated about them. Their fame spread. Their feats of arms, if they were warrior-dervishes, grew prodigious. If they were hermits, the wild beasts of the forest were said to have eaten out of their hands. And at last their real lives vanished under a conflation of hearsay and fantasy, until they were believed to have whispered into the ear of God Himself.

In many a tumbledown graveyard some fenced-off sepulchre shows signs of intermittent veneration: a few candles, a piece of cloth. The grave of one folk-saint—for a reason I could not discover—is surrounded by water-bottles. Some of these tombs attract both Muslim and Christian worshippers. Women stand with their hands opened upwards in an ancient attitude of supplication, knocking on the grille to attract the saint's attention, kissing it and whispering petitions. Often they ask for specific things—above all, for the health of a relative: the saints are the physicians of the poor. To a woman, in particular, they are more approachable than is the remote, cosmic God before whom her menfolk kneel. A saint, after all, was flesh and blood like her. He listens, he understands.

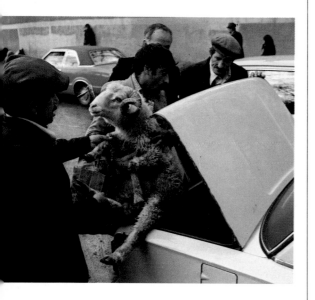

In north-west Stamboul, the tomb of Rahine, daughter of a 16th-Century dervish, is visited by women seeking a husband. I once saw a whole group of teenage girls there, offering up desultory pleas, followed by two portly spinsters who did not seem to have lost hope. Near Sariyer, up the Bosphorus, is the grave of a folk-saint called Telebaba, to which brides go after their weddings. This saint appeals to middle-class Muslims, who arrive in motorcades. The bride's car is bedecked with ribbons and carnations stuck on with tape, while a monstrous doll (an image of the longed-for baby) squats on the bonnet. Upon the saint's grave the bride leaves a little tinsel from her head-dress, as a prayer for fertility.

Even men may sometimes find it easier to circumvent God and canvass the favour of a saint instead. "It's hard to ask God directly for things," an old man explained to me. We were walking in a cemetery above the Bosphorus, where I had come for quiet, and he for prayer. "Why should God answer us?" His face, frosted by a walrus moustache, looked sad. "So I get the saint to ask for me. That way I have a better chance." Under his dusty trilby hat, he looked like a long-jobless civil servant. Around us, among cypress trees, the tombstones leaned and tumbled like crowds of dissolute dancers, overgrown with brambles and pink roses. The headstones of the men's graves stood tall and rounded, like clubs, topped by carved turbans and fezzes. Those of the women were sculpted with flowers.

The old man pointed out different graves to me. "Here's a minister. You can tell by the type of turban. You can tell each of these men's station like that, just as if they were alive." He walked up a brambled path. "Over here there's a princess. Look, you can see the date." We strayed through a museum of stone headgear, upright, tottering, fallen: turbans of pasha and eunuch—all the hierarchy of Ottoman administration. The slabs laid flat over the graves were pocked with small cavities to catch rainwater for the birds: a last charity of the dead. Their headstones were carved with epitaphs in decorative Arabic scripts.

The old man paused at some modern graves. "Look at that writing. It's so ugly. It just gives names, dates." Then he gestured at a slab carved in Arabic. "But the old work is beautiful. I was brought up to understand this writing." His eyes began to water as he read:

> *"What is destiny?*
> *Before a half of my desires' fulfillment*
> *I was taken from the world.*
> *That is destiny—*
> *But God will resurrect!"*

He smiled faintly. "A woman's grave. And that's a proper inscription!"

Such small cemeteries are touched by a benign neglect. Even the larger ones may be little tended, and many of the imperial tombs themselves are forgotten jewels, locked up and decaying.

Yet around other sultans' tombs, such as that of Süleyman the Magnificent, a cult almost of emperor worship persists. Süleyman is buried in a flower-filled cemetery behind the Süleymaniye Mosque. His tomb is a tall, octagonal chamber, such as the Turks built all over Asia Minor. Inside, its walls are cased in fine tiles, its ceilings painted in intricate patterns of black, gold and dark red, set with winking slips of glass.

At the tomb entrance I came upon a group of men in carefully pressed suits, crouched in the wind and praying; while within, beyond a rope barrier, an old peasant moved in reverence counter-clockwise around the grave.

The caretaker was furious with him. "Stop! Come out! Don't you know? You're not meant to pass the barrier. You're not meant. . . ."

But the old man merely completed his circuit, then slowly, as if still in the presence of majesty, walked out backwards.

In a smaller and still lovelier tomb nearby lies the woman known to the West as Roxelana—a graceful creature, probably Russian by birth, who from the multitudes of his harem captured Süleyman's heart and became his sole consort. Her influence was sinister—she caused the sultan to execute his first-born son—but the deepness of Süleyman's regard for her is witnessed by their marriage (only rarely did a sultan marry) and by the proximity of her tomb to his. Staring through its windows (the door is firmly locked) I saw that its walls, rising to a height of 28 feet, were covered with a paradise-garden of tiles, bright as the day they were laid. On either side of the entrance, they showed skeletal trees that flowered into white blossoms with red hearts, while the lunettes above the windows shone with stylized feathers and peacock eyes.

The shrine of Mehmet the Conqueror, which stands behind his mosque, is another centre of pilgrimage. It was at the Conqueror's first-built tomb

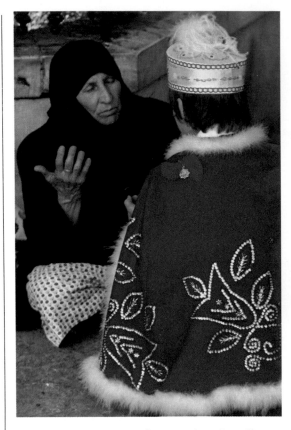

**Dressed in the ceremonial cape and cap he will wear during his circumcision the next day a Muslim boy observes local custom by communing with a fortune-teller. Every Islamic male must undergo circumcision, usually at the age of 10 or 11. The rite is performed at home and is the occasion of a joyous party attended by friends and relatives.**

that the triumphant Ottoman armies used to hang their battle trophies. But the tomb was thrown down by an earthquake in 1766; and in its place I found a heavy baroque mausoleum, its inner walls and ceilings painted in a splendour of dimmed gold and silver, crimson and blue. In the gloom an unlit chandelier glistened like a cluster of icicles. I waited in the entrance while an old woman pushed past, her body folded over her walking stick and her mouth quivering with prayer. The caretaker was reading the sports news inside. Entering, the old woman murmured as if in panic fear, over and over: "Ah God, God. Ah God, God, Thou art great. Ah God, great God. . . ." I heard her grey-stockinged feet shuffle to the head of the grave and there she froze, as if transfixed, for a full 10 minutes.

Such prayers are often misdirected. In the stone-flagged garden by Sancta Sophia I saw men worshipping at the grave of Selim the Sot, the dissolute son of Süleyman and Roxelana, who died after slipping in a drunken stupor and smashing his skull on the floor of his baths. In the same tomb are buried his five youngest sons, strangled, according to the Ottoman custom, to ensure the rule of the eldest, Murat III. Nearby, in the tomb of Murat himself, the tiny cenotaphs of 19 of his own sons, strangled according to the same custom, lie pathetically among the graves of their happier sisters, who died of natural causes.

Certainly there are holier places of pilgrimage. Up the polluted inlet of the Golden Horn, where boats and landing-stages rot side by side, lies the sacred quarter of Eyüp. Here is the reputed grave of the standard-bearer of the Prophet Muhammad; and it was here in Ottoman times that the sultans, on their accession, were girded with the sword of Osman, founder of their house. Now the district, filled with funerary mosques and tombs, has become the garden of the pious.

Through these sad and beautiful avenues of death, I entered the courtyard beside the standard-bearer's grave. I found it to have a charm all its own. Against its tottering plane trees hung pigeon-cotes, whose inhabitants, fed by the faithful, covered the courtyard floor. Herons had slung their nests in the branches high above, and filled the air with sad cries; while round about, and in the hollow clefts of the trees, weary-looking storks stood on their crooked red legs, one apiece, like wounded soldiers. Storks, in particular, are favoured in Islam, because they migrate southwards over Arabia and are thus believed to make the pilgrimage to Mecca every year.

I came into a hushed inner court. On one side rose a mosque, a baroque building full of light; on the other, the tomb-chamber, crowded with worshippers, where the grave of the standard-bearer was encased in silver. This is among the holiest shrines of Islam. The pilgrims, massed before the grave, made no sound. I watched them with awe. Their prayers were so quiet that I heard only the distant passage of an aeroplane, like a meteor from another world, and the soft, distressed cries of the herons.

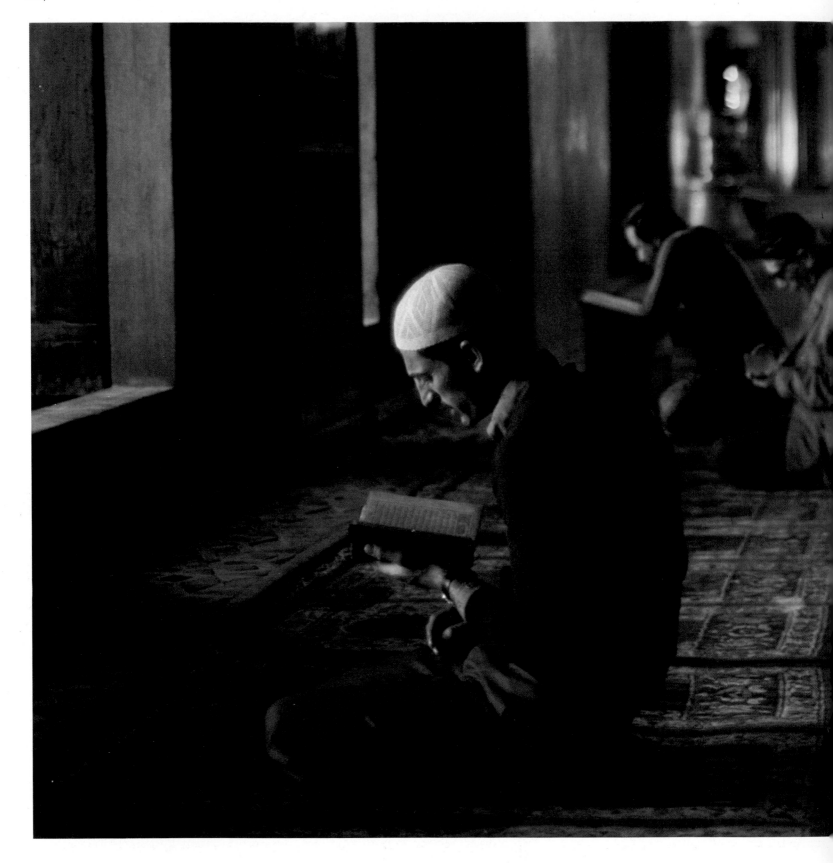

# Oases for the Faithful

PHOTOGRAPHS BY MARC RIBOUD

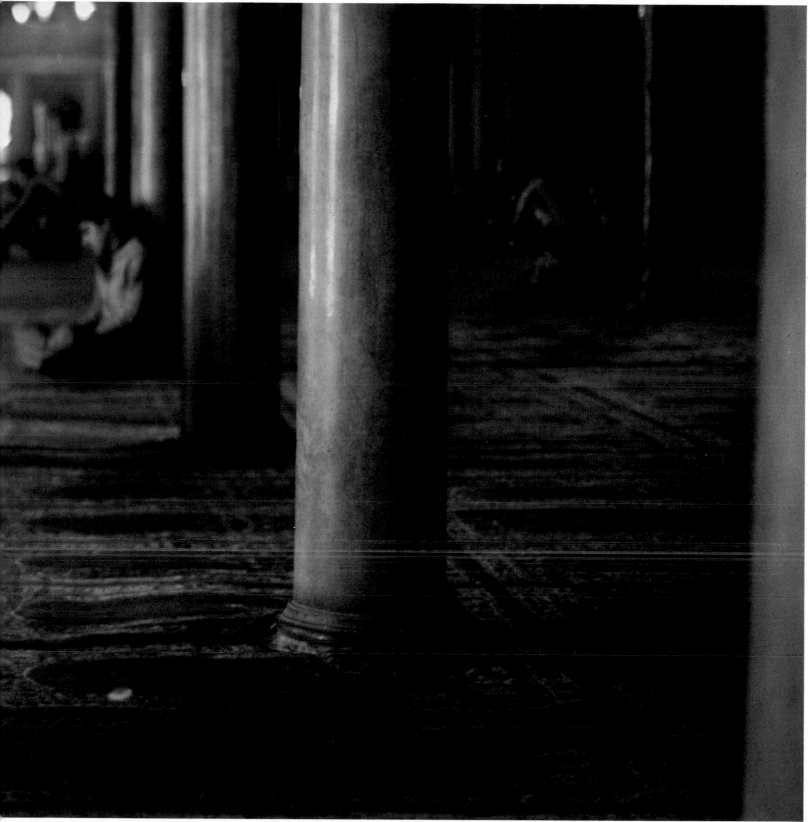

**Meditating on the Koran in the Blue Mosque, devout Muslims sit facing Mecca, where the Prophet Muhammad lived and preached during the 7th Century A.D.**

Like oases in the desert lands where Islam arose, Istanbul's mosques are focal points of the world around them. Every mosque has a courtyard and water-taps or a fountain where the faithful perform ablutions before entering the house of worship for the simple, but all-important, ritual of prayer. This ceremony —performed five times a day by devout Muslims—can be enacted alone or in congregations that are guided by an official called an imam. At the beginning of the prayers, a Muslim stands with his palms turned upwards and says, "God is most great". Then, bowing and prostrating himself, he recites passages from the Koran, Muhammad's record of divine revelations. Finally, sitting on his heels, the worshipper pronounces the *shahada*, a creed that crystallizes his faith in two ringing phrases: "There is no god but God, and Muhammad is His Prophet."

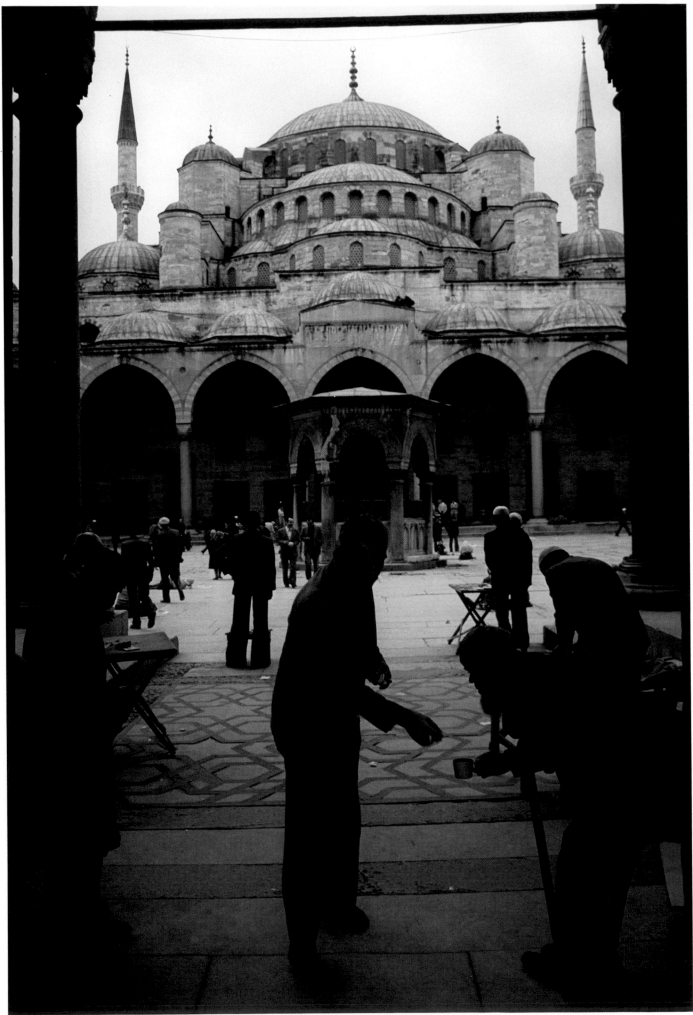

At the western gate of the Blue Mosque, a crippled beggar accepts alms. Altruism is one of the prime duties of every Islamic believer.

Muslims wash their hands, feet and faces at a row of taps before entering the Yeni Mosque to say their prayers.

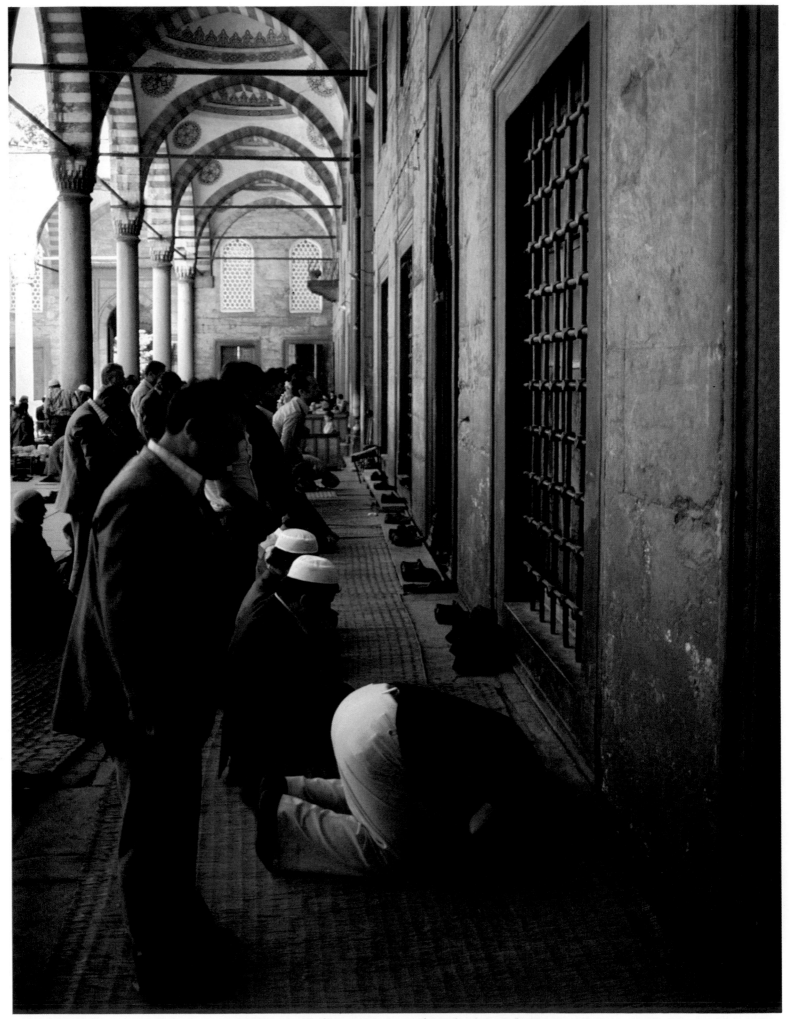

After respectfully removing their shoes, worshippers recite their prayers in a colonnade of the Eyüp Mosque, filled to capacity for a noontime service.

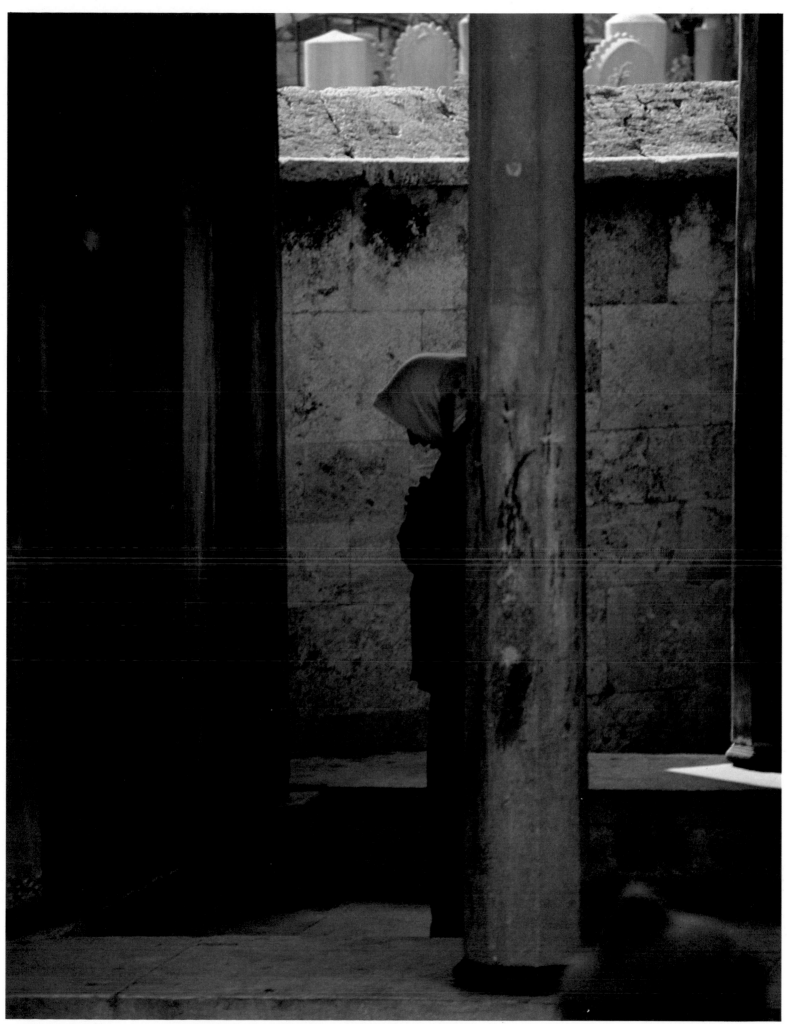

A woman makes private supplications behind a courtyard pillar of the Eyüp Mosque. Within a mosque, women sit together at the back or in the galleries.

In the vast interior of the Blue Mosque, worshippers prostrate themselves at a service during Ramadan—a month of strict fasting prescribed by the Koran.

# 6

# Lives Washed by the Sea

Istanbul is a child of the sea. Few cities are invested so totally, so intimately, by water. It laps the twin shores of the Stamboul peninsula, defines the blunt head of Beyoğlu across the Golden Horn, washes the long front of Asian Üsküdar. The sea, perilous and rich with the flux of trade and war, has always been the city's chief highway. As for anchorage, the water is so deep around the city that ocean-going liners berth cheek-by-jowl with streets and markets; and huge freighters, when they need repair, back their sterns without trouble on to shore.

This juggling of land and sea plays romantic conjuring tricks with the eye. Lines of smoking funnels glide between landlocked chimneys. Masts linger among rooftops. And the ends of a hundred winding streets are sealed not by suburbs, but by a sparkling curtain of waves. "You are accustomed to the gondolas that glide among the palaces of St. Mark," wrote the English traveller Alexander Kinglake in the 19th Century, "but here at Stamboul it is a 120-gun ship that meets you in the street."

At the centre of the city's sea traffic is the ramshackle, 70-year-old Galata Bridge, connecting Stamboul to Beyoğlu across the mouth of the Horn. The bridge, floating on half-decayed pontoons, swings open early each morning to usher shipping into the inlet. Closed again, it rocks with the swell of the water and with the flow of the 90,000 cars and 40,000 pedestrians that cross it every day. Beneath the roadway, close above the water, run passageways lined with makeshift stalls and restaurants. But the bridge's days are numbered. Polluted waters, harsh winds, and the endless crash and rub of ferry-boats have corroded it to the danger point.

At this bridge, Istanbul's three waterways—the Bosphorus, the Golden Horn and the Sea of Marmara—collide with an eccentric glamour. The sea is ploughed and churned by an embroglio of ships. Hooting, belching, whistling, whooping, groaning, they slide and bump in disorder between one another, miming the insane turmoil of streets not far away. At some moments, in morning or early evening, the whole sea seems to convert itself into a maritime Place de la Concorde or Piazza Venezia, where crashes are avoided only by hard-won expertise and perpetual horn-blowing—while overlooking all, as from the tiers of an amphitheatre, the steep shores are thronged with mosques, palaces, banks, offices, bazaars.

A lover of ships can dawdle here for days. They range through a hundred types and ages. On the northern side of the bridge the deep-water anchorage of the Karaköy district is filled with the liners of the world. From its southern side, snout-nosed car ferries oscillate between Europe and

**Trays of freshly caught palamut—an abundant local fish—make a tempting display for commuters and housewives passing a Golden Horn wharf. Istanbul, situated between seas that yield a catch of some 200,000 tons each year, is the centre of Turkey's fishing industry.**

Asia, and the wharves are crowded with passenger-boats of the national-ized Turkish State Line that journey along the Bosphorus and among the villages of the Marmara and the Princes' Isles. Even these boats are dis-similar. The diesel-powered modern ones, their yellow funnels blazoned with red anchors, are mimicked by sluggish ancestors—coal-burning warriors that steam in of a morning with their bows almost under water, listing under hordes of commuters.

It is not, in fact, the grander boats that lend most flavour to these waters, but rather a blackened and scurrilous riff-raff—a whole *demi-monde* of caiques and barges and bossy little tugs stuttering and stammering on a thousand minor missions. These need not wait for the Galata Bridge to open, but are small enough to sail beneath it into the Golden Horn. Lounging on the bridge, you may stare down on Black Sea skippers, perched high at their wheels, steering between the pontoons while their crews laze among their nets. The holds of mechanized barges show gravel, timber, stone. The caiques are full of fruits from the Asian mainland and they dip their masts quaintly, as if saluting, as they pass under the bridge.

Within the Horn the tumult subsides. The Bosphorus and the Sea of Marmara are highroads; but the Horn is a dead end, and is utterly still. Over its glassy waters go the cripples and veterans of the sea: super-annuated skiffs and yawls trafficking in who knows what; and jaunty, leaking water-buses, holding 15 or 20 passengers, that move up the quiet inlet to small landing-stages of their own.

For most of Istanbul's history, the Horn was the focal point of com-mercial life. A superb natural anchorage, its wharves and warehouses were the entrepôts upon which the capital's prosperity was founded. Today Istanbul is still Turkey's largest export harbour, but most of its business is carried out in deeper waters to the east of Galata Bridge. The Horn itself has become silted and filled with the refuse of the factories that line its banks. Large ships moor at its mouth; they enter only to dry-dock.

Of the old wharves, only those of Stamboul, near Galata Bridge, remain. During the decline of Byzantium, they were leased to the ravening mari-time republics of Italy: Venice, Genoa, Pisa and Amalfi. Today the old Venetian wharf is the main wholesale fruit-and-vegetable depot for Stam-boul. Called the "Prison Gate", after a Byzantine tower immured nearby, its landing-stage is lined by caiques heaped with produce from the countryside. These rotted and romantic monsters look as if each has been hammered together from the flotsam of six shipwrecks. Their sails have been replaced by engines, but their curved prows and wide bellies—coloured in peeling stripes of sky-blue, red or yellow—lend them a time-less and dilapidated glory. Heavy with cargo, they move like coloured cradles across the sea. Their masts and rigging swing with pulleys and dusty lanterns; and in the sterns, where enormous rudders reach from deck to sea, brightly painted cabins look as if a breeze would whisk them away.

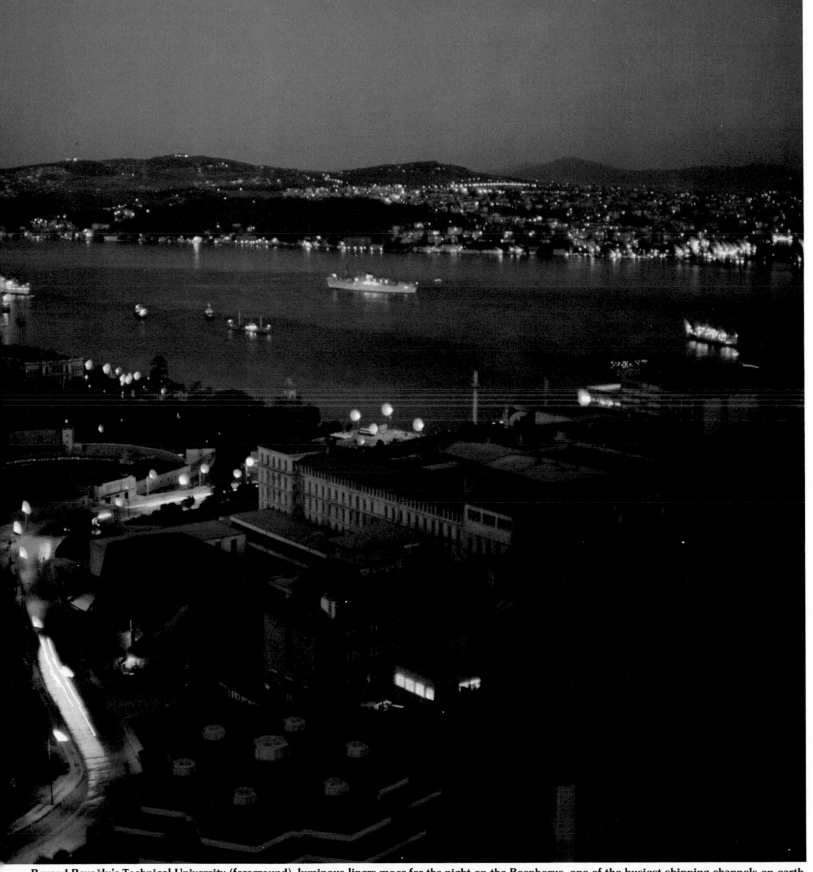

Beyond Beyoğlu's Technical University (foreground), luminous liners moor for the night on the Bosphorus, one of the busiest shipping channels on earth.

On the wharves where the caiques leave their cargo, a pitiless human transport prevails—the Stamboul *hamal*, or porter. One old tourist handbook states loftily that the hamal is stupider than the beasts of burden whose role he performs. But in a city where unemployment chronically runs into the hundreds of thousands, a man has little choice of work. Bent double like congenital cripples, their backs strapped with leather saddles or wooden frames, the hamals—often slight and elderly—totter under immense burdens. From the caiques they first make their way into steaming emporia where clerks scribble beside weighing machines. From there they manoeuvre their freight into the road to a medley of lorries, carts and three-wheeled trucks, sometimes blundering through traffic to reach the far side. A terrible strain shows in the faces of even the younger men; and the old look white-faced and have been known to fall stone dead under their loads. Only at lunchtime do they relax among stacked crates of strawberries, cherries, medlars, a farrago of vegetables—there to eat a frugal meal and joke together.

As for the Horn itself, its beauty is no longer even in the eye of the tourist. It has been replaced by a *déclassé* seediness. Up to the last century it was lined by the palaces and gardens of the wealthy; there is still a spot called the Archery Field, high on the north bank, where the sultans practised bowmanship and left behind little marble pillars in memory of perfect shots. But its waters are now so polluted by factory effluent that fishing is forbidden there. Industrial premises and hovels shoulder each other along shores crusted with garbage. At the Horn's end, where the Ottomans used to picnic among orchards filled with nightingales, two little streams still called the Sweet Waters of Europe lisp into the inlet with a stink of sewers.

Along the dry-docks on the northern shore, dozens of freighters lie half out of water, like stranded whales. A stench of fired metal fills the stores of ship's chandlers. This is a grim area of harsh, hereditary occupations: of tumbledown workhouses and booths stacked with cables, pulleys, ropes, oilskins; of an endless crashing and dinning. The sterns of cargo ships, their rudders sunk in mud, loom 30 feet above the shacks. In forges all around them, hirsute men tend machines where gargantuan slabs or pillars of iron are lopped and sawed, gouged and trimmed, like so much pastry. For this is a land of improvisation. If finished spare parts are not available, somebody creates them. And if this fails, there are always other men, second-hand dealers, who sit all day like sleepy wizards in grottoes of hanging iron—rusty cogs, springs, wheels, chains—waiting for calls.

Beyond these wharves to the north-west spread the state docks of Azapkapi—literally "the Gate of the Marine"—and farther beyond again, the district of Terşane, the site of modern naval docks. When I last visited it, a white-uniformed marine band was practising Viennese waltzes on its landing-stage. Two Turkish frigates and a submarine nuzzled together beneath the slow swing of cranes.

A doughty steamer, laden with passengers collected at villages along both shores of the Bosphorus, ploughs beneath the Bosphorus Bridge on its way to Istanbul. The six-lane bridge is the only road link between non-communist Asia and Europe, and it has already siphoned off almost all the truck traffic that formerly crossed the straits by ferry. Within 28 months of completion in 1973, tolls had made up the entire $35 million construction cost.

Nothing is left of the Ottoman shipyards that once stood here; but in the 16th Century they could handle 120 men-o'-war on dry land, and were the wonder of Europe. The Ottomans, like the Arabs before them, were quick to master the sea. By the time of Süleyman the Magnificent, Turkish fleets commanded or threatened the whole Mediterranean. They sailed the Red Sea, hunted Spanish galleons beyond the Canary Islands, and fought the Portuguese in the Indian Ocean. The Golden Horn was filled with their brilliant white sails and tiered gunnery. Gilded lions and eagles glared from their prows; they were manned by turbaned crews whose sashes were stuck with an armoury of daggers and cutlasses; and the sharp-prowed galleys of their even fiercer confederates, the corsairs of North Africa, often moved with them.

It was from the ranks of such corsairs—drawn from many nations—that the empire took its experienced captains. The greatest Ottoman admiral, Khair ed-Din Barbarossa, was himself the son of a renegade Christian from the Greek island of Lesbos. He overhauled the whole imperial arsenal in 1533. For years he sailed unconquered through the Mediterranean, ravaging Italy and the Aegean, spreading terror even to Rome. His tomb still lies in northern Beyoğlu, across a paved square lapped by the sea; close by, his statue reveals a ferocious elder statesman standing beneath his galleon's prow. It is the only fine public statue in the city.

These were the years when the city's shipyards could build a whole fleet in a single winter. In 1571, after the Ottomans lost 230 ships and some 30,000 men to an allied Christian fleet at the Battle of Lepanto, 158 new galleys were immediately laid down in the arsenal. When Kiliç Ali, the sultan's chief admiral, enquired how enough anchors and rigging could be found for such a resurrection, the grand vizier told him that "the wealth and power of the empire are such that, if it were necessary, we would make anchors of silver, cables of silk, and sails of satin". Within eight months the new fleet was sailing the Mediterranean.

The naval quarter is still scattered with fountains decorated with carvings of ships' lanterns—the insignia of the admirals who built them—and by the mosques and tombs of distinguished seamen. Piyale Paşa, who commanded the Ottoman armada against the Christian enclave of Malta in 1565, had his own mosque built by the great architect Sinan, to a curious and unique design. With a single minaret rising from the centre of its porch, the building dimly resembles a wide-pooped galleon bumping its way through the surrounding trees. It is said that the window grilles were forged from the iron of Christian bells captured in the admiral's campaigns.

The mosque and tomb of Kiliç Ali, who reconquered Tunis from the Spaniards 10 years after Lepanto, and who died in the arms of a concubine at the age of 90, is by contrast conservative: a small-scale replica of Sancta Sophia. Tradition has it that when he approached Murat III for a site on

Thick with flotsam and scraps of refuse, oil that has spilled from boats sailing the Golden Horn forms an unsightly crust beside a quay. Because the pontoons of the Galata Bridge block the cleansing currents of the Bosphorus, the inlet is polluted by shipping effluent and industrial waste from the factories that are concentrated at the upper end of the Horn.

which to construct it, the miserly sultan replied that he could go and build it in the sea. So the old admiral did, filling in a cove on the Bosphorus to support it. And although perpetual silting has stranded it many yards inland now, it still overlooks the straits towards Üsküdar.

By the end of the 16th Century, Ottoman sea-power was already declining—not shattered through war, but stagnated by peace. The Christian powers were busy fighting each other. In the gentler centuries that followed, Terşane became a home for the sultan's caiques, whose crews and guards were lodged nearby. Sometimes, if the sultan sailed to Friday prayer, 40 oarsmen would drive the sleek-prowed royal boat over the Horn like a white-and-gold shark; while behind it, in another caique, the Great Turban Bearer inclined the sultan's turban left and right to a populace prostrated on the shore. Early in the 18th Century, we hear of Ahmet III, the Tulip King, reclining on a poop under a canopy of scarlet and gold as he sailed up the Bosphorus or the Horn to the gardens and lakes that he had created on their shores.

No sultan would recognize today's inlet. Only by night, when the anchored liners become illumined palaces, are the old waters startled into beauty. Then the ferry-boats throw their searchlights over the calm; the red and white lanterns of the caiques wander disembodied, and Topkapi Palace is lit in a greenish glow of floodlights. From the suburbs overhanging the Horn, you may look down on the moving passenger-boats as if at a theatre. Through the foreshortening darkness they seem close at hand. Only in the small hours do the waterways fall quiet. And even then, from time to time, some ship's horn moans in its sleep, echoing against the banked shores of the city, and is answered by howling dogs and by the cries of awakened peacocks in the sultans' old parklands.

The Ottoman historian Evliya Çelebi, who loved to recount legends, tells how Alexander the Great subdued an army of demons by piling mountains on them. Later the great conqueror ordered these fiends to guard the waters about Byzantium, but perversely they scooped out a passage into the Black Sea, which flooded through into the Marmara and drowned them.

This explanation for the birth of the Bosphorus, though unacceptable to geologists (who say it is an old river valley penetrated by the sea) is a measure of the wonder that the narrows have always inspired. A neck of water never more than two miles wide, it separates two continents and joins two seas, and is one of the great strategic waterways of the earth.

All year it is thronged with traffic. You may see tiny fishing smacks sailing through; Turkish destroyers with their missile warheads covered; a Swedish or a Japanese liner; and rowdy tugs—sea-dwarfs, pouring out filth through their obstreperous funnels. Sometimes a great black submarine noses its way into the straits, flying no flag. And snub-nosed Russian tankers appear, bouncing the fishing craft in their wakes like babies.

At first sight, its waters—flowing towards Istanbul between hills 200 to 300 feet high—may seem as calm as the stream of some pastoral valley. But this peace is deceptive. A powerful surface current, surging out of the Black Sea into the Mediterranean, sometimes turns the whole waterway into a mill-race. Every bay and promontory alters its speed and direction, sending out fierce eddies; and around two headlands its strength is such that in earlier days oared vessels were pulled around the points by teams of men with ropes. When hurricanes buffet down the passage, the current can quicken to almost nine knots, sweeping away caiques and fishing boats like driftwood.

Yet some 20 fathoms beneath the surface another, brinier current, which the Turks call *kanal*, pulls strongly in the opposite direction, flowing towards Russia. And when southerly gales blow, the wind sometimes joins forces with this bottom current to reverse the whole surface flow.

Even in tranquillity, the straits may be treacherous. Often dense fogs descend and ice-packs have been known to move south out of the Black Sea. In the winter of A.D. 763 a giant iceberg blocked the whole strait, then floated down and breached the Byzantine sea walls.

The fishermen who hunt these waterways are a law to themselves, just as the waters are. Some ply only a modest trade, and fry and sell their catch in boats along the Golden Horn. But many more engage in deep-sea fishing. Turkey's fishermen land 200,000 tons per year—only a moderate catch, of which less than 10 per cent is exported. But Istanbul itself is a great consumer of fish and its fishing populace permeate it much as gondoliers permeate Venice. The districts in which they live are not only scattered around the fringes of the city, but line the Marmara and the Bosphorus. Fishing, after all, is the city's oldest profession.

A few of these fishermen are Turks whose grandfathers were farmers from the northern hinterland, not hereditary seamen at all. Others are Greeks and Armenians. But most belong to the mysterious people called Laz, a tribe of unknown stock who came from the region of Trebizond by the Black Sea, and spread over the Marmara and Istanbul two or three generations ago. They are dark and slender-featured, with a reputation for ferocity. Their sea-jargon, like that of sailors over all the eastern Mediterranean, is Italian, a legacy of the Venetian maritime empire; and they sail far into the Black Sea and the Aegean in 60-foot steel boats.

The whole Bosphorus is a lane along which migratory shoals move, sometimes in immense numbers. Seasonal myriads of mackerel, turbot and blue fish (the Turkish *lüfer*) move between the Mediterranean and the Black Sea. Other fish are more sedentary: red and grey mullet, sea-bream, tunny, rays, weevers and wrasses, as well as lobsters, oysters and mussels.

As long ago as Roman times, the geographer Strabo wrote how crowds of tunny were swept into the Golden Horn from the rocks of Üsküdar, and could there be caught by hand. At one of the most violent capes, crabs

Under a freighter's looming bow, a waiter from a waterfront café delivers a glass of tea to one of the fishermen who have tied up along a Golden Horn jetty. Some 10,000 Stamboullus earn their livelihood by fishing the Bosphorus, the Black Sea and the Sea of Marmara.

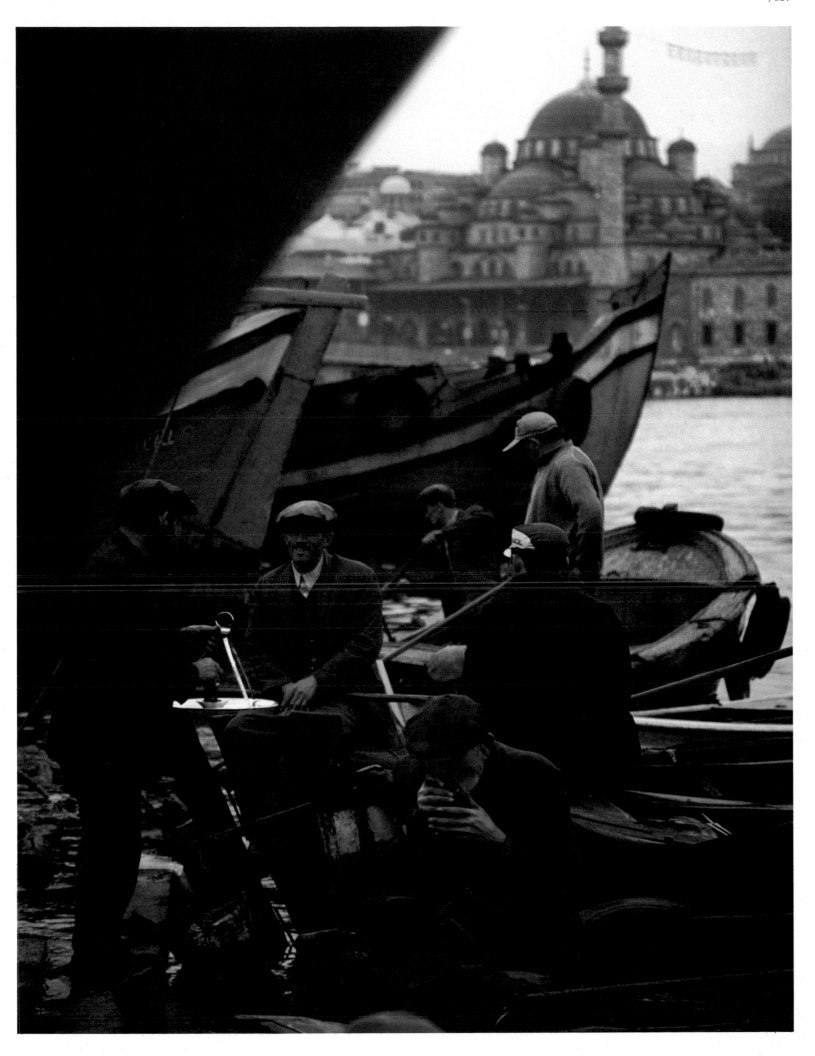

would abandon the sea altogether and walk overland across the promontory, where they eventually wore a path in the rocks. Around the same headland today, grey mullet sometimes swarm so thick that they can be speared from the shore. Often, off Seraglio Point, I have seen the water black with fishing smacks covering some unseen multitude; and the Galata Bridge itself occasionally swarms with men pulling up sprats as fast as they can dip in a line. Even the jellyfish, feeding on rubbish, become so numerous that when the swell of a passing oil tanker washes them over the coastal roads, they dry there in a thick, crusty carpet.

Faced with such prey, the fishermen are rarely idle. Even when docked, they busy themselves spreading their heaps of red-dyed nets over the wharves and stand for hours mending them. Ageing women, widowed by the sea, sit helping them, earning a living in the way they remember, with penknives and bone needles in their mittened hands.

"So you're writing a book?" laughed an Armenian widow with a tanned, brazen face as I wandered along the wharf of Kumkapi: "Write about our troubles then!" She flashed a mouthful of gold teeth in a rueful smile. "We've worked since the day we were born, that's our trouble!"

But the men are taciturn. (Why, I wonder, does the sea turn men so quiet?) Under their peaked or woollen caps the faces appear sober, self-reliant. A group of skippers, relaxing in a tea-house near the wharf, looked at me with disinterest as I sat nearby. They were all Laz—medium-built men with slight moustaches—and each owned a boat. They spoke of the Bosphorus currents as a phenomenon less to be feared than to be used. In their minds the whole channel was a changing map of shoals. They use nets at many levels—for all but the dogfish and the swordfish, which nets cannot hold—and each of them had seen sharks and packs of seals.

"In the spring the shoals start to swarm up into the Black Sea to spawn. They're on their way up now," said one man. I was scrutinized by vivid eyes in a predatory face. "In winter they flow down again to the Mediterranean." He arranged the teaspoons on the table between us to create a makeshift Bosphorus. "But at the moment we're after a shoal of sea-bream deep under Seraglio Point. There's a whole army down there." He placed a lump of sugar between the forks. "There, we have to wait for the current around the Point to change, perhaps for as long as a week. Then they'll come up."

The others nodded, harbouring their little glasses of tea, spoonless now, in dirt-engrained hands. The predatory-looking man seemed to enjoy prestige among them. But each was dressed as shabbily as the next in a hard fraternity.

"Last year there were *lüfer* down there," said another man with a simian face black as a coal miner's. "We waited for them, too. When they surfaced, there were so many you could spit on them. For months afterwards Istanbul was eating *lüfer.*"

"But *lüfer* are best caught at night," the predator declared. "Like sprats. You hang a lantern in the prow and its light is refracted in the water.

The fish get confused and don't see the nets." He dismantled his culinary Bosphorus and dropped the sugar-lump into his tea.

On autumn nights, I remembered, the Sea of Marmara is sometimes covered with the lanterns of these fishing fleets, trailing in dim constellations far out to the Princes' Isles.

"Different fish are trapped in different ways," he said. "I'm one of those who hunt the swordfish. In spring, when the sea begins to warm, they swim to the surface and get caught up in the current. You see them streaming along, bathing in the warm water, half asleep." He closed his eyes, as if dozing on an imaginary slipstream. "When you spy them just under the surface, you choose your harpoon-head—about two and a half inches long—and shoot them from above."

"And sell them for a pittance," added a heavy old pessimist.

"We hunt the dogfish too," the man went on. "That's a hard fish, very strong. You catch it by line, and it's dangerous. Sometimes it gets in the nets and panics, tears them up, and you lose everything."

"Everything." The pessimist stared into his tea. "A fisherman's life isn't a life." His slow-smiling face was glazed in white bristles, and he wore a plastic hat like basketwork, through which his bald head shone. When I asked him about the Black Sea storms, he replied stoically that a man had to ride them out. He himself had been kept at the helm for days and nights at a time.

"But it's good to sail in international waters." The predator drew vigorously on his cigarette. "The big fish. That's living. If you want to get the sheath-fish—he's a pink monster—you have to go outside the 12-mile limit. So sometimes we poach in Russian preserves in the Black Sea." He reassembled the spoons into two separate territories, and slid his oil-grimed fingers in and out of them. "The Russians are fishing for sturgeon, of course—for caviar—which finds its way into our waters. And we're after the sheath-fish, which swim in Russian waters. So what do we do?" His eyebrows lifted, his forehead broke into cunning wrinkles, and his trailing fingers slunk round the spoons and met between them. "We gather outside the 12-mile limit and exchange catches. Sometimes, of course, we get caught. But that's life, too."

Around the Marmara islands, following the shoals into the Aegean, and for 800 miles as far as Cyprus, the Laz live the lives of sea-gypsies. Their women, traditionally harvesters of tea and hazelnuts by the Black Sea, find no such work when they move to Istanbul. They sit at home.

"Sometimes they have to wait three months for us to return." The simian man grimaced. All his features seemed to have been beaten and smudged into one another by the sea, and he was crowned by a woollen cap from which brambles of grey-black hair flowered.

"So when you return there's a celebration?"

The circle of faces creased and split into smiles. "Yes, a celebration."

In earlier times the mystic guardians of Turkish seamen were Jonah and the Seven Sleepers of Ephesus, mythical beings who are related astrologically to the Great Bear and who—for this reason, perhaps—busy themselves over navigation. In the days before air mail the name of the Sleepers' dog, Kitmir, to whom the Koran has awarded a place in paradise, used to be inscribed on envelopes to ensure the letters a safe sea passage. Noah, too, was a patron of Istanbul's sailors. In Ottoman times a legend arose that the south-east doors of Sancta Sophia were built from the wood of the Ark, and the seamen would bow to them before a voyage, reciting a prayer for the repose of Noah's soul.

But when I asked the Laz about this, they did not understand. "Noah? Who's Noah?" Then the predator, unwilling to be found at a loss, added: "Ah, Noah. He's dead now, but his brothers are in the business."

The business remains a hard one. The Laz are nearly alone in fishing now. The Greek and Armenian sea-communities are dying out. Those who reap the largest profits are probably not the fishermen at all, but the middlemen, who own refrigerated store-rooms and often resell the fish at 30 times the price they paid for them. "If the markets are flooded," the pessimist told me, "the price goes down, and what we can't sell goes to fish-paste manufacturers for a trifle. We've no protection." He scratched his head under the perforated hat. "That's why our sons don't follow us. Once they get education"—he pointed upwards—"they go in that direction. Without education"—he stabbed downwards—"it's into the engine oil with you, and out to sea."

For the seamen, operating costs are high. A ship's new engine, I was amazed to discover, might cost the equivalent of $70,000. So fishing remains the calling of a tightly-knit few—men with both the circumspection and resilience of professionals. Two lean years may mean bankruptcy.

The Bosphorus, theatre of the lives and deaths of the fishermen, is integral to Istanbul. Administratively it is part of the city, and thousands of workers commute across it daily. In summer, the rich flock to villas on its shores to escape the heat, and others can taste its beauties from one of the passenger-boats that ply its waters.

As the boat leaves the mouth of the Horn, its churning motor sends a wave of rotted fruit and dead fish against the Galata Bridge. A faint breeze rises while the vessel enters the confluence of the straits. To the right, the Marmara is littered with ships. In front, an island tower—now a signal station—has inherited the classical legend that the youth Leander drowned here when swimming across to Hero, the woman he loved.

The waterway is pervaded by such myths. Its very name commemorates the legendary wanderings of the sad nymph Io, beloved of Jupiter, who tried to rescue her from the jealousy of Juno by disguising her as a heifer. But the goddess tormented the heifer with a gadfly, until it sought escape

As a warship noses up the Bosphorus, sentries at the 19th-Century Dolmabahçe Palace—now used for state banquets—file past a gateway by the water's edge.

by plunging into the waters that separate Europe from Asia, and thus bequeathed to them the Greek name, Bosphorus, "the Ford of the Cow".

As the boat turns north, and Stamboul fades to a shadow-play of domes and minarets behind it, the buildings of more recent legend crowd the western bank. These are the palaces—mockeries of baroque Europe— that were built by the last sultans. The Dolmabahçe, a pompous imperial confection, covers the Beyoğlu shore for 400 yards. The home of most sultans after 1853, it is now used for the state functions of the Republic. Farther inland, in the kiosks of the palace-park of Yildiz, the last Ottoman despot, Abdul the Damned, lived in a seclusion more extreme than that of his ancestors. Within the park's double walls roamed ferocious guard-dogs; secret passages connected half the palace chambers and corridors; and in every room lay a loaded revolver, to be used against assassins. Yet the proprietor of this stronghold was no conquering sultan, but an old, neurotic hypocrite in a frock-coat, who ruled through a veil of corrupt eunuchs and a legion of spies, until at last he was forced to abdicate by the Young Turks in 1909.

Beyond, standing on the shore in another act of this imperial drama, is the fire-gutted Çirağan, last of the baroque palaces, where Abdul's predecessor, Murat V, lived in squalor for 29 years, after he was deposed for insanity in 1876. A roofless ghost, abandoned half a century ago, its gaping windows are covered in a weft of flowers; it is less like a building than the fantasy of some romantic painter.

By now the boat is in full sight of the new Bosphorus Bridge, a six-lane suspension completed in 1973. Its span is superb and a little unreal; the cars crossing it look like running ants. Almost a mile long, with a clearance of 210 feet, it is the largest bridge in Europe or Asia. The boat passes under it as into the valley of a great river. Yet the charm of the valley is hard to define. The steepness of the surrounding land haunts and exaggerates the waters. Above the antiphony of bay and headland, the hills show undulating silhouettes. A light haze covers them. Here and there a tributary valley gives a glimpse of deeper greenness, or some more distant hill, untouched by any building, shadows the peopled shore.

But in the past decade these slopes have greatly altered. Pink-roofed houses and apartment blocks mount them on all sides. Old Bosphorus-lovers are horrified by a blaze of hotels and factory chimneys that now covers them. Only where summer embassies of European powers keep their parks unchanged can you see how richly clothed were many of these hills. A dense curtain of trees lifts from water to sky. Cedar, cypress, terebinth and chestnut mingle in the gardens to create a private and variegated beauty, while umbrella pine and mauve-flowering Judas-trees foreshadow the rain-softened vegetation of the Black Sea.

Vanishing, too, are the Ottoman *yali*, waterside mansions whose mellow charms—columns, balconies, lace-like friezes and lattices—are built only in the perishable architecture of wood. Once such palaces covered the shores, but fires have reduced them. The last yali keep a tottering, old-world charm. Their owners often cannot restore them; but the government has forbidden their demolition. Now, mostly shuttered and decaying, they stoop over the waters with their balconies askew and occasionally let fall a slat or a roof tile. So close are they to the shore that more than one yali-dweller has awakened to a terrible crash and found the prow of a freighter intruding into his bedroom.

Halfway to the Black Sea, on the European shore, the cylindrical towers of Rumeli Castle muscle out on two strategic hills. Built by Mehmet the Conqueror, in 1452, to choke Constantinople from the north, the castle is powerful still, looping its walls across the valley and down to the sea.

As the passenger-boat zig-zags between Asia and Europe, it touches at many villages, rounding blunt headlands where fishing nets are staked out in the water. Some of these villages are fashionable, but in most of them a halcyon sleepiness prevails. On the creaking wharves and landing-stages, and in the squares nearby, men doze in the shadows, while in the water round about, umbrella-like jellyfish—"mothers of the sea", as the Turks call them—are dozing too.

Out of the greenish shallows and across the grey-blue, the boat moves again into the main current and the long intertwining of deep sea and tall land. Sometimes, crossing a wide bay to the farther side, you imagine yourself in a land-locked lake, where colossal boats sail unexplained. The water sparkles towards you. A light wind stirs. And at last, where a Byzantine castle circles the hills with ruin, you glimpse, far away, the misted vacuum of the Black Sea.

This castle marks the beginning of solitude. Here the passenger-boats turn back, and anybody who wants to go farther must bribe a skiff captain to take him. The shores rise empty on plinths of rock, and sandy coves appear. But they belong to a military area, where it is forbidden to land.

Here, where the straits merge with the sea, their tension often slackens. Opaque patterns glide over the water, and flocks of black-and-white shearwaters—said by Turks to be the souls of the damned—skim low over the surface. For the first time, Istanbul ceases to haunt the Bosphorus. All around, the slopes fold on one another in a sculptural desolation, and the waters, no longer constricted, spread flat and shining under the sun in an unbroken sheet of steel.

# A Dynamic World Afloat on the Horn

PHOTOGRAPHS BY JOHN GARRETT

**Ferries that ply the Horn lie beside Galata Bridge in the early morning. In the foreground are red trays on which fish vendors will display their catch.**

For all-round utility on a grand scale, few structures can rival the quarter-mile-long Galata Bridge that spans the entrance to the Golden Horn—the inlet separating Istanbul's two European districts of Stamboul and Beyoğlu. Built in 1912 upon 45 giant pontoons, the bridge has become a tumultuous, floating magnet for the citizens of the metropolis. During rush hours, its sidewalks and five-lane highway churn with commuters—some 40,000 pedestrians alone making a twice-daily crossing. Throughout the day, tea-houses, restaurants and shops on the lower level do a thriving trade. And well into the night, ferries that serve communities along the Golden Horn or Bosphorus continue to pick up or disgorge passengers at quays alongside the bridge. Only in the quiet hours between 4 a.m. and dawn does Galata open its iron midriff and allow waiting ships to pass.

At the peak of the morning rush hour, dense crowds and nose-to-tail traffic flow in both directions across Galata Bridge. On the lower level, at far right, commuters clog a broad quay that is attached to the bridge.

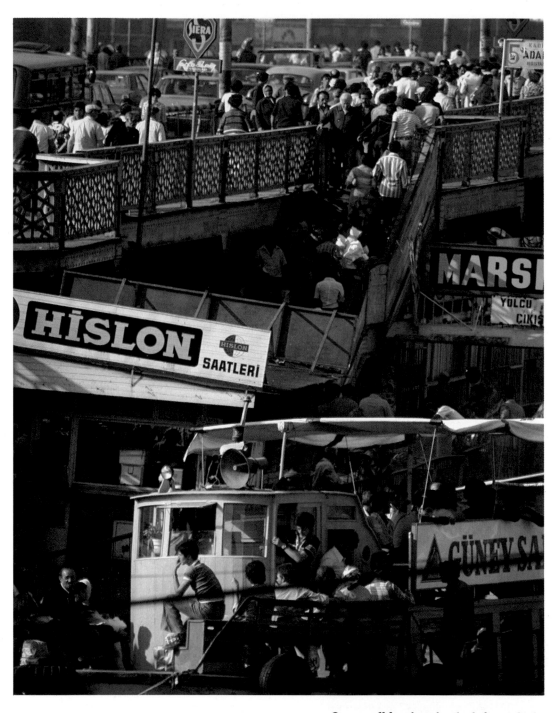

On a small ferryboat berthed alongside the bridge, passengers patiently wait for the next trip out to the Asian side of Istanbul. A steep iron staircase beyond gives quick access from the landing on the quay to the upper level.

A fruit-and-vegetable vendor (right) pushes a
barrow across Galata Bridge towards his regular
selling-spot near Sirkeci Railway Station on
the Stamboul side. Some 50,000 Stamboullus
make their living as street-vendors, selling
anything from roasted nuts to nylon stockings.

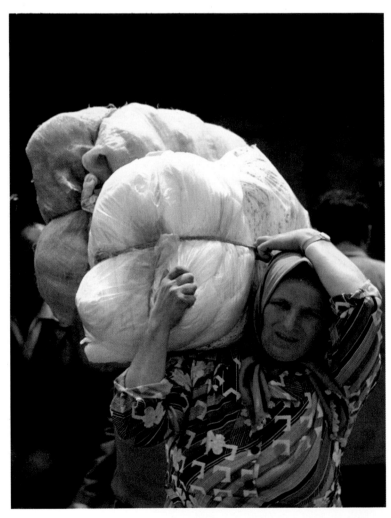

With professional ease, a woman crossing the
bridge on her way home from a shopping
expedition carries a hefty bundle of bedding on
her shoulder. Many streets in the city are too
narrow for vehicular traffic, making it more
efficient for people to haul goods themselves.

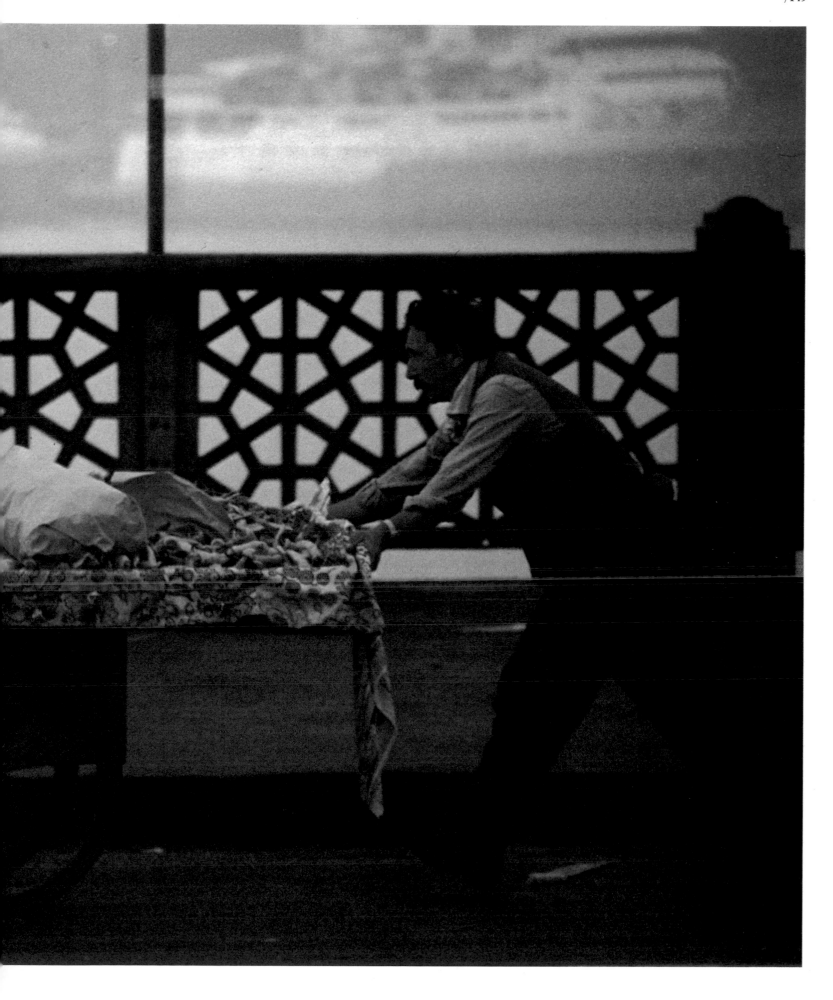

Bobbing in the chop on the Bosphorus side of the bridge, two fishermen (right) grill a panful of palamut cutlets that will be stuck into rolls and sold as snacks to passers-by. The palamut, a large species of mackerel, is one of 60 types of edible fish caught in the vicinity.

A party of friends, seated in one of the two floating fish restaurants tied up on the side of Galata Bridge, enjoy a meal accompanied by bottled water. Stamboullu patrons have discerning palates, and restaurateurs pride themselves on the freshness of their fish, which they buy from neighbouring markets.

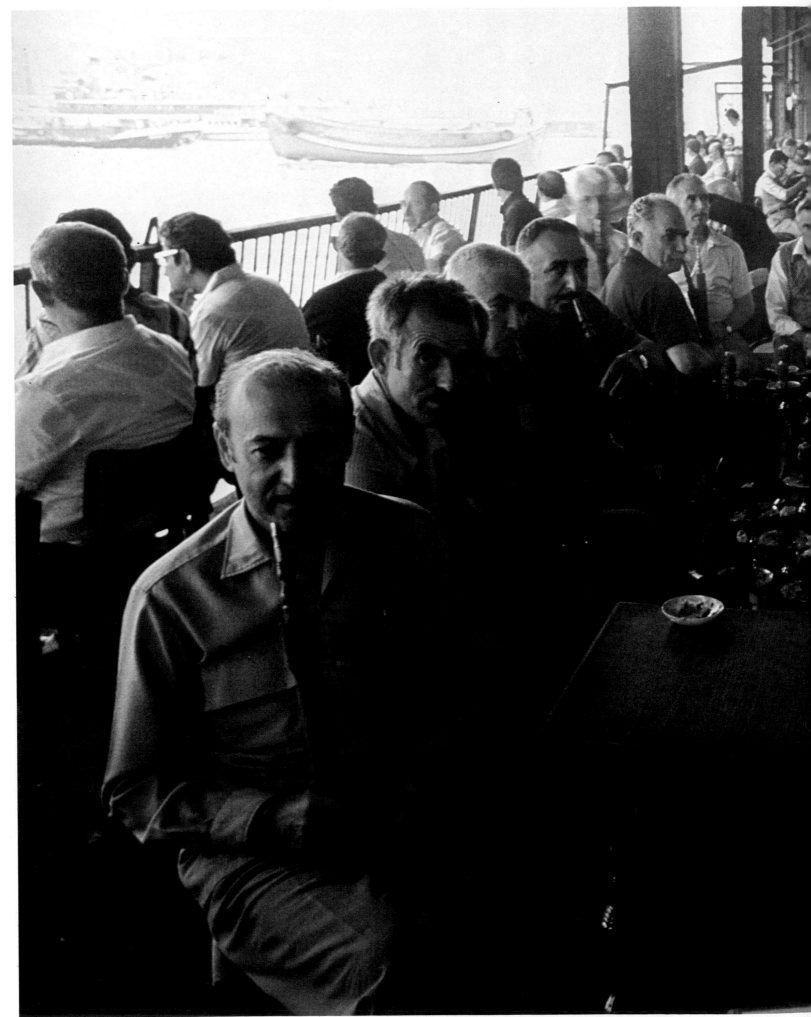

On the lower level of the bridge, commuters and loungers pass the time with the aid of hookahs—Oriental pipes that draw tobacco smoke through a bowl of water.

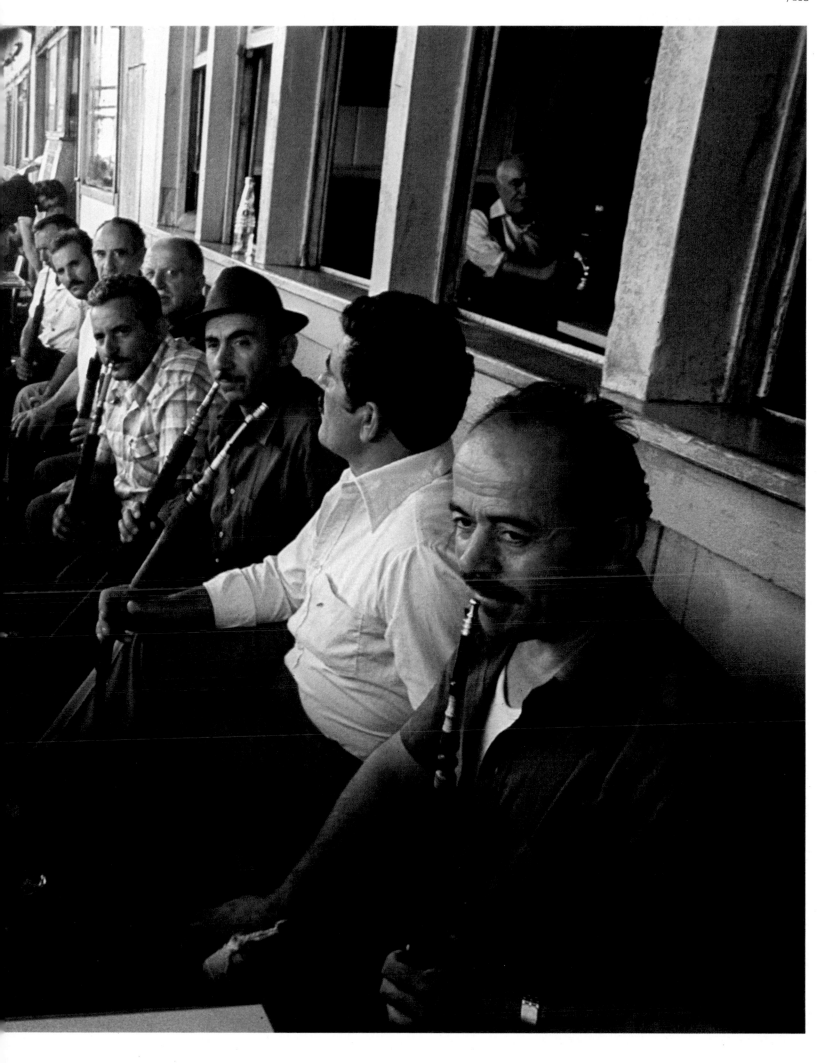

With the pivoting central span floated clear to let ships through, blazing lights illumine Galata Bridge's internal girders in the early morning. A guard and striped railings are positioned on the roadway to deter unwary motorists.

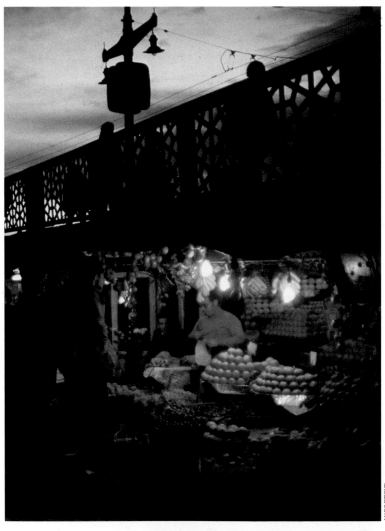

MARC RIBOUD

A fruit stall, located under the Beyoğlu end of the bridge, attracts customers heading home in the evening. Most of the citrus fruit arranged here in trim displays has been grown along Turkey's Mediterranean and Aegean coastlines.

# 7

# Treasure-House of Trade

By a timeless irony, religion, which speaks of brotherhood, has divided man; whereas trade, the vehicle of his self-seeking, has united him. Throughout history, nations that repudiated one another's God remained addicted to each other's spices or horses or slaves; and with these, almost unnoticeably, came a commerce of thought and habit.

The prosperity of Constantinople, of course, was founded on trade. In Byzantine centuries its merchants travelled the known world, from India to the Atlantic; and the empire's unit of currency—the golden *nomisma*— was accepted as legal tender even in central Asia.

During Ottoman times, the boundaries of empire were pushed to the Caspian Sea and to the Persian Gulf, but Constantinople remained the natural focus for Eastern luxuries. Its herbs, spices, silks, carpets and dried fruits were coveted by European merchants, and travellers reported that the city's markets were as finely provided as any in the world.

Under both the Byzantine emperors and the Ottoman sultans, the city's internal economy was controlled by a tight and clannish network of guilds, which set conditions of employment, supervised standards of workman- ship and controlled prices. Membership was compulsory and hereditary: a father's trade devolved automatically on his son. Guildsmen were bound by ties not only of trade, but often of race and religion. For some 1,500 years—until the present century—this elaborate and rigid system con- trolled every detail of Constantinople's daily work.

At the zenith of the Ottoman Empire there were more than 700 such guilds. Every half century, in a moving census of the city's commercial and military strength, the guildsmen would mass in a colossal procession, heavily armed and 200,000 strong, and march from dawn to dusk past the review pavilion of the sultan's palace. The chronicler Evliya Çelebi in 1638 described how this census disrupted the whole city for three days.

From the 500 sherbet-sellers to the 7,000-strong guild of beggars, the whole texture and pageant of the Ottoman world could be seen in a prodigious fantasia. The bakers went past, led by quaint, ox-drawn floats that carried a windmill, an oven, and boys who baked and kneaded flour and threw little cakes among the crowd; behind them marched the whole guild, with pies and pastries balanced on their heads. The furriers' floats quivered with stuffed animals; the farmers marched by wearing garlands of corn and sweeping their scythes; the guild of watchmen blew whistles and rushed in and out of the crowds, pretending to catch pickpockets. And the Captains of the White Sea—officers of the sultan's Mediterranean

At a makeshift stall in gardens near Sancta Sophia, one of Istanbul's army of street traders decants perfume into used bottles for sale to tourists. Petty retailing of this kind, requiring little outlay for stock and none for rent, becomes a way of life for the large percentage of the city's labour force that is otherwise perennially without steady employment.

fleet—wheeled along enormous ships with jewelled oars and muslin sails, then clashed with a "Christian fleet" in front of the imperial pavilion, finally boarding the infidel galleons in a cannonade of smoke.

Numberless strange guilds featured in these carnivals. In Evliya's day, 500 nightingale dealers went by. There were ice merchants, whose wares, used to refrigerate food, came from the heights of Asia Minor, and were sailed across the Marmara in 300 boats. The sultan's lion-keepers marched by, leading their charges gingerly and quieting them with gazelle meat steeped in opium. The keepers of lunatic asylums paraded their patients in gilded chains, and two thousand slave merchants herded along a flock of magnificently dressed girls. Last of all came the tavern-keepers—Greeks, Jews and Armenians (alcohol has always been officially forbidden to Muslims)—who marched in armour, their faces masked, and poured out raspberry juice from crystal and porcelain cups.

And what became of this giant procession that marched through 200 years of celebrations—in Evliya Çelebi's words—"like a thundering sea"? Even as he described it, the seeds of decline were being sown. By the mid-16th Century—after the discovery of the Americas and of the seaway around Africa—the whole economic balance of the world was changing. Inexorably, trade began to flow away from the Mediterranean to the powers of the Atlantic's European shores: Portugal, Spain, Holland, France, Britain.

By the mid-17th Century the Turks had lost control of the Mediterranean. Maltese and Tuscan privateers roamed at will; and the Barbary corsairs, once the servants of the sultans, slipped the Ottoman leash and began pillaging for themselves. By the late 19th Century Turkey's rulers could avoid bankruptcy only by selling concessions to European traders, who bought up the raw materials of Asia Minor cheaply in Constantinople, and in exchange sold expensive finished goods to the wealthier citizens.

Nothing evokes more poignantly the empire's decline than the enormous emporiums, called hans, that still stand foursquare among the city's bazaars. In its heyday, the han was both inn and market—the haven of travelling merchants who could lodge there and store their wares in the rented rooms that were ranged in tiers around fountained courtyards.

Some dozen of these caravanserais survive in the city—great empty bellies that have received nothing for half a century past. Their timber gates, plated with iron, are wedged apart by layers of dust. Their court-yards have grown deformed with the years. Trees twist up through the pavements. Wigs of creeper top the colonnades. The fountains are broken or earthed in; and the upper chambers and galleries where the merchants slept have been commandeered for workshops, their spaces now halved, quartered, tortured to fragments, until they become mazes where men move like insects in some riddled cabinet.

The decline of Turkey's trading position, leading to near-bankruptcy in the early 20th Century, meant that the nation had to create fresh sources

In a detail from an illuminated manuscript, a procession of the guilds that dominated the economy of Ottoman Constantinople winds through the city in 1720. Grouped around floats representing their trades, and accompanied by musicians and dancers, the entire workforce was periodically reviewed in this way by the sultan.

of revenue. The man responsible for setting its new course was Atatürk. He diagnosed the lack of native factories as the cause of his country's economic stagnation. To cure it, he devised a form of state capitalism propped up by government-controlled investment banks whose role was to encourage industry. Some of the state-aided industries were nationalized; others continued in private hands. And this model of a government-supervised economy has been followed ever since.

Atatürk's economic policies have had conspicuous results. New factories sprawl among the outlying areas of Istanbul—in Üsküdar, on the fringes of Beyoğlu, and west of the walls of old Stamboul. More than 40 per cent of Turkey's gross national product is now generated in the city's foundries, textile plants, breweries, cement works, mills and distilleries—mostly for internal consumption. Yet lack of management expertise (and of foreign investment) has restricted growth at every step.

With new industry a new workforce has developed: a restive proletariat organized not in guilds (which remain only for craftsmen) but in trade unions. The right to strike was written into law in 1963. Union leaders now negotiate regularly with employers and with the government. The combined efforts of the country's largest labour confederation, Türk-İş, and of its younger and more radical rival, DISK (the initials represent the Turkish for Confederation of Revolutionary Workers' Unions), as well as of a host of smaller unions, ensure that industrial wages do not drown in Turkey's inflation—averaging 20 per cent annually through most of the 1970s. A worker in Istanbul may now earn up to four times as much as his cousins in the smallholdings of Asia Minor.

In spite of government investment, this unionized world of modern factories cannot employ even half of Istanbul's workers. So the greater part of the city's unskilled labour has been absorbed by small workshops, employing groups of eight, or five, or three. Divided and subdivided minutely into makeshift enterprises, this workforce sweats at the loom and the forge, producing anything from coats to kettles.

Even these labyrinths of ateliers have not consumed all of the city's jobless. In the mid-1970s, 16,000 newcomers from the provinces were arriving every month. Unemployment filled the cafés of working quarters with rootless men, and semi-employment became endemic.

The business of selling, too, has been fragmented among tens of thousands of self-employed. They wander the city with a handful of cigarettes, or wheel small carts of penknives and combs along the lanes. There are mendicant carpet-sellers, lottery-ticket vendors, black-market money-changers. Men selling drinks by the roadside are legion. Lemon and cherry fruit juices, sweetened or weak, are dispensed from booths, with a cold, soured goat's milk called *ayran*. The *salep*-seller strolls the markets with a silver samovar strapped to his back, pouring out a cold and harmless brew

In the Stamboul market district, a shabby panoply of signs advertises small businesses—mostly selling building materials—that have yet to open for the day.

of orchid roots; while other men, generally old, push trolleys of venemously coloured pickle-waters in jars, from which they mix *turşu suyu*, a beverage of throat-searing acidity. Half the poorer working populace buys its lunch from hawkers—timeless vendors of sesame-sprinkled bread or of *lahmacun*, circular sandwiches smeared with tomato, peppers and onions.

More grand and settled merchandise occupies huge areas of the city, and has its heart between Galata Bridge and Beyazit Square in the district of Stamboul. In this area—Istanbul's market centre since Byzantine times —the city's chaos develops a logic of its own. Entire streets and districts are devoted to a single ware or craft. A blind man could walk from place to place with ease, scenting where he was. The fragrance of the wood-turners' shops pervades whole alleys, then merges with a stench of smelted metal or the musty aroma of leather.

Many of these markets have kept their character over half a millennium or more. The 15th-Century Mosque of the Scale-Makers, west of Galata Bridge, is still hemmed in by shops piled with scales and balances, even bathroom weighing machines. The vine-shaded courtyard of the second-hand booksellers—where Turkish novels and crudely-bound Korans stand beside translations of Marx or Harold Robbins—occupies the site of the Byzantine book market, near Beyazit Square. But other ancient markets have disappeared, leaving only a name—the Street of the Sword-Makers, the Street of the Pearl Merchants—that throws an empty splendour around their decay.

Strolling into this enormous district from Galata Bridge, you come first upon the covered Spice Market, which is still pervaded, curiously, by the smell of sandalwood and gum, although there is scarcely a spice booth left in the place; instead the stalls offer everything from beads to smoked mutton. Beside it, the tomb of Ahmet III—the Tulip King—overlooks the Flower Market, where cut flowers and potted plants are still for sale. On a pavement nearby, the second-hand clothes bazaar, which used to disseminate diseases through the Ottoman Empire, is a forum for barter in kind, where the city's poor exchange one shabbiness for another.

Further up the slopes, beyond the fruit markets—avenues of musk-melons and water-melons, strawberries red or white, summer figs, mulberries and pomegranates—the lanes grow steeper, darker. You approach the clothes bazaars: lanes choked with barrows. Awnings meet overhead. You rummage through a creepered jungle of dangling dresses and pants. Laden porters are the only traffic. Beyond, above other streets, the sky is shut out by impenetrable regiments of shop signs obliterating one another. And at last you plunge into an entire, self-contained city—gated, walled and domed—that is still, perhaps, the largest single concentration of merchandise in the world: the Grand Bazaar.

Ever since Mehmet the Conqueror established it here in 1461, and despite appalling fires, the Bazaar has continued to occupy the same area.

His service announced by the traditional cylindrical spouts on his handpainted container, a water-seller waits for customers near Galata Bridge. The spouts are no longer functional; a modern faucet has been fitted to the container's far side. In the past, such men were often employed to transport water from fountains to private homes. Today, most houses in Istanbul have running water, and the water-sellers simply supply cheap and convenient refreshment in the city's main streets.

It has been computed to contain 4,399 shops, 2,195 workshops and 497 stalls, as well as many little mosques and fountains. The shops are small, every one, and are closed at night by sheets of corrugated iron pulled down and padlocked to the pavement. So densely are the cubicles packed together that they almost conceal the stone tissue of the Bazaar itself, whose 67 streets are interconnected by a myriad lanes, some so small that a well-fed Stamboullu can barely squeeze through.

Overhead, the jungle of shopsigns is neon-lit even at noon. Windows, high in the passageways, seem to cast down only pools of shadow, while far below the merchandise shines in artificial light. Here, as in the markets outside, each trade congregates in its own area. This exclusiveness, and the oriental custom of bargaining, spring from a world in which time is less important than money. A woman may walk two miles to buy a ribbon. But the ribbon she buys will be taken from the Street of the Haberdashers, at a competitive price, after a sharp exchange over terms.

On my first visit here, I wandered in dreamy stupefaction. Between spangled and cascading slippers I passed down the Street of the Haberdashers, lichened with hanging colours like a Walt Disney forest; then I moved into farther streets, deeper lanes, enticed always to some chamber of light beyond, winking with intimated riches. I collided with staring countrywomen in sequinned headscarves. All around, the brilliance and intricacy of merchandise weakened the eyes and increased the sense of walking through a self-created world—an oriental fairy-tale. Salesmen ravened fruitlessly around me, shouting their wares or whispering special prices. Along the banked blaze of goldsmiths' and jewellers' shops, past a pale marble fountain, I became lost among streets of copperware and wandered into a geologist's cave of alabaster and green onyx ornaments. The next moment I found myself in a long, colonnaded passageway whose every surface was hung with carpets, glowing delicate and wine-red or heaped together in a confused Ali Baba splendour.

But little by little the fantasy subsided, the drug thinned in my veins. Sleepily I opened one critical, undazed eye, then two. The antiques, I noticed, are mostly fake. The ceramics parody an old beauty. Even craftsmanship in jewellery has declined. The silversmiths beat every surface into flowers or cupids. And other craftsmen, defecting to Western taste, produce pure horror, whether it be lamps and brass tortoises studded in coloured glass, or the white wedding dresses of the bourgeois, tumbling in pink muslin flowers.

At the very heart of the Bazaar is the Old Market, a domed hall that was for centuries the lodestar of travellers, who went there to buy inlaid weapons and damascened armour, gems and seal-rings. Immured like a fortress in the centre of a city of merchandise, it can be locked off from the rest of the Bazaar at night. Now its giant hall is so contorted with wooden and glass partitions that you barely notice the domes and arches that tower overhead. Its antique shops mingle fake and genuine inextricably. A weird confusion of artifacts covers the shelves—leftovers and parodies of the French taste that beguiled the Ottoman aristocracy through the 19th Century: Empire-style clocks draped with lounging nymphs, Bohemian crystal, pseudo-Sèvres porcelain. Here and there, 18th-Century icons appear—after some emigrating Greek family has sold its treasures—or woodwork with a rich inlay, now blurred and burnished, of ivory, silver and brass. Old, turquoise-studded jewellery is for sale (but has been mimicked subtly by the new). Solid silver purses hang on hooks. Along the floor, glass hookahs idle in lines, like cashiered troops.

A sickening of such luxury is best cured in the Street of the Copper-Workers, which abuts on Beyazit Square at the Bazaar's southern end. Coppersmiths still sell their goods there; and beside them, in a dusty flea-market, other vendors squat in their lairs under a deluge of long-broken watches, religious medallions, cow-bells, plate cameras, antlers, phonographs, stuffed lambs' heads, roller-skates and ancient opera glasses. You may buy or sell anything, and bargaining can be elongated into hours.

I watched a man haggling for half an hour over a second-hand umbrella. He was a courteous old Stamboullu of the kind that seems constantly to be dying out, yet is constantly renewed. Under a dark blue beret his spare features were pinched into an expression of delicate concern, while the round-faced storekeeper gazed at the umbrella, stroked it, named it the prince of umbrellas, and quoted 50 lira (about three dollars). The old man tilted back his head and puffed disdainfully into the air. The etiquette of bargaining includes outright disparagement.

"It's not worth a dung-beetle," he said. "Look. Its cover is split on two sides."

The storekeeper came down to 40 lira. It was a work of art, he declared. The next tourist would take it for any price he quoted.

The old man offered ten lira in a tone of disgust. The storekeeper should take the money now, he said, before the umbrella fell to bits in his hands. Anyway, he added, who wanted an umbrella in Istanbul these days? It hadn't rained for weeks. It would probably never rain again.

"It will make a fine sunshade," the storekeeper replied. "Ten lira wouldn't buy the handle off it."

Five times the old man wrinkled up his face at the slandered umbrella and marched away up the street, while the storekeeper lolled against his doorway in a posture of well-rehearsed indifference. Five times the old man sauntered back and stopped abruptly, as if his eye had just fallen on the umbrella. The storekeeper came down to 25 lira. The old man went up to 15, and complained that the umbrella did not open properly. The owner opened it with a flourish. It was the finest umbrella in the Grand Bazaar, he said. The Grand Bazaar must have fallen on bad times, the old man answered. He went up to 17 lira; the owner came down to 19.

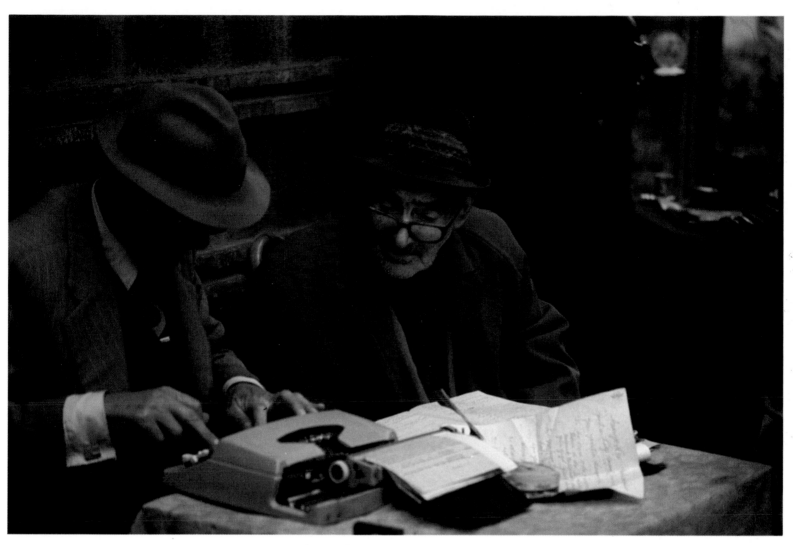

An elderly man dictates a letter to a public scribe in the market area of Stamboul. In a city whose illiteracy rate hovers at about 30 per cent, scribes find a continuing demand for their services, particularly in dealings with officialdom.

It was as if the two were chipping away at a block of stone, defining its eventual shape by a slow attrition.

The shape they arrived at was 18 lira. The shopkeeper beamed. The old man crooked the umbrella over his arm with a look of quiet delight, and then, with old-world politeness, he handed the storekeeper a 20-lira note and did not wait for the change.

The sales technique of the rug merchants, who sell their wares—old and new—from a fine colonnade in the Bazaar, is very different. They offer the rugs a little as if in love with them, rolling them at your feet and murmuring of their beauty. "Feel it," they will say. "That's the wool of six-month-old lambs. What could be softer? It's like the skin of a woman. . . ."

Many of these richly handsome carpets were woven by young girls in the villages of Anatolia for their trousseaux. But this custom is dying; and gazing at the intricate patterns as they flood over the merchant's floor, you trespass on the thoughts and longings of women now old or dead. In the sea of their abstract designs—lozenges, arabesques, concentric borders—the merchant descries another language. "You see the scorpion?" he asks. "And the crab? You can't see it? Look. It's a sea-crab. See how he swims with his tiny claws!" He may point out lamps, tulips, water-pitchers, turtles, amulets, stars. For although the portrayal of life is forbidden by Islam, there presses up, close beneath the designs, a half-expressed underworld of living nature. Inexplicit, bodied out in pure pattern, it trips along the edge of heresy. And in every carpet the bride has left a single mistake, indistinguishably slight, to avert the Evil Eye, which is thought to fall, like the ancient Furies, on any object of perfection.

In today's workshops the traditional vegetable dyes are no longer used, except in rugs of pure wool. They have been replaced by chemicals that are washable and more varied, but lack some last depth and lustre. The even spread of hues betrays them, for a vegetable colour continually softens or intensifies over the surface with a life of its own. The double-knotting of the pile, which gave to earlier rugs their durability and dense smoothness—like a flow of water under the hand—is no longer always used.

But the finest modern rugs can yet be magnificent, because many towns and villages keep their weaving traditions. The work is done by girls as young as eight years old—but for profit, not trousseaux.

As the merchant's enthusiasm mounts, your senses are alternately ravished and bemused by the heavy blaze of Konya carpets from Anatolia, or the thinner, often silkier delicacy of rugs from nearby Kayseri. Caucasian designs flare and glow; Hereke silk weaving—from a village 50 miles east of Istanbul—is so fine that a square centimetre can hold a hundred knots.

Yet the number of girls who give themselves to this arduous work is declining. In 20 years, perhaps, such precious carpets will no longer be produced. A craft older than record, already ancient when Turkish carpets were coveted by medieval Europe, will then be preserved only in these too-perishable forms, and in the gorgeous counterfeits that Renaissance artists painted beneath the feet of a saint or a prince.

Unlike the rug-sellers, the leather workers of the Grand Bazaar sometimes make their own goods. Countless stuffy workrooms are filled with serious-faced men crouched at long tables, snipping and joining leather with the ubiquitous Singer sewing-machines.

A proprietor caught me trespassing in his premises; but instead of pushing me out he demanded that I drink tea with him. He had the craggy face and ferocious eyebrows familiar in pictures of Atatürk (perhaps it's patriotic to train up eyebrows that way).

"Leather? You won't find better leather than here," he boomed. "It's cured in the Yedikule district, outside the land walls, just as it always was. And they're still a tough lot down there, believe me. The stink of the tanneries would drive a normal man insane. Down there you could hold a skunk to your nose and not know it." He began measuring me with his eyes. "We make jackets to measure in 24 hours. They fit like a skin."

A tea-seller appeared, dangling a brass tray with tiny cups. Tea-sellers exist for such courtesies; they are summoned in and out of shops and offices all day and paid with plastic counters purchased in advance.

The proprietor picked a jacket off a hook and threw it in my lap. "Feel that. That's the best Istanbul leather for you." It was soft, pliant. "The leather from Asiatic Turkey is never quite like that. Always a bit coarser." He laughed, showing broken teeth, and pointed at a hanging row of furs: rabbit, kid, jackal, fox. "Everything's coarser over there, even the jackals."

At an open-air market that operates daily just outside the Byzantine land walls, Stamboullus meander among impromptu displays of goods ranging from fresh food to old clothes. Such markets, frequented by the city's poor, occupy many tracts of undeveloped land in Istanbul.

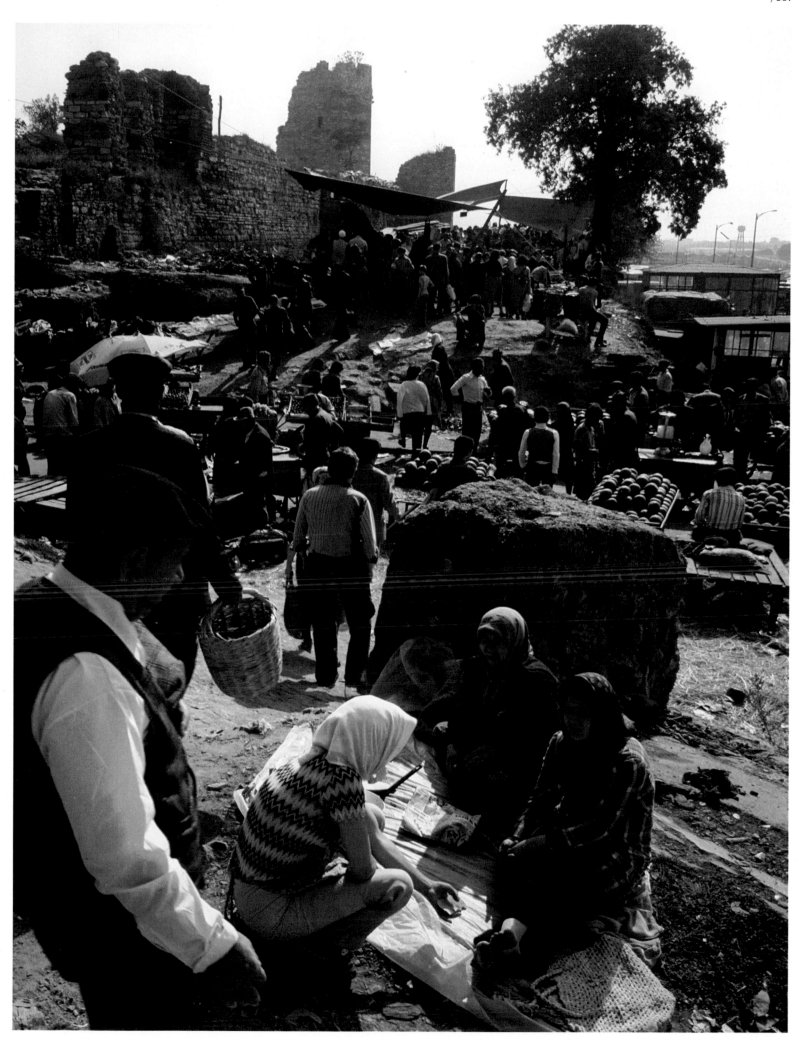

Even in 24 hours such leather workers could produce a handsome suede coat or jacket cheaper than anywhere else in Europe. The proprietor himself cut the pattern out of cardboard, bullying the shapes into life with thundery frowns and knottings of eyebrows. He tyrannized over a devoted band of seamsters, and when customers come to be fitted, he bullied them too.

"I want the coat split at the back," announced a comfortably proportioned woman. "It'll hang better."

"No it won't," scowled the tyrant. "It'll just pull open. It'll go in and out."

"I prefer a split."

"No." He gnashed his teeth on his pen. "It won't hang better at all. It'll just look as if you've been stabbed."

In the face of such intransigence, the customer can only surrender.

This pride and independence are typical of the older type of craftsmen, who may work in conditions as exacting as those of 300 years ago. Unlike the unionized worker of the factories, they are still organized in their old guilds, many of which trace their history back to the time of Evliya Çelebi, or earlier.

Among the proudest and most independent of these communities are the shoemakers. Tradition has it that in the reign of Süleyman the Magnificent they offered their services to the sultan when he was threatened by a Janissary revolt. The Janissaries at once returned to loyalty and the grateful sultan repaid the shoemakers by granting them exemption from civil law; instead, the guild's officers were given the power to try offending members, whom they could sentence even to death.

Curious to see how this once-proud organization had survived, I sought out the guildmaster in his office near the Grand Bazaar. I found a lightly moustached man in an open-necked shirt and jacket, seated behind a bare desk. From the walls the photographs of earlier guild-masters, turbaned and lapped in white beards, stared at us palely out of their unimaginable past.

"We have 12,000 members now," the man said, "and it's obligatory for workshop owners to belong. We run training courses every year, we arrange insurance for master-craftsmen, and we look into complaints." His hands shifted uneasily over the desk. "Sometimes we even take our own members to court in the interests of good shoe-making.

"One of our most important duties is to test the stretchability of leather." He gestured at a giant machine—an arcane creation of hammers and spikes—that stood behind me. "We have to do this because there are no other controls here—nothing. And as for the four or five principal factories. . . ." He stopped, leaving the bitter sentence unfinished.

Later he guided me through a whole hive of small shoemakers near his office. Like most other craftsmen, they worked not in factories but in tiny rooms, usually two or three artisans together, sometimes only one.

Some of the ateliers were so squalid that they seemed to be in ruin. Their walls were sombre with grime and plastered with pictures of nudes. And no people could less have resembled the ferocious Turk than these small, grey-faced craftsmen in spectacles, bent like gremlins in the half-light, who hammered and stitched and chiselled in fetid isolation.

An elaborate hierarchy interconnected them. Under the supervision of the *usta*, the master, at least 10 men joined in the making of one shoe. The *kalepçi* made the shoe-last (often from Italian patterns). An apprentice called a *çirak* roughed out the lowers. A more skilled colleague, the *kalfa*, trimmed them. In one den I saw the *sayaci*, who stitched together the upper parts of the shoe, which lay about him like black and brown intestines. In another sat the *firâze*, the master who made the bridge and body of the shoe and who had beneath him his own retinue of *çeraks* and *kalfas*. Then there was the *ayakkabici*, who presented the final product, polishing the leather over a flame; and a whole undergrowth of other men who spent all their lives attaching rubber soles or planing wooden heels.

I suppose that somewhere this dizzying hierarchy accommodated the wizened figure I found in the deepest cell of the labyrinth. He was minute, delicate. His ancient wrists were little thicker than another man's fingers. Without a machine, and with no tools but a scalpel and a strong needle, he was stitching together shoe-leathers by hand in the glow of a gas lamp. Around him on the walls dangled black thongs, which he greased and strengthened with clumps of beeswax. He peered at me through tiny blue eyes—an archetypal craftsman, proud of his trade and sceptical of anything that might make it easy or new.

His voice was high and plaintive, like the squeak of a very old mouse. He told me that he refused even to use the stitching machine that the other men employed. "How can you give a shoe shape that way? No, you can't tighten or stretch it as you like. You can't do anything." His whiskered head trembled with disdain.

And it is true that the shoes that at last emerge from this maze are neither very beautiful nor long-lasting. The man sighed. Shoes were better in the old days, he said, when there were no machines at all.

# The Ultimate Marketplace

PHOTOGRAPHS BY JOHN GARRETT

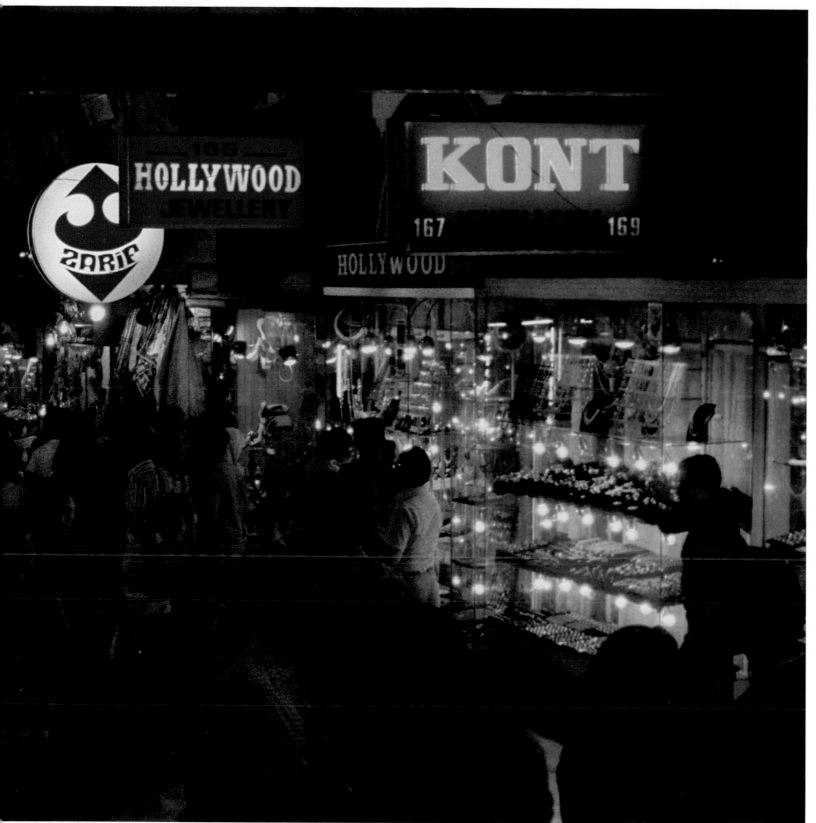

Western-style neon signs and brightly lit display windows cast a rich glow over crowds parading past shops along one of the main arcades in the Grand Bazaar.

At exactly 8 a.m., six days a week, the Grand Bazaar in Istanbul's old quarter of Stamboul swings open its 8 iron gates and draws the public into a labyrinth of merchandise that has no equal anywhere in the world. Today the great covered market, established by the Ottomans five centuries ago on a site that may have served for an earlier Byzantine emporium, encompasses more than 4,000 shops within its 50-acre expanse of domed halls and vaulted arcades. Many of its merchants are multi-lingual and expert at bargaining with the tourists who come in search of jewellery, onyx ornaments, old coins, copperware and hand-knotted Turkish rugs. But the majority of dealers make their living by selling clothes, hardware, fabrics and other mundane goods to Istanbul's own citizens—an army that pours through almost half a million strong each day.

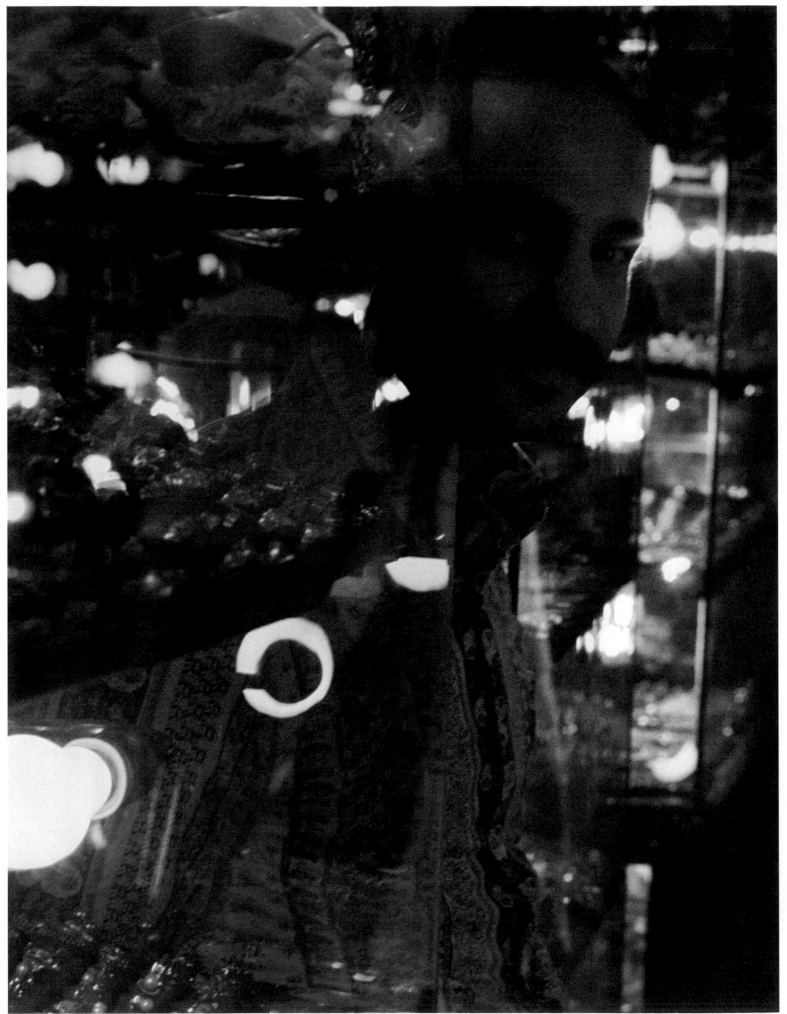

Stationed at a corner of his display case, a jeweller keeps an eye peeled for prospective customers. Almost 500 jewellery shops do business in the bazaar.

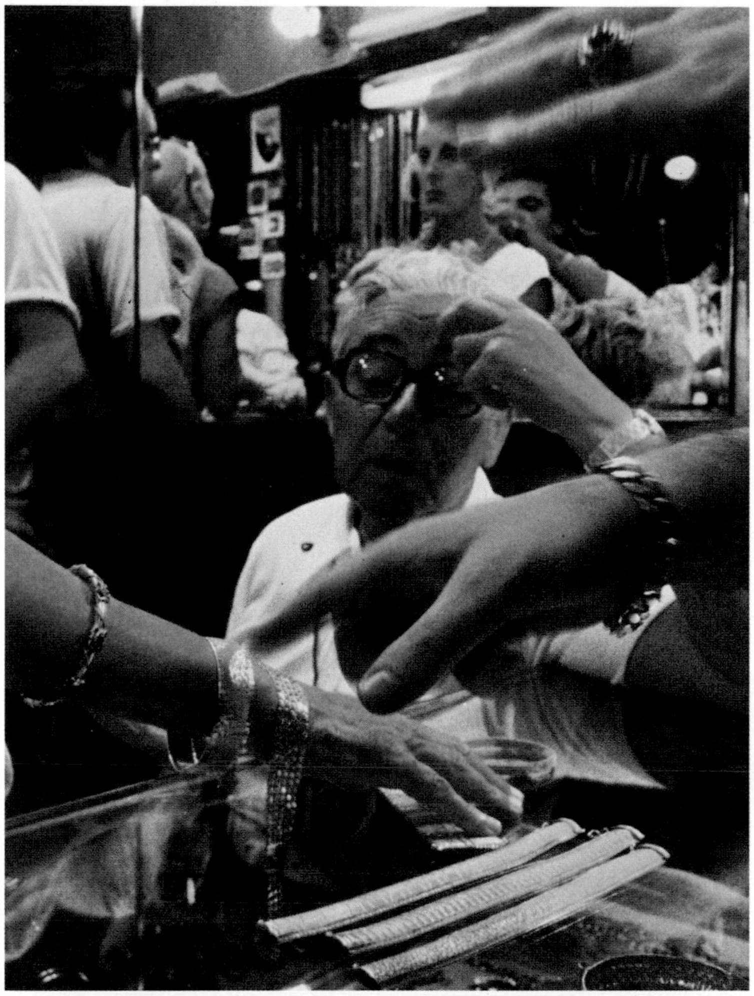

A visitor puzzles over the choice of bracelets being offered to his wife.

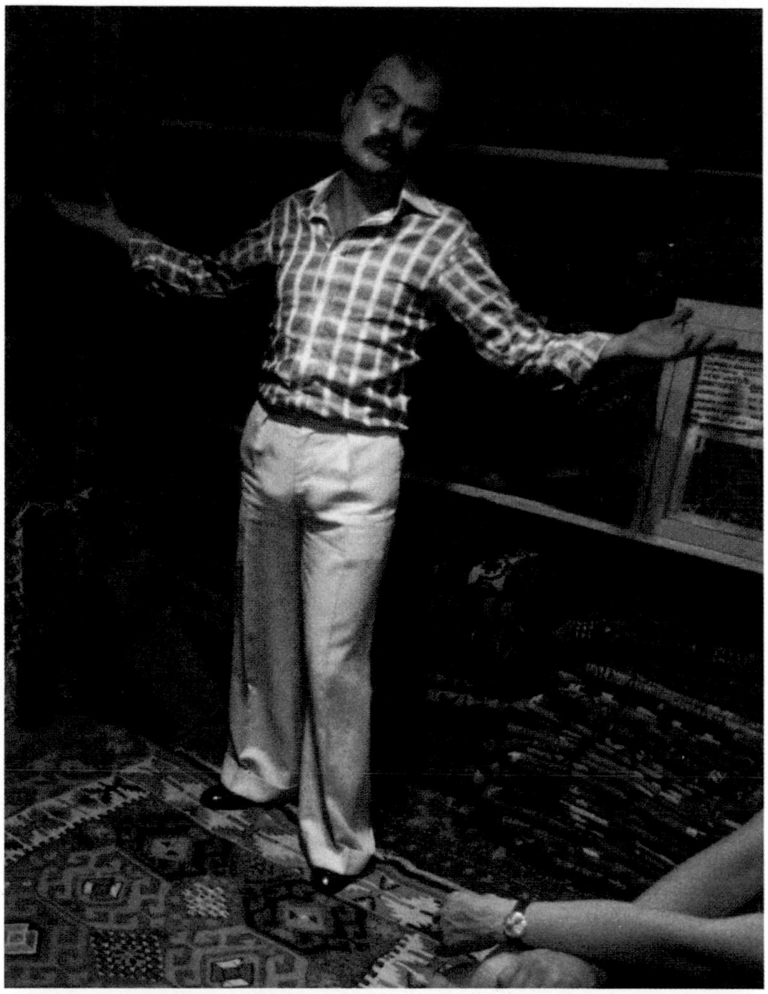

Arms outstretched, a carpet merchant feigns disbelief at a patron's offer.

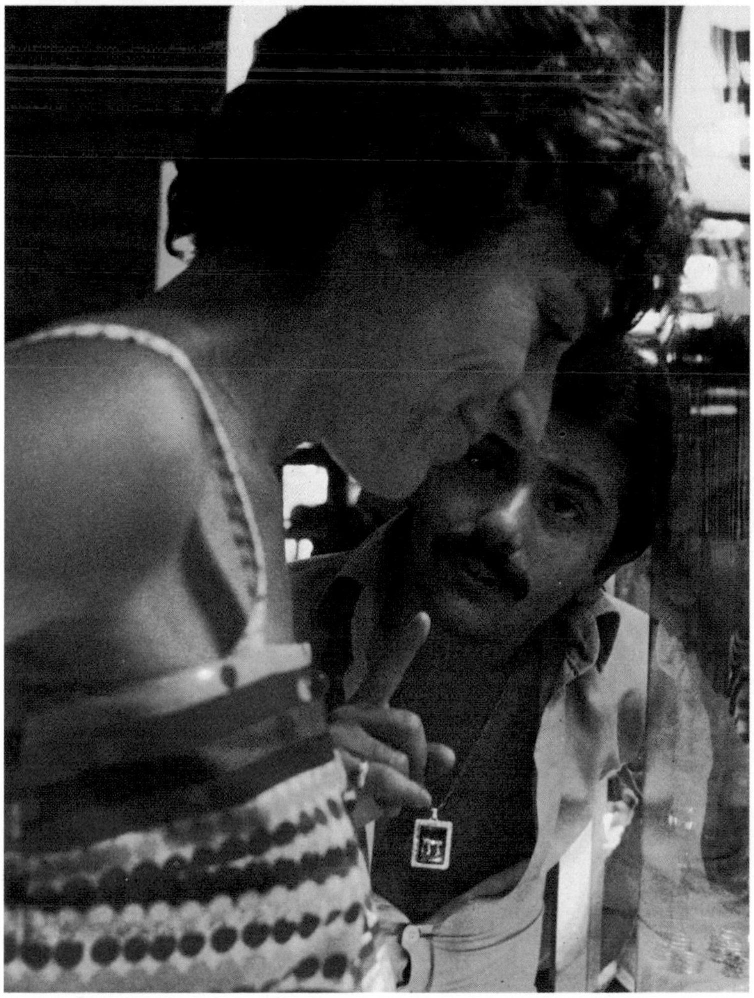

Earnest advice from a jeweller helps to sway a tourist into choosing a gift.

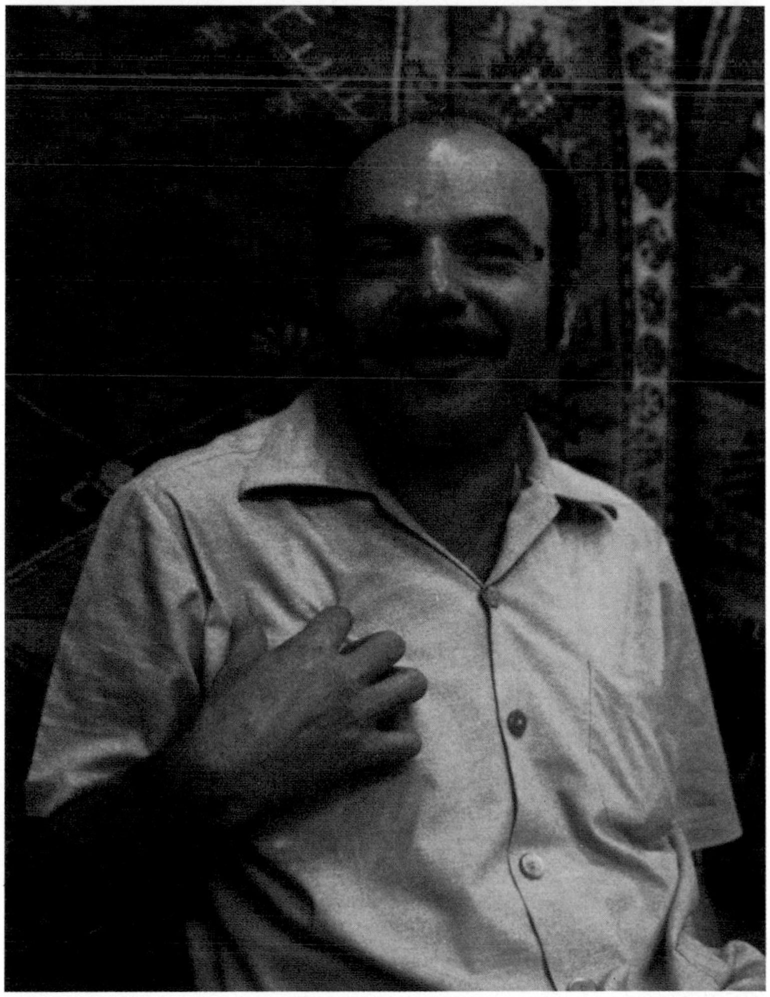

With a confident smile, a rug dealer suggests his prices could not be bettered.

In a fantastical cave of cotton, a merchant displays rolls of fabric selected from the vast stock lining the walls and held against the ceiling by wire mesh.

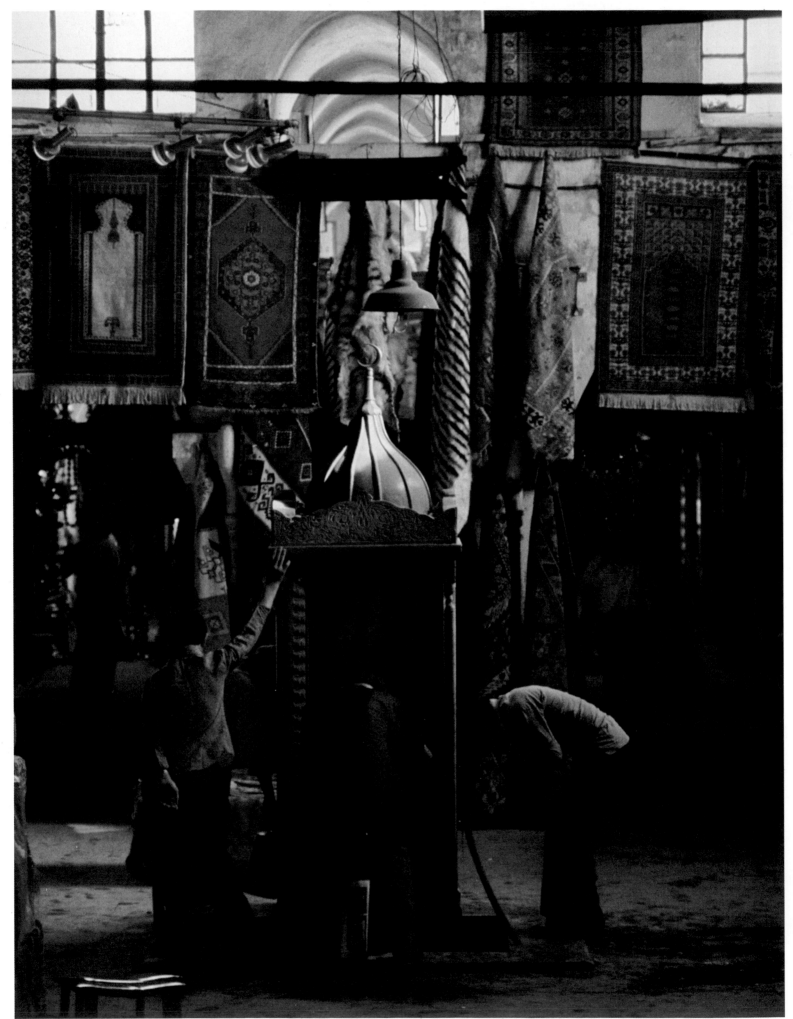

A domed fountain at an intersection provides water for the thirsty—and for Muslims to perform ablutions before entering one of the bazaar's several mosques.

**Dressed for shopping in a visored bonnet, a girl drinks from a cup that is chained for safe keeping to a fountain.**

In a gloomy hall dating from the 17th Century, Turkish carpet dealers bid at the bazaar's weekly auction of second-hand rugs—many of them destined for export.

# PARIS
# MÜNCHEN
# ATHENS

SNFC FRANCE-CARS

## east and west

ATHENS ⟶
AMSTERDAM
PARIS ⟶
MUNICH ⟶

batareur - S.M. FRANCE-CARS
Uluslararası Otobüs işletmesi
Türk - Fransız işbirliği
ISTANBUL - PARIS - ISTANBUL
TARİFELİ OTOBÜS SEFERLERİ

GET
YOUR
FREE
COPY
INSIDE

WE CAN ARRANGE A
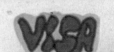
BULGARIAN
VISA FOR
YOU

# 8

# A Troubled Cosmopolis

When Constantinople fell to the Ottomans in the 15th Century, it seemed to Europe as if the great city was lost forever—not only to Christianity but to civilization. Yet Mehmet the Conqueror was no barbarian. He considered himself on the one hand to be leader of the Islamic world, God's vice-regent on earth, and on the other as heir to Byzantium and the Caesars; and he dreamed of ruling as they had—as a universal sovereign over many faiths and nations.

So the cosmopolitan character of the ancient city was preserved under his reign. Greeks, Jews, Armenians—peoples who had inhabited Constantinople since ancient times and whose life was inseparable from commerce—settled again in the city and were soon flourishing as middlemen between the Ottoman Empire and Europe. Foreign merchants also arrived—representatives of the European powers. At first, in the age of Süleyman the Magnificent, they were treated with a grand condescension; but slowly, as the Ottoman Empire declined, the whole city and empire became a pawn in the power-politics of Europe.

Today the fierce nationalism of Turkey and a surge of Muslim immigrants from the Asiatic mainland have unsettled these timeless minorities. Reluctantly they are filtering away—to Athens, to Israel, to the Americas. But all over the city their polyglot legacy continues: in dozens of enclaves, in smatterings of near-forgotten languages among half-integrated sects, in unexpected physiognomies, different skin textures, even quirks of architecture.

The home of foreigners in the city has traditionally been the district, loosely called Beyoğlu, that covers the northern shore of the Golden Horn, and that confronts the sober heart of old Stamboul across the inlet with a barrage of wealth and tawdriness. Whereas Stamboul is the city of tradition, of the poor and of religion, Beyoğlu has a hybrid tradition of its own—and its religion is money. At night its dense offices, topped with advertisements for the big Turkish banks, blaze across the water at the dim-lit older city: commerce staring at religion. "Osmanli Bankasi", "Akbank", "Yapi ve Kredi Bankasi"—the signs glow like a ghoulish publicity stunt, aimed at those who have nothing to invest.

The origins of this mammoth suburb are ancient, but its distinctive character stems from medieval times, when the Byzantines, as their power declined, all but ceded the area to the Genoese, one of the great trading peoples of Italy. Ruled by a governor appointed from Genoa, it grew into the powerfully fortified sectors that now constitute the core of Beyoğlu—Galata, on the Golden Horn, and Pera, which covers the heights beyond.

**Signs cluttering the window of a Stamboul travel agency reflect Istanbul's role as a crossroads between Europe and Asia—the key to the city's commercial importance and cosmopolitan character since ancient times.**

Few reminders of Genoese rule have survived in these quarters. So smudged and grimed together are their buildings that the old towers and walls are all but smothered. The handsome governor's palace still stands in Pera, but its interior has been split into workshops. At the summit of the slope dominating the Horn, where the rapacious Genoese extended their walls in 1348, an imposing bastion—the 220-foot Galata Tower—still lifts to heaven like a bullying finger. But now an elevator has been installed in it and on successive floors it offers a café, a restaurant and a night-club.

After 1453, the Ottomans confirmed the privileges of the Genoese. But the power of the Italian republics declined; Pera and Galata were infiltrated by Greeks and Armenians and by the trading companies of Europe. Over the next 400 years, the population proliferated into an amazing farrago of peoples. To the district's first minorities were added Arabs and Moors, who settled here as early as the 15th Century, after the Christian conquest of Spain. Later, as the empire shrank, Albanians, Slavs, Hungarians and Tartars who had thrown in their lot with the Ottomans arrived in the city as refugees—along with a host of commercial predators from Europe. Late in the 19th Century, Rumanians, Bulgarians and Serbians followed them, as well as Persians and Maltese, who came to trade.

Almost since the Conquest, this Tower of Babel has been decried as a haunt of lechers and drunkards; and for centuries its inn-keepers and pimps were the outrage of pious Muslims. Even into the 20th Century, its population was reputed to be the most depraved in Europe. "Pera has all that is odious of the Levant," wrote an English visitor at the turn of the century; "impudence, ostentation, slyness, indelicacy, uproar, a glittering commonness. It is like a blazing ring of imitation diamonds squeezing a fat and dirty finger." In those days one Turk might moan of another that he had "gone to Pera", as much as to say that he had gone to the dogs. It was the sewer and counting-house of a bankrupt empire.

As I climbed the lanes of Beyoğlu on my last visit to Istanbul, the district's personality seemed little altered—only more decrepit, perhaps, even its false glitter dimmed. Up from the Golden Horn the alleys wormed in refuse-littered steps or cobbled ramps—dingy passes, between cliffs of offices and workshops, threaded by porters and cats. High above, among buildings of indeterminate age and progeny, a 19th-Century mansion might thrust out tiers of bay windows framed by Corinthian pilasters and topped by mouldings where carved heads leaned with flaking smiles. It was as if the construction of some bombastic palace had stopped short and had left its vanity in fragments here and there, to be shored up all around by modern tenements.

Beyond these twisted lanes, the Grande Rue de Pera, renamed Istiklâl Caddesi (Independence Street) after Atatürk's revolution, is as tawdry as ever it was—a stringy intestine of a street, whose nondescript buildings have broken out into a fantastic fungus of billboards and streamers. On

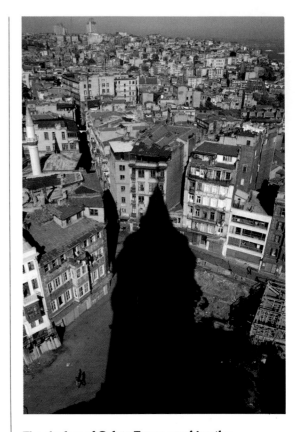

The shadow of Galata Tower, marking the border between the Galata and Pera quarters of Beyoğlu, leads the eye across tenement rooftops to the Bosphorus beyond. After the settlement of Galata by Genoese traders in the 13th Century, Jews, Greeks, Armenians and other non-Muslim peoples flocked into the waterfront area, spread to the higher ground of Pera, and took a major part in the city's commercial life.

either side short, featureless alleys run off it, and dim passageways lead to unfrequented shops, cinemas showing sex films all day and all night, and taverns where out-of-work residents play backgammon.

Istiklâl Caddesi might be personified as one of its own tradesmen. He lounges in the doorway of his business, watching the street with flickering and jaded eyes. A thickening stomach pushes apart his styleless suit and his plump hands fondle beads or dangle a cigarette in an ostentatious holder, which he occasionally draws to his mouth with narcissistic indulgence. He speaks French, or Greek; he may have travelled a little, no doubt on business; he sees the present sharply, the future dimly, and the past not at all.

Along this street, and in lanes about it, are some of the oldest reminders of the city's link with Western Europe: Roman Catholic churches whose missions have stood here for centuries. The Franciscans appeared as early as 1219, while St. Francis was still alive; and the Dominicans and Benedictines followed soon after.

Mingled with such monasteries and churches are the leftovers of a more aggressive Europe. In 1854 Turkey was bullied into hostilities by the Russians; and Britain and France rallied to her side in the arena of glory and blunder called the Crimean War. The Crimean Memorial Church in the heart of Beyoğlu still stands, sombre-stoned, turreted, but no longer in use. Together with a forbidding barracks in Üsküdar, where Florence Nightingale ministered to the war-wounded (and where her rooms are preserved), only this church commemorates the victory over Russia that brought 20 years' respite to the dying Ottoman Empire.

In these years, Pera and Galata were havens for exiles, and seethed with expatriate gossip and intrigue. The diseased Ottoman Empire, playing poker with the European powers for its survival, had by then accorded such immunities to France, Britain, Russia and Austria that their communities in the city were all but autonomous. Their ambassadors held court like petty kings and their embassies were palaces.

Even today the grandiloquent pageant of these buildings multiplies around Istiklâl Caddesi behind stately wrought-iron gates. The Italians commandeered the old palace of the Republic of Venice, whose Lion of St. Mark still prances grumpily on its façade. In the former British Embassy—a Roman *palazzo* set in a Victorian garden—the ambassador, Lord Stratford de Redcliffe, entertained Sultan Abdül Mecit at a ball in 1856—a diplomatic coup of sonorous prestige, for no sultan had accepted such an invitation before.

In their chandeliered and marble-paved expanses, too huge for present needs, the once-great power of these establishments seems formidable still. From the elegant Maison de France—then the embassy of Turkey's oldest European ally—to the former Russian Embassy, from which the Tzar's ambassador-extraordinary, Prince Menshikov, provoked Turkey into the war of 1854, they breathe a time in which the empire's fate hung on the scheming of a few foreign statesmen. "Who is to have Constantinople?" demanded Napoleon as early as 1808. "That is always the crux of the problem."

The palaces are merely consulates now. They have come down in the world. And so have the great hotels of Beyoğlu, whose rise accompanied theirs. At the turn of the century foreigners arriving on the Simplon-Orient Express originating in Paris would disembark into the pseudo-Moorish splendours of Sirkeci Station, and an hour later would be seated under the chandeliers and gilded staircases of these Victorian homes-from-home, exchanging international scandal. Everybody knew, of course, that the hotel manager might be a spy in the service of the German ambassador, that the headwaiter was in the pay of Britain, and that the middle-aged Jewish lady descending in the silver-painted elevator was the ex-mistress of Count V——, who was not a Russian exile at all, but. . . . And the sultan's own spies were as ubiquitous as aspidistras.

Nowadays foreign visitors generally arrive at Yeşilköy Airport, west of the city. The Simplon-Orient ran its last train in 1977. The hotels are tottering to their end. Plump caryatids still press up the balconies of the Londra, a Victorian survival standing on Meşrutiyet Caddesi; but inside, cracks crawl across its moulded ceilings and the red carpets are torn and stained with the passing of a century. Nearby, the Bristol is closed, and the Alp demolished into a car park. ("I'm the Alp Hotel now," the attendant told me.) Only the dowager of them all—the six-storeyed Pera Palas near the British Consulate—still keeps about it something of that age of delusory grandeur. Across a lake of plush and marble, among the ormolued lamp-stands and the dark-wooded chairs of the lobby, an elderly clientele still idles and gossips—but no longer of Balkan politics, only about the servant problem and the price of rose-leaf jam.

It was the First World War, of course, and Atatürk's War of Independence, that swept away this theatre of European privilege. As the diplomats and businessmen left the city, other and more tragic expatriates arrived. Sixty-five thousand White Russian refugees, fleeing from the Bolsheviks after the 1917 Revolution, brought chaos and music to the city. They set up their dance-halls and restaurants on the upper reaches of Istiklâl Caddesi, and their women caused scandal on the Marmara beaches by the cut of their bathing-dresses. The last of their restaurants, the Rejans, a haunt of aristocrats, passed to other hands in 1976 when its proprietors —three ex-dancing girls—went into belated retirement. It is hard to tell how many Russians remain in the city. Even language is not a sure clue. A person who speaks French socially and Turkish to the porter may break into Russian in anger. But only one small chapel remains to them in the city, served by a Bulgarian priest; for most of these popular and resilient refugees have moved on to France and Canada.

Not far from the minarets and domes of the Yeni and Süleymaniye Mosques, the mundane routine of commerce goes on at Sirkeci Station, where freight cars are loaded on to a ferry to cross the Bosphorus. Sirkeci was the eastern terminus of the world-famous Orient Express until the service was discontinued in 1977.

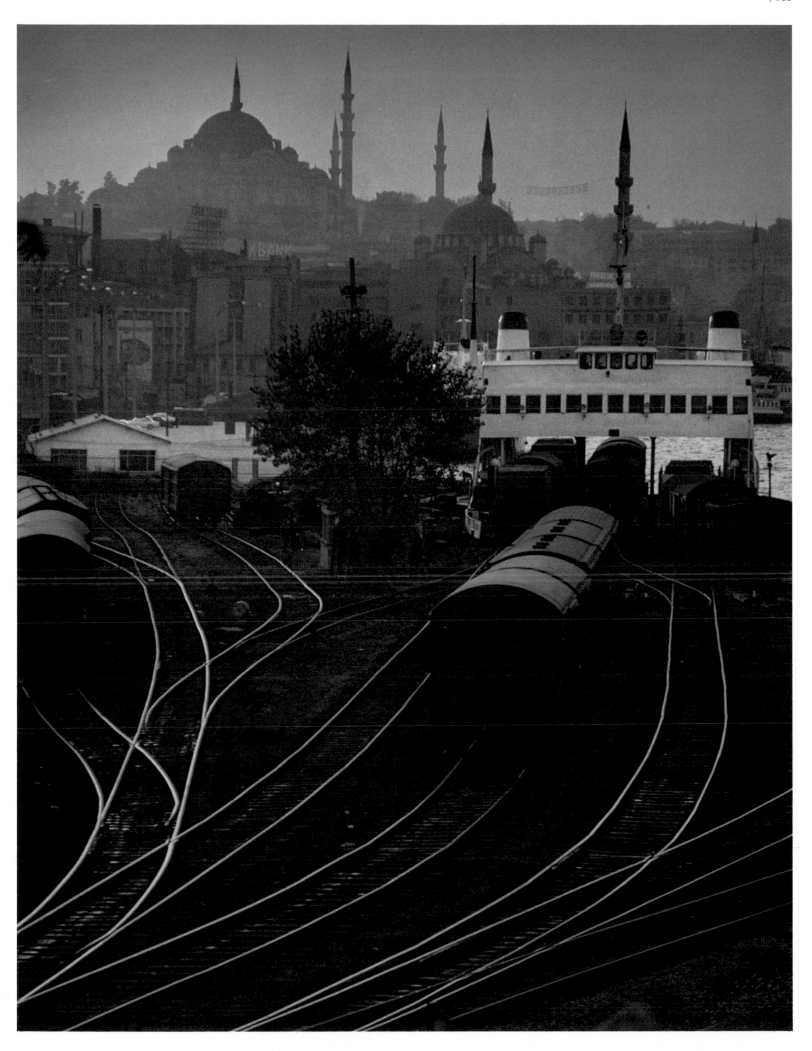

The fate of Istanbul's older minorities—Greeks, Armenians, Jews—has mirrored that of the expatriate Europeans. The growth of Western prestige in the 19th Century enhanced the status of these Western-orientated peoples, while the resurgence of Turkish nationalism after Atatürk's revolution has brought about their isolation and decline. Even as late as 1950 the minorities comprised nearly a quarter of Istanbul's population. But now their numbers have shrivelled pitifully and the city is less theirs, perhaps, than at any time in its history.

The largest of the minorities has traditionally been that of the Greeks, who for centuries after the Ottoman conquest occupied the district of Phanar (the Turkish Fener), high on the Stamboul bank of the Golden Horn. When Constantinople fell, the local fishermen voluntarily surrendered the quarter to Sultan Mehmet, who granted them the protection of their lives and religion. Over the centuries his promise was forgotten or ignored, and many of their churches were confiscated and turned into mosques. But it was into Phanar that the surviving Greek community gradually coalesced. Here, in a sad counterpoint to the mighty harmonies of Islam, they continued to worship in discreet subjection. While the great mosques were rising on the hills of Stamboul, their churches—to which domes and bells were now forbidden—sheltered behind courtyard walls.

But the people were tenacious. By the early 16th Century, the Greeks numbered 25,000 in the city's population of 80,000. Their knowledge of seafaring, their commercial flair and their contacts with European powers brought them increasing prosperity. Soon dynasties of merchant princes rose among them, claiming descent from the Byzantine aristocracy. They became the bankers and financiers of the empire, bribed favours at the Ottoman court, supplied doctors to the sultan, and grew powerful enough to be appointed governors in the northern Balkans.

The houses of these great families—known, from their district, as Phanariots—clustered around the palace of the Patriarch, lonely heir to the glories of Byzantium and spokesman of his people. Ever since 1054, when the Christian Church was formally split between Catholic and Orthodox branches, the primacy of the Patriarch of Constantinople among the Orthodox bishops has tinged him with the aura of a Pope. Paradoxically, his powers were increased by the arrival of the Ottomans. He was granted civil as well as religious authority over all the Orthodox peoples of the empire. He kept an intrigue-ridden court, placating the sultan, conniving at Greek nationalism. The Phanariot families manoeuvred for influence around him, and he around them.

But his triple role—as leader of the Greek community, head of the Orthodox Church, and servant of the sultan—brought contradictions that came to a head during Greece's War of Independence against the Ottomans in 1821. As soon as the Greeks rebelled, Sultan Mahmut II took his revenge by ordering the execution of Gregory V, the Patriarch of the day, who was seized while celebrating Easter Mass and hanged. The secular power of the Patriarchs was removed—although they retained their sacred office—and the Phanariot merchant empire began its decline.

Phanar is quiet now. It is haunted by the waters of the Horn, which shine grey and lustreless beyond its houses. Along the shore the Byzantine sea walls, tumbling among shrubs, wind among wood-and-tin shacks. A feeling of closure and emptiness lingers. Here and there show the window-less walls of a church courtyard, whose doors have sunk beneath the level of the modern street. On Sunday mornings you may see the few Greek families left, respectably dressed, picking their way to Mass along the refuse-strewn lanes. Sometimes, too, among the working jumble of wharves and hovels, you may glimpse a merchant's old mansion that has been patched and pulled almost to bits, and turned into a warehouse or a tenement. The carved decorations above its blocked-up windows remain, perhaps, like surprised eyebrows in a blind face. But mostly these handsome brick and stone dwellings, with their subtle marquetry and conical fireplaces, have vanished altogether.

The Greeks, I found, had almost abandoned the district. No more than 30 families remained; and these were poor. Among all their churches from Byzantine years, only St. Mary of the Mongols—founded by a 13th-Century Greek princess married to a Mongol prince—remains in use. One Sunday, staring into it, I saw the priest and a lay reader celebrating the liturgy; they had no congregation at all.

Little by little, since the beginning of the last century, the people have moved to wealthier neighbourhoods in Beyoğlu, on the more cosmo-politan side of the Golden Horn; and from here, after the rebirth of Greece in 1821, they began emigrating to Athens. Wars between Turkey and Greece—in 1897, 1913, and between 1920 and 1922—made their position delicate. In 1955 there were anti-Greek riots; there was violence again during the Turkish invasion of Cyprus in 1974. The Greek popula-tion, once more than a third of the city's inhabitants, dwindled from 100,000 in 1960 to less than 10,000 by the mid-1970s.

The Greeks dream of regaining Constantinople. This is a fading vision, but its aura lingers. There is a legend that when the conquering Turks broke into Sancta Sophia, the priest carrying the consecrated Host vanished into the wall above the pulpit and there bides his time. The church's great altar, it is said, was placed on a ship that sailed west but went down in a storm on the Sea of Marmara. The ship now rests on the bottom of the sea, whose waters are always calm above it. A strange fragrance rises from them, with the sounds of singing, and there the altar waits to be reclaimed when the Greeks win back Constantinople.

But the dream recedes. The buildings of the Patriarchate are now iso-lated in Phanar. Ever since the murder of Patriarch Gregory, the central gate has been kept locked and sealed with pitch—a symbol of Greek unforgivingness. Even today, visitors enter by a side gate, into a terraced garden with ivy-covered trees. Inside the Patriarchate office, I found two deacons counting the Easter offertory and a few male secretaries in glass cubicles. Their sad eyes scrutinized me. When I talked to them, they were circumspect, distantly kind. Hanging outside the office, in nervous patriotism, was a Turkish banner.

This place, I had to remind myself, is the Vatican of the Eastern Church, the lineal descendant of the great patriarchal palace that stood by the Sacred Palace of the emperors in Byzantium's heart. The Patriarch—rich in revenues, his power limited only by the emperor and the Holy Synod that appointed him—once governed a vast and convoluted hierarchy of officials. Today's Patriarch is still the nominal leader of the big Orthodox communities in Western Europe and the Americas, but in his own city he is almost a prisoner.

His flock has dwindled about him. One Sunday, when I went to the Patriarchal church, even the singing sounded frail, repeating the *Kyrie Eleison* in an endless plea for forgiveness, as if the sins of the fathers were still visited upon the children. The Patriarch—a dark Olympian, his beard dashed with grey—sat in gold and purple robes on a high-backed throne. Before him, in the timeless drama of the liturgy, yellow-vested priests went pacing and repacing, resurrecting the lost paradise. But the congregation was heart-rendingly small—a dozen or so people, mostly old, sitting in passive loneliness. Even the saints seemed to stare from their darkened icons with a remote misgiving.

The Armenian community, scattered through Istanbul, has suffered more terribly than the Greek, but its members have no free homeland to which they may escape. Some of them manage to emigrate to Canada, America or France; but many remain.

Long before the 11th Century, when their ancient kingdom in the Caucasus was submerged by the Seljuk Turks, Armenians had flourished at Constantinople, providing soldiers, architects and even emperors for Byzantium. During Ottoman years, they made their fortune in banking, and as entrepreneurs in the silk trade between Persia and Italy. With the regeneration of Greece after 1821, they moved into many of the positions that the now-distrusted Greeks had once enjoyed, until even the Treasury and the Mint were in their hands.

But between 1894 and 1896, in atrocious punishment for separatist agitation among them, Sultan Abdül Hamit II engineered a series of massacres that ended with the slaughter of some 7,000 people in Istanbul. And in 1915, in an act of calculated ruthlessness, almost a million Armenian men, women and children were butchered in the eastern provinces.

Defensively, the Armenians of Istanbul have kept their blood and language pure. Some 45,000 still remain in the city, and their flair for

An old woman sweeps up rubbish from a cobbled street in the Galata quarter of Beyoğlu. The doorway behind her suggests Galata's former role as the home of wealthy foreign merchants. With the exodus of minorities from the city since the First World War, the area has become a dingy warren of warehouses, workshops and crowded apartments.

commerce gives them an importance greater than their numbers. The Armenian Apostolic Church, whose rite resembles that of Orthodox Christianity, has maintained its independence over nearly 17 centuries of alternating persecution and triumph. Its local headquarters is a mellow wooden Patriarchate in the Kumkapi quarter of Stamboul. Its services, like those of the Greeks, continue with a shambling and depopulated pomp. East and West are helplessly mingled. Its Patriarch, dazzling in white vestments and globular crown, resembles an oriental king. But the long-aisled church looks European; and beyond its altar, banked with candles and vases, the painted Christ is no Byzantine despot, but rises like a Titian saviour through the incense-laden light.

The Armenian massacres contrasted tragically with the Turks' traditional tolerance of their minorities. In early Ottoman times, for example, a wave of Sephardic Jews, fleeing from Spanish persecution, found refuge in the city, settled in the Stamboul quarter of Balat on the Golden Horn and intermarried with the older Jewish community. By the mid-16th Century the city's Jews numbered some 40,000—a tenth of the population—and because the Turks trusted them, they preceded the Greeks and Armenians as bankers, physicians and interpreters, and eventually gathered most of the empire's trade into their hands.

But in 1666, a rabbi of Smyrna, called Sabbathai Levi, proclaimed himself Messiah and ignited Jews all over the Ottoman Empire and Europe. When he came to Constantinople, the vizier threw him into prison and offered him the choice between Islam or impalement. He chose Islam and exchanged the Kingdom of Heaven for a post as doorkeeper in the sultan's palace. He continued to seek converts—no longer to Judaism, now, but to Islam—and to Islam his more devoted disciples followed him. These strange crypto-Jews, called *dönme*, still exist in Istanbul—their religion officially Islamic, their blood Jewish—occupying a twilight between the two faiths and accepted by neither.

Through the 18th Century, with no foreign support or protection, the Jews of Balat lost their wealth to the Christians. The few Jews who immigrated from Europe held themselves aloof from their declining brethren, settling in Beyoğlu instead. Slowly the old learning and culture brought by the Sephardim were forgotten. Nineteenth-Century travellers left pathetic descriptions of the Jews' poverty and squalor. They lived, it seems, as traders in second-hand goods, as lapidaries, or as dealers in scrap metal, and their quarter was a labyrinth of disease.

Today the only Jews who remain in Balat are the poor. Along its shore, half-derelict houses are walled with beaten-out cans; rotting balconies sag like old stomachs; even the children are listless. But walk a little inland and you enter a tiny enclave, almost countrified, of vine-garlanded lanes where women go in flowered trousers and Nazarene headscarves. Among eccentric homes in many shapes and sizes, you see a well-kept synagogue or two, and street fountains that still flow.

Some Jews, who have grown rich in business and shipping, still live comfortably in Beyoğlu. But the huge majority left early in the 1950s for an infant Israel. Today, perhaps 10,000 are left in the city. The synagogues, like the churches, are empty.

The only minority increasing in the city is that of the Syrian Christians, who number 25,000 and have cornered much of the jewellery trade. Legend has it that they are descended from the ancient Assyrians—a legend that they themselves believe. In fact, their origin goes back to the 5th Century A.D., when they separated from Orthodox Christianity during its hair-splitting controversies over the nature of Christ. They are clever, with an Arab opportunism, and speech as well as religion sets them apart. They talk in Syriac, a branch of the Aramaic language, and to listen to them speaking together is to feel as if time itself were countermarching —for this was the tongue of Christ.

These eddies from the mainstream of Christianity are not all old. The city's Bulgarians, who number 2,000, established their independence from the Greek Orthodox Church in 1871, and signalled their victory by erecting a curious structure on the Stamboul shore of the Golden Horn. Tall, slender, immaculate, it rises from its gardens as if modelled in clay. Walking here, you stare up with astonishment at grey-blue domes and turrets, friezes of seraphim and garlands, deeply-incised capitals, pilasters, tiny crosses. The whole church, you feel, must have been built a year, not a century, ago—so crisp is it, so untouched. Then the gardener, intrigued by your visit, takes your hand and knocks it against the church

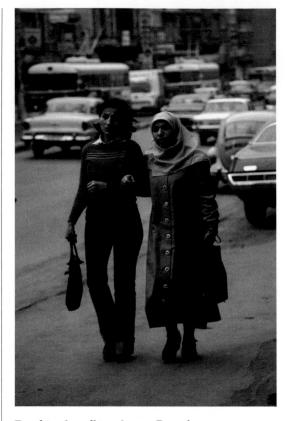

**Two friends walking down a Beyoğlu street present a contrast in contemporary Turkish dress styles. One sports the casual sweater-and-jeans outfit familiar to urban young people everywhere. The other is modestly wrapped in a maxi-coat, and covers her hair and neck with a headscarf—a lingering reminder of the custom of veiling the face, a practice that was condemned by Atatürk in the 1920s.**

wall. You hear a clang. The gardener smiles. Iron! From its sham painted marble to its smallest cross, the church was prefabricated in cast iron in Vienna, floated down the Danube into the Black Sea, then landed and erected here a hundred years ago.

The saddest element in the city's populace came from the absorption of fleeting minorities through the slave trade. This traffic continued far into the 19th Century, even into the 20th, although it was officially abolished in 1846; and it seems at its end to have been managed, ironically, by the ladies of the imperial harem.

Century after century, the strong peoples of central Africa and the beautiful ones of the Caucasus were driven into the city and sold for kitchen labour, bedroom pleasure, or both. The size of the traffic is impossible to know, but in 17th-Century Constantinople alone there were 2,000 slave-dealers. In these years, men who could not afford a free-born wife—and the custom of marriage-gifts was financially crippling—would purchase slave-girls instead. Deprived of family support, such women would be more submissive, and were very likely more handsome, than a girl of the man's own standing. Strict laws governed sale and ownership; but the would-be purchaser, wrote a Victorian worthy, "may fix his eyes on the lady's face, and his hands may receive evidence of her bust".

The smouldery good looks of the Caucasus Georgians were especially desired, until Russian conquest of the region stopped the supply in 1801. But their Black Sea neighbours, the fair-skinned Circassians, were still herded into the city—you may hear Circassian spoken even now—and became the most coveted odalisques in the empire. If a concubine bore her owner a child, the man would generally marry her. She could then enjoy the privileges of an Ottoman matron and her offspring would inherit.

A cheaper and more menial trade—not for the bedroom, but for the kitchen—was carried on in black slaves from central Africa, mostly women. A century ago, even families of modest means would keep a black woman for housework, and there were some 30,000 in the city. Often they were cruelly treated. Many passed through 10 or more owners and were released only in old age, to roam the streets as beggars.

Their only protection lay in curious societies that they formed—lodges to which they offered whatever they could steal from their masters. Over each lodge ruled a priestess—despotic and sacred to her outcast people —who walked in a fantastic regalia of pearls and golden sequins. Her followers believed her to be the incarnation of an African demiurge called Yavrube, with whom she sought communion in frenzied, trance-like worship. Sick and homeless slaves might find refuge in her home, and she sometimes managed to purchase the freedom of those who were ill-treated by their masters.

Some black women were eventually granted their liberty and married, a few with the poorer whites; yet scarcely a trace of their blood remains today. Often they must have won their freedom too late to bear offspring; they were frequently divorced; and their children, born into squalor, died as infants. Rarely can you detect their legacy in the skin or features of the crowds of modern Istanbul, and the one apparent black to whom I spoke said that he did not know why he was so dark, but thought that his people had come "from the south".

Last and most despised of the minorities, credited with no religion or God at all, are the gypsies. There is a Turkish story that when God ordered the peoples of the world to inscribe for Him their respective creeds, all did so in stone except the gypsies; they wrote theirs on a cabbage leaf, which was at once eaten by a donkey. It is said, too, that they live under the curse of incest, and that their women command invisible spirits.

Standing midway down the length of Stamboul's land walls, the gypsy village of Sulukule has an evil reputation. In the 1960s the government even levelled it to the ground; but shabby vestiges of it have risen again. Great ridges and seams of refuse furrow it, haunted by dog packs. Some dwellings are hollowed out of the decaying fortifications. Others, at the foot of the Byzantine towers, are no more than patchwork, heated by wood-burning stoves whose rusty nostrils project between the entrance flaps. Nearby, cramped in cages, dancing bears lie curled up asleep.

The gypsy women, handsome in their youth, make money by palmistry or flower-selling, or work as mendicant belly dancers. Sometimes the small girls—only 10 years old, perhaps, but lascivious in rouge and lipstick—wander among Istanbul's taverns with lute or violin, their faces already aged. The men are scavengers, pickpockets, or leaders of the dancing bears, which they accompany with tambourines.

The exodus of the minorities from Istanbul has been more than counterbalanced by the influx of peasants from Asia Minor. Twenty-five years ago, the city had little more than a million inhabitants. Today there are four and a half million, and the native-born Stamboullus have become a minority in their own metropolis. Every year 200,000 more peasants stream in from the country. Mechanization of agriculture, soil erosion, and the minute fragmentation of old peasant holdings have reduced employment on the farms and turned the drift to the cities into a torrent. So crowded is Istanbul that electric power cuts are endemic, even in modern areas, and the water supply is frequently shut off.

"The city's changed utterly," said a silversmith—a delicate, nervous-looking man. "In the old days, I remember, it was almost quiet. I was brought up in Fatih [in western Stamboul], which was a pleasant place to live then. My family used to picnic by the sea. We'd lay out carpets and enjoy ourselves." He smiled miserably. "But now these people are always about—country people—making noise, picking quarrels."

"How do they find jobs?" I asked.

In the late afternoon, a gypsy street entertainer leads his dancing bear home to the ramshackle district near the city's land walls where several hundred of his people reside. The history of Istanbul's gypsy community can be traced back as far as the 15th Century.

**In trim attire marking them as modestly prosperous members of Istanbul's vast population of former peasants, an elderly couple pass the hours in a café.**

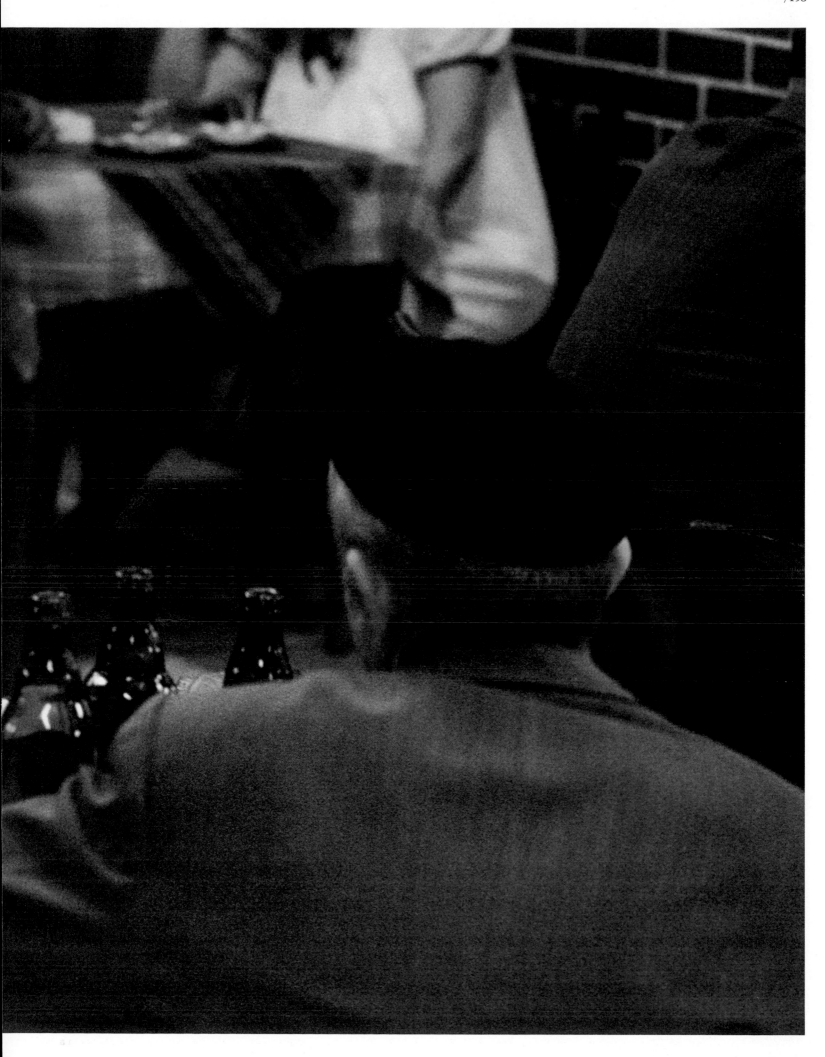

"Jobs?" The man shrugged. "They don't seem to have jobs. They just gamble and drink and create trouble." His look was of helpless disapproval. "Nowadays everyone wants to be the equal of everyone else. If you try to work a bit, save a bit, you become the enemy of these people. They want to get what you have. That's what they call equality." He was wringing his soft hands. "I always go home before dark now, so as not to be attacked. If you're wearing anything gold—a watch or a medallion— that may be the end of you." This petulant outburst suddenly stopped and he demanded: "Haven't you noticed them? How they stick their elbows into you? They stick knives too!"

The rough manners and harsh voices of the country people permeate the whole city. They are trying to survive in an environment that offers them no security. The newcomers find themselves exposed to a host of bewildering forces. Leaving behind the customs and ethics of the country-side, which were absolute but unquestioned, they enter a world in which they are unknown and must make their own way. Old allegiances vanish and, in the hard, impersonal metropolis, nothing replaces them, except allegiance to self. So the peasants enter the dark valley—of how many generations?—between rural integrity and urban refinement.

They build their houses of anything that lies to hand, on ground belonging to somebody else, or to nobody. If a house can be roofed between dusk and dawn, it must be legally accepted. So some families, in a frenzied concert of energy, rush up a dwelling overnight, while others go through subterfuge to conceal their half-built homes during the day, disguising them as ruins or as legal construction sites. So intense has been this activity, and so thick the deluge of immigration, that almost half of Istanbul's people now live in these lodgings, often without electricity, water or sewerage. The Turks call them *gecekondu*, "night-built" houses, and they infiltrate even the city's heart. Many are surprisingly sturdy, and all are individual. But many more are merely clay earthworks mounted by tottering skeletons of wood, and roofed with matting or corrugated iron. Sometimes vines are trained over them, or tiny gardens formed of plants in rusted pots—a country nostalgia.

"Of course it's tough. If you can't work, you starve," an immigrant told me. He had arrived from the southern village of Cennet two years before. A strain of Tartar blood showed in his widened nostrils and cheek-bones, and in the set of his eyebrow ridges. "When I first arrived, the city's rush and crowds terrified me. I'd never seen so many cars. I didn't even know how to cross a street." He passed a hand over his eyes. "In those days I couldn't afford to eat even once a day in the cheap cafés. I'd buy some bread and an egg." He laughed. "But no, I don't regret coming. Because Istanbul's a special city. International, I suppose. It's not like the rest of Turkey. I think I was asleep before I came here. It taught me about life. I've met all sorts of people. I've done all sorts of jobs—some I'm not proud of." He looked at me wryly. "But to tell the truth, I want to go home to Cennet. Here the talk is of money, nothing but money. But I don't want money. I just want enough."

You will often hear this said by Turks, very simply, as if ambition was for fools.

Yet likely he will not go home. The rural invasion never slackens. The brimming city overflows. In the fears and grumblings of the older Stamboullus, as in the thinning chant of church and synagogue, there sounds unmistakably the receding tide of Europe. Once again the city is invaded from the East, and its old alloy is changing. When the suspension bridge between Europe and Asia was opened in 1973, half a million Turkish peasants converged on it in fascination and there were fears that the bridge itself might collapse.

Such fears continue: dread that East will smother West, that the ancient cultural bridge will fall. But rural immigration has a long history here. It perplexed the Byzantine emperors. The Ottomans were so alarmed by the rise in crime and the paucity of water supplies that they set up check-points in the vain hope of preventing the influx.

Nor can one forget the old, absorbent subtlety of this polyglot capital of empires. Throughout its history, the city has civilized the peasant; the peasant has not barbarized the city. On the contrary, it has often needed him: his vitality, his anger. Istanbul, even now, is sometimes reminiscent of a degenerate but still beautiful sultana, lolling on her corrupted past. Her very domes and minarets, throbbing like an opium dream, compose a too-glorious obituary around the uncertain present. In one generation, or perhaps in two, today's peasant harshness will start to succumb. The city's witchery, its tendency to over-refine, is itself a talisman for the future—a promise that blood and climate will work their old miracle, and that the bridge will stand.

# Bibliography

**Arnott, Peter,** *The Byzantines and Their World.* Macmillan, London, 1973.

**Atasoy, Nurhan, and Çagman, Filiz,** *Turkish Miniature Painting.* R.C.D. Cultural Institute, Istanbul, 1974.

**Bury, J. B.,** *History of the Later Roman Empire (2 vols.).* Dover Publications, New York, 1958.

**Coles, Paul,** *The Ottoman Impact on Europe.* Thames and Hudson, London, 1968.

**Creasy, Edward S.,** *History of the Ottoman Turks.* Constable, London, 1961.

**Cuddon, J. A.,** *The Owl's Watchsong, A Study of Istanbul.* Barrie and Rockliff, London, 1960.

**Davis, Fanny,** *The Palace of Topkapi in Istanbul.* Charles Scribner's Sons, New York, 1970.

**Devereux, Robert,** *The First Ottoman Constitutional Period.* The Johns Hopkins Press, Baltimore, 1963.

**Diehl, Charles,** *Constantinople.* Librairie Renouard, Paris, 1924.

**Downey, Glanville,** *Constantinople.* University of Oklahoma Press, Norman, 1960.

**Dwight, H. G.,** *Constantinople: Settings and Traits.* Harper, New York, 1926.

**Ebersolt, J.,** *Sanctuaires de Byzance.* Editions Ernest Leroux, Paris, 1921.

**Evliya Çelebi,** *Narrative of Travels in Europe, Asia and Africa in the Seventeenth Century (3 vols.).* Oriental Translation Fund, London, 1834, 1846, 1850.

**Foreign Area Studies, The American University,** *Area Handbook for the Republic of Turkey.* U.S. Government Printing Office, Washington, D.C., 1973.

**Hearsey, John,** *City of Constantine (324-1453).* John Murray, London, 1963.

**Hotham, David,** *The Turks.* John Murray, London, 1972.

**Inalcik, Halil,** *The Ottoman Empire.* Weidenfeld & Nicolson, London, 1973.

**Jenkins, Romilly,** *Byzantium: The Imperial Centuries (A.D. 610-1071).* Weidenfeld & Nicolson, London, 1966.

**Karpat, Kemal,** *Social Change and Politics in Turkey.* E. J. Brill, Leiden, 1973.

**Kinross, Lord,** *The Ottoman Centuries.* Jonathan Cape, London, 1977.

**Kinross, Lord,** *Ataturk, The Rebirth of a Nation.* Weidenfeld & Nicolson, London, 1964.

**Levey, Michael,** *The World of Ottoman Art.* Thames and Hudson, London, 1975.

**Lewis, Bernard,** *Istanbul and the Civilization of the Ottoman Empire.* University of Oklahoma Press, Norman, 1963.

**Lewis, Raphaela,** *Everyday Life in Ottoman Turkey.* Batsford, London, 1971.

**Liddell, Robert,** *Byzantium and Istanbul.* Jonathan Cape, London, 1956.

**Maclagan, Michael,** *The City of Constantinople.* Thames and Hudson, London, 1968.

**Mathews, Thomas F.,** *The Early Churches of Constantinople: Architecture and Liturgy.* Pennsylvania State University Press, University Park, 1971.

**Mayne, Peter,** *Istanbul.* Phoenix House, London, 1967.

**Merriman, R. B.,** *Suleiman the Magnificent 1520-1566.* Harvard University Press, Cambridge, 1944.

**Mundy, Peter,** *Travels in Europe and Asia, Vol. I: Travels in Europe (1608-1628).* Cambridge University Press, Cambridge, 1907.

**Ostrogorsky, G.,** *History of the Byzantine State.* Oxford University Press, London, 1956.

**Penzer, N. M.,** *The Harem.* Spring Books, London, 1966.

**Pereira, Michael,** *Istanbul.* Geoffrey Bles, London. 1968.

**Procopius,** *Of the Buildings of Justinian.* Palestine Pilgrims' Text Society, London, 1888.

**Rice, D. Talbot,** *The Byzantines.* Thames and Hudson, London, 1962.

**Rice, D. Talbot,** *Constantinople: Byzantium-Istanbul.* Elek Books Ltd., London, 1965.

**Runciman, Sir Steven,** *The Fall of Constantinople, 1453.* Cambridge University Press, Cambridge, 1965.

**Runciman, Sir Steven,** *The Great Church in Captivity.* Cambridge University Press, Cambridge, 1968.

**Runciman, Steven,** *Byzantine Civilization.* Edward Arnold & Co., London, 1933.

**Shaw, Stanford J., and Shaw, Ezel Kural,** *History of the Ottoman Empire and Modern Turkey (2 vols.).* Cambridge University Press, Cambridge, 1976, 1977.

**Schneider, A. M.,** *Konstantinopel.* Mainz, Berlin, 1956.

**Sherrard, Philip,** *Constantinople: Iconography of a Sacred City.* Oxford University Press, London, 1965.

**Sherrard, Philip,** *Byzantium.* Time-Life Books, Amsterdam, 1967.

**Smith, John Holland,** *Constantine the Great.* Hamish Hamilton, London, 1971.

**Sumner-Boyd, Hilary, and Freely, John,** *Strolling through Istanbul.* Redhouse Press, Istanbul, 1973.

**Vogt-Göknil, Ulya,** *Living Architecture: Ottoman.* Oldbourne, London, 1966.

# Acknowledgements and Picture Credits

The editors wish to thank the following for their valuable assistance: Maria Vincenza Aloisi, Paris; Josephine du Brusle, Paris; Godfrey Goodwin, London; Mehmet Ali Kislali, Ankara; Rose Lockwood, Cambridge; Mimi Murphy, Rome; Frances Middlestorb, London; Ann Natanson, Rome; Betula Nelson, London; Dr. R. C. Repp, Oxford; David Sinclair, London; Norah Titley, London; Turkish Embassy, London; Turkish Tourism Information Office, London; Giles Wordsworth, London.

Sources for pictures in this book are shown below, with the exception of those already credited. Pictures from left to right are separated by commas; from top to bottom by dashes.
Cover—John G. Ross-Rapho, Paris. *Front end paper*—Steve Herr, courtesy of *The Sunday Times*, London. Page 4—Marc Riboud from Magnum Photos. 7—*Yanki Haftalik Haber Dergisi,* Turkey. 8, 9—Ara Güler, Istanbul. 12, 13—Map by Hunting Surveys Ltd., London, (Silhouettes by Norman Bancroft-Hunt, Caterham Hill, Surrey). 15—Marc Riboud from Magnum Photos. 17—John Garrett, London. 18, 19—Steve Herr, London. 23 to 35—Engravings from *The Beauties of the Bosphorous* by Miss Pardoe, George Virtue, London, 1861. 36—Ara Güler, Istanbul. 38, 39, 42—Marc Riboud from Magnum Photos. 43—John Garrett, London. 45—Scala, Florence. 46, 47—Marc Riboud from Magnum Photos. 48, 49—Ara Güler, Istanbul. 51—Photo Bibliothèque Nationale, Paris. 52—Scala, Florence. 54—Marc Riboud from Magnum Photos. 57—John Garrett, London. 58 to 65—Marc Riboud from Magnum Photos. 76, 79—Ara Güler, Istanbul. 82, 83—Sonia Halliday Photographs, England. 84, 85—Steve Herr, London. 86, 87—Sonia Halliday Photographs, England. 88, 89—The Rodney Searight Collection, London. 90—Sonia Halliday Photographs, England. 94 to 101—Courtesy of *The Sunday Times*, London. 102, 105—Marc Riboud from Magnum Photos. 106—John Garrett, London. 107—(top) Steve Herr, London, Marc Riboud from Magnum Photos, Sonia Halliday Photographs, England—(middle) J. Rufus, Robert Harding Associates, London, John Garrett, London, J. Alex Langley, Aspect Picture Library Ltd., London—(bottom) left, centre, John Garrett, London, Marc Riboud from Magnum Photos. 109—Klaus D. Francke, Hamburg. 110, 111—John Garrett, London. 112, 113—Marc Riboud from Magnum Photos. 114, 115—Jack Stanley, Art Directors Photo Library Limited, London. 116 to 118, 128 to 131—Marc Riboud from Magnum Photos. 133—John Garrett, London. 134, 137, 140, 141—Marc Riboud from Magnum Photos. 156—John Garrett, London. 159—Ara Güler, Istanbul. 160, 161—John Garrett, London. 162—Steve Herr, London. 165, 167—Marc Riboud from Magnum Photos. 180, 182, 185—Marc Riboud from Magnum Photos. 189—John Garrett, London. 190, 193—Marc Riboud from Magnum Photos. 194, 195—John Garrett, London. *Last end paper*—Ara Güler, Istanbul.

# Index

Numerals in italics indicate a photograph or drawing of the subject mentioned.

Colour reproduction by Irwin Photography Ltd., at their Leeds Studio.
Filmsetting by C. E. Dawkins (Typesetters) Ltd., London, SE1 1UN.
Printed and bound in Italy by Arnoldo Mondadori, Verona.